The Changing Role
of the American Prosecutor

The Changing Role
of the American Prosecutor

Edited by

John L. Worrall
and
M. Elaine Nugent-Borakove

State University of New York Press

Published by
State University of New York Press, Albany

For information, contact State University of New York Press, Albany, NY
www.sunypress.edu

Production by Ryan Morris
Marketing by Fran Keneston

Library of Congress Cataloging-in-Publication Data

The changing role of the American prosecutor / edited by John L. Worrall and M. Elaine Nugent-Borakove.
    p. cm.
  Includes bibliographical references and index.
  ISBN 978-0-7914-7591-1 (hardcover : alk. paper)
  ISBN 978-0-7914-7592-8 (pbk. : alk. paper)
1. Public prosecutors—United States. 2. Prosecution—United States—Decision making.
3. Criminal procedure—United States. I. Worrall, John L. II. Nugent-Borakove, M. Elaine, 1966–

KF9640.C43 2008
345.73'01—dc22

                                                                      2008000574

          10   9   8   7   6   5   4   3   2   1

Contents

Illustrations

Tables

Figures

PART I

Background

Chapter One

Prosecution in America
A Historical and Comparative Account

JOHN L. WORRALL

Introduction

Prosecutors are important officials within the American criminal justice system. They (mostly district attorneys, their equivalents, and their deputies) respond to various crime problems through the efficient process-ing of criminal cases. They decide, based on police reports, who is charged and ultimately whether a case will go to trial or be pled out. For the most part, the image of the American prosecutor is one of a diligent professional who represents the government in criminal trials for serious felonies. Indeed, many (perhaps most) aspiring prosecutors have ambitions of argu-ing high-profile cases before juries and removing dangerous felons from the streets. But there is much more to prosecution than the prosecution of crim-inal cases.

Prosecutors have received relatively little attention by social scientists. The sheer number of studies dealing with policing issues, for instance, dwarfs those aimed at prosecution. This may be because of the visibility of the polic-ing profession; cops are without a doubt the gatekeepers to the criminal jus-tice system. Another reason prosecutors have received scant attention by researchers is perhaps a misguided assumption that they are little more than case processors. A view that prosecutors only charge criminals may lead researchers to believe that there is little to learn about prosecutors; they do one thing. Nothing could be further from the truth, however. American prosecutors are part of a rich, interesting progression in criminal justice, and the dominant prosecution paradigm is starting to shift.

The goal of this introductory chapter is to place the American prosecutor in both a historical and comparative context. Prosecution represents one of the few criminal justice institutions the United States did not import from Europe. In many respects, the American prosecutor is a unique actor on the world's criminal justice landscape. What is more, the case-processing conception of prosecution is becoming inadequate. The American prosecutor is changing in response to emerging crime problems, political pressures, and other developments in crime control and prevention.

The Prosecutor

The American prosecutor has no equal throughout the world. This is especially true of local district attorneys. They straddle a line that separates courts from politics. As Jacoby (1980, p. xv) put it, "[t]he prosecutor is established as the representative of the state in criminal litigation, but either constitutional or statutory mandate, and yet is directly answerable to the local electorate at the ballot box." District attorneys' subordinates do not directly answer to the voters, but they nonetheless serve at the pleasure of the elected district attorney (DA). Likewise, U.S. attorneys are political appointees with certain loyalties and ideological connections to the president, who is responsible for their status. State attorneys general, while not considered prosecutors in the traditional sense, also are elected officials.

American prosecutors also are somewhat unique in the sense that they perform a number of different functions. The most obvious role is representing the government in court, executing the law, and upholding the federal and state constitutions. On top of that, though, prosecutors have the potential to influence law enforcement activity as a result of their screening function. They can alter both the quality and nature of law enforcement investigations by deciding not to press charges against offenders. Prosecutors, and particularly their interest groups (such as the National District Attorneys Association), also work to change procedures and legislation to work in their favor. The electorate also influences prosecutors, as will be evidenced by this book, such that trials are but one part of the story.

Despite their unique position and many hats, prosecutors are largely unknown. Davidson's (1971, p. vii) observation rings true today:

> The Prosecutor, reviled, unloved, unknown—except for the occasional Tom Dewey or Frank Hogan. On television and in fiction generally he's the ruthless Cromwell to the defense attorney's dashing King Charles. In

the movies most often he's the plodding Watson to the super-detective Holmes. In the press, the F. Lee Baileys and the Edward Bennett Williamses outscore him ten to one in paragraph space. . . . Yet though he and legions of experts he commands are the cornerstone of the democratic American system of justice and law enforcement—what the prosecutor does and how he does it are almost totally unknown to the vast majority of the American public.

Roots

There is no one wellspring of American prosecution. Instead, most historical accounts paint American prosecutors as having arisen from three separate European predecessors (Kress, 1976). Like the Dutch *schout*, the prosecutor is an official of local government. Like the French *procureur publique*, the prosecutor has total authority to file criminal charges. And like the English attorney general, the prosecutor has the power to terminate a criminal prosecution at any time. But there also are profound differences between American prosecutors today and those from whom they appear to have descended. For example, neither the *procureur* nor the *schout* was a primary law enforcement official within a specific jurisdiction but instead worked underneath a higher-level centralized official. Also, the discretion enjoyed by American prosecutors is unmatched.

Prosecutors' current authority was not always in place, however. Throughout American history, the prosecutor "evolved" through several stages, from a weak figurehead to a powerful political figure. Jacoby (1980, p. 6) has identified four forces that have contributed to this progression. The first was political; Americans chose a system of public instead of private prosecution. The second was legal; Americans' pursuit of democracy begat local government systems. The third was an outgrowth of the second; prosecutors became elected (as opposed to appointed) officials out of popular sentiment—consistent with democratic ideals. Finally, a desire to separate judicial and executive functions all but guaranteed an executive branch function for prosecutors.

From private to public prosecution. Perhaps the most unique feature of American prosecution is that it is public. Public prosecution is not a result of our British common law heritage. As Kress (1976, p. 100) put it, the district attorney seems to be "a distinctive and uniquely American contribution . . . whereas Americans typically describe their legal system as based upon English common law, in terms of both its procedural attributes and substantive state penal codes, the public prosecutor is a figure virtually unknown to the English system, which is primarily one of private prosecution to this day." Others have called public prosecution "largely an American invention" (Miller, 1969). While England has moved toward a system of public prosecution (e.g., in 1879 the office of the director of public prosecutions was formed), that was not the case at the time prosecution emerged on the American landscape. Kress (1976, p. 100) described the practice of private prosecution at common law:

> In common law [in England], a crime was viewed not as an act against the state, but rather as a wrong inflicted upon a victim. The aggrieved victim, or an interested friend or relative, would personally arrest and prosecute the offender, after which the courts would adjudicate the matter much as they would a contract dispute or a tortuous injury.

More recently, police officers have stepped in to initiate prosecutions, but even then the officer acts with a mind-set that the crime is an offense against a victim, not the state. The tension between private and public prosecution has long flourished in English history, but it was not as much of an issue in the American colonies. Private prosecution ran counter to the democratic process. By 1704, Connecticut adopted a system of public prosecution, and other colonies soon followed. To be sure, there are some traces of private prosecution in the United States. An example is the grand jury, but even grand juries are intimately tied to public prosecutors (prosecutors present evidence to the grand jury). The logic behind having a public prosecutor was laid out in a 1921 Connecticut court decision:

> In all criminal cases in Connecticut, the state is the prosecutor. The offenses are against the state. The victim of the offense is not a party to the prosecution, nor does he occupy any relation to it other than that of a witness, an interested witness mayhaps, but none the less, only a witness. . . . It is not necessary for the injured party to make complaint nor is he required to give bond to prosecute. He is in no sense a relator. He cannot in any way control the prosecution and whether reluctant or not, he can be compelled like any other witness to appear and testify. (*Mallery v. Lane*, 1921, p. 138)

From centralized to decentralized prosecution. The American colonists shunned all aspects of centralized British government. The desire to place government authority in the hands of locals, coupled with the geography of the early colonies, and ultimately the United States, gave rise to decentralized prosecution, another unique feature of the American system of prosecution. Add to that the distance between population centers and the relative isolation people enjoyed in a largely unpopulous land and decentralized government was critical. The legal system and many of its functions bore close resemblance to English common law traditions, but similarities ended there. Yet another explanation for this is the relative neglect by the British government of the colonies:

> The British government claimed the sole right to create courts, and the early courts except in the charter and proprietary colonies, were created by executive action. However, after the initial settlement, the judiciary received little attention from the King, and colonial courts were left to evolve without much thought, or consideration. England never tried to make the judicial system in the colonies uniform. (Surrency, 1967, p. 253)

Given the isolation of the colonies, several experiments with prosecution began and flourished throughout the 1600s, many of which retained some element of private prosecution. Interestingly, Connecticut became the first colony to use county attorneys as prosecutors. And in 1704, it became the first colony to totally abandon private prosecution. The statute providing for public prosecution stated that "Henceforth there shall be in every county a sober discreet and religious person appointed by the county court to be attorney for the Queen to prosecute and implead in the law all criminals and to do all other things necessary or convenient as an attorney to suppress vice and immorality" (Van Alstyne, 1952). The American revolution solidified the progression from private to public prosecution.

From appointed to elected status. Public prosecutors were first appointed. This continued in the postrevolutionary era when the first Congress created the office of the attorney general and the U.S. Attorneys, both uniquely American creations. The role of the U.S. Attorney, for example, was spelled out in the Judiciary Act of 1789 statute "to prosecute and conduct all suits within the Supreme Court of the United States in which the United States might be concerned" and to give advice and opinion on legal matters for the president and other officials of the executive departments. U.S. Attorneys' offices also were created as a result of the act. The attorney general and U.S. Attorneys enjoyed relatively little power in following the revolution. Primary control over prosecution continued to remain in the hands of local prosecutors. Beginning around 1820, though, during Andrew Jackson's presidency, there was a push for increased democratization, including a push for elections rather than political appointments:

> In the colonial period, and for some decades thereafter, the prosecutor's office was in fact an appointive one, appointive being in some cases by the governor and in others by the judges. . . . As with judicial offices, however,

appointment almost everywhere gave way to popular election in the democratic upsurge of the nineteenth century; and it became the universal pattern of the new states. (Mayers, 1964, p. 413)

Closely tied to the emergence of elected prosecutors was the judicial election process, because while prosecutors are now considered executive officials, they often were defined as judicial figures. In fact, many states had prosecutors listed in the judicial articles of their constitutions. Leading up to and following the Civil War, however, prosecutors increasingly found their way into the executive articles of state constitutions. As judges started to see themselves elected, then, so too did prosecutors, because both officials were regarded as closely tied to one another. By 1821, the first prosecutor was elected in Ohio and served Cuyahoga County. In 1832, Mississippi became the first state to include a constitutional provision providing for the election of prosecutors. "By 1859 the trend was clear and irreversible—the prosecutor was a locally elected position" (Jacoby, 1980, p. 38).

From limited to almost limitless power. While prosecutors were relegated to the judicial articles of states' constitutions, their powers were somewhat secondary to those of the courts. They were not listed as executive officials, or even as local government officials. The prosecutor was, "in the eyes of the earliest Americans, clearly a minor actor in the court's structure" (Jacoby, 1980, p. 23). Instead, the sheriff and coroner were given greatest deference (they also were the first judicial officers to gain independence and elective status). As the prosecutorial function shifted to the executive branch, however, and as prosecutors saw themselves being elected, their powers increased. They went from having very limited power to almost limitless power. This signaled the fourth step in the emergence of the American prosecutor.

By the early 1900s the prosecutor became perhaps the most powerful figure with respect to criminal law. While perhaps not as visible as the police, the prosecutor was regarded as having significant, if not total, power over the ultimate enforcement of the law: "In every way the Prosecutor has more power over the administration of justice than the judges, with much less public appreciation of his power. We have been jealous of the power of the trial judge, but careless of the continual growth of the power of the prosecuting attorney" (National Commission on Law Observance and Enforcement, 1931a, p. 11). More recently, the National Association for Attorneys General reported that "there is little probability that the basic pattern (of increased power and prestige for local prosecutors) will be changed; there is every indication that it will be strengthened" (National Association of Attorneys General, 1971, p. 103).

Courts even began to recognize the surge in prosecutorial power. The Illinois Court of Appeals reached this conclusion: The prosecutor ". . . is charged by law with large discretion in prosecuting offenders against the law. He may commence public prosecution in his capacity by information and he may discontinue them when, in his judgment the ends of justice are satisfied" (*People v. Wabash, St. Louis and Pacific Railway*, 1883, p. 263). In several important historical cases, courts have gone so far as to compel the prosecutor to pursue charges, but none have succeeded. The court in *Wilson v. County of Marshall* (1930) said, for instance, that the prosecutor has "absolute control of the criminal prosecution." Another declared that "[t]he remedy for the inactivity of the prosecutor is with the executive and ultimately with the people" (*Milliken v. Stone*, 1925, p. 399).

At about the same time, prosecutors started to draw the attention of legal scholars and, importantly, crime commissions. We will take up the issue of crime commissions, particularly their influence on prosecutorial evolution, later, but for now it is clear that the American prosecutor reached a certain "level" in the 1920s. At that point, prosecution in America was quite unlike anything else in the world. So unique and powerful has the American prosecutor become that certain commentators have expressed concern. Baker (1932, p. 934) made this observation: "The people of the United States have traditionally feared concentration of great power in the hands of one person and it is surprising that the power of the prosecuting attorney has been left intact as it is today." In the end, though, the courts have spoken most vocally; countless decisions have upheld prosecutors' control over life and liberty (e.g., *People v. Berlin*, 1974; *State v. LeVien*, 1965; *People v. Adams*, 1974). As Jacoby (1980, p. 38) pointed out,

> The final authority was conferred by the courts, which upheld his discretionary power. This completed his development because it made him the chief law enforcement official in his community. As a local official he was free to apply the laws of his jurisdiction as he felt best served his constituency. As an elected official given discretionary power by the constitution or by state statutes, his decisions were virtually unreviewable. This freedom of choice was, in the end, what truly set him apart from all other members of the criminal justice system.

Defense Developments

One of the most significant developments in American history with implications for prosecution is a string of Supreme Court decisions granting rights to criminal defendants. As early as 1932, in *Powell v. Alabama* (1932), the Court called attention to the constitutional basis for a defendant's right to counsel. The watershed decision, though, was *Gideon v. Wainwright* (1963), where the Supreme Court incorporated the Sixth Amendment right to counsel, ensuring

that criminal defendants are to be represented by counsel in state criminal trials—not just federal trials. *Gideon* dealt with felonies, however. In *Argersinger
v. Hamlin* (1972), the Court extended the right to counsel to defendants who,
if found guilty, faced prison terms. Other decisions, such as *Miranda v. Arizona*
(1966), extended the right to counsel to police interrogation.

   These cases significantly altered the prosecutorial workload. In particular, the Supreme Court's decisions meant that prosecutors suddenly needed to
be present at many more stages of the criminal process. More accurately, prosecutors felt compelled to be present at these important stages due to the
Supreme Court's decisions requiring the presence of counsel at critical stages
(e.g., the preliminary hearing). Prosecutors now must prepare themselves to
deal with defense attorneys from initial processing all the way through to the
appellate stage. Concerning the Supreme Court's defense counsel decisions,
Jacoby points out that they make ". . . the average criminal case longer and
procedurally more complex. Defendants [are] more likely to file motions, to
demand rather than waive preliminary hearing, and to institute postconviction
proceedings and appeals" (1980, p. 101).

   A parallel development was the passage of various speedy trial laws at
both the federal and state levels. These laws added additional pressures, making the prosecution function all the more difficult:

> Greater care had to be taken to provide prompt and suitable protection
> of the rights of indigent defendants, both by informing them of their
> rights at all stages of the process and by insuring that the state's case was
> instituted before proper deadlines. Having defense counsel in all cases
> would now exert pressure on the police and prosecution to perform to the
> letter of the law. (Jacoby, 1980, p. 101)

   In sum, today's prosecutor looks a great deal different than the prosecutor of old. Population growth and the prominent role of the criminal defense
bar (due to the Supreme Court's many defense decisions) have made prosecution difficult. For the typical urban prosecutor, more work needs to be done in
less time. There is most certainly more to the current state of prosecution than
population growth and defense attorneys though. What prosecution looks like
today owes a great deal to important developments early in our nation's history. Foremost among those were democracy and decentralizing, which gave
birth to a uniquely American form of prosecution.

✳ Evolution in the Prosecution Role

Thus far we have summarized the history of prosecution in America, about
how it came to pass. All along we have assumed that the prosecutorial func-

tion is one of processing criminal cases. To be sure, prosecutors continue to prosecute criminal cases, but there is more to the story. The prosecution role has changed over time, especially recently. Early understandings of the prosecutorial role were naïve and largely uninformed concerning the realities of processing criminal cases. Then researchers "discovered discretion." Now we are arguably on the cusp of a new prosecution paradigm.

Progressive Naïveté

The Cleveland Survey of Criminal Justice (1922), the Wickersham Commission (National Commission, 1931b), and early 20th-century commission reports (e.g., Illinois Association for Criminal Justice, 1929; Missouri Crime Survey, 1926; see also Walker, 1980, pp. 169–180) provided the basis for what has been called the "progressive era" of criminal justice. The authors of these reports were reformers intent on removing corruption and political influence from criminal justice operations. The reports sought to learn how criminal justice was operating at the time, and the authors offered up a number of recommendations for improvements intended to professionalize the administration of justice. The problem, though, was that they failed to dig deeply into the real-world operations of the criminal justice system, especially prosecution. For example, the crime commission investigators relied only on official data and did not directly observe criminal justice operations:

> The treatment of prosecution demonstrates most clearly how methodology and conclusions about the administration of justice were shaped by an a priori set of ideological assumptions. All of the crime commissions expressed alarm over the "mortality" of cases, noting that few arrests ever resulted in prosecution, trial, conviction, or imprisonment. . . . The crime commissions assumed that the "mortality" of cases was evidence of a "failure" to punish wrongdoers. (Walker, 1992, p. 53)

The "ideological assumptions" to which Walker referred were beliefs on the reformers' part that the criminal justice system consisted of several semiautonomous agencies whose employees applied the law in a neutral, impersonal, and evenhanded fashion. Quite simply, reformers felt the law could be followed to the letter, and that anything less was evidence of failure. As Walker (1992, p. 54) later observed, ". . . this reform strategy seems hopelessly naïve. It shows no awareness of the phenomenon of discretion, or of its underlying dynamics." In other words, the commissions totally ignored day-to-day operations and pressures facing criminal justice officials. Heavy workloads, case backlogs, public pressures, turf wars, self-serving interests, and other "realities" of criminal justice administration were totally ignored. Nevertheless, the progressive era paradigm was one of "textbook" criminal justice—a fully functional, competent, and effective "system." Reformers felt prosecutors should enforce the law by prosecuting all cases and taking all offenders to court. Anything less was regarded as a failure. This view was quickly dispensed once discretion was discovered.

Discovering Discretion

The progressive "systems" paradigm was quickly replaced following Frank Remington's 1956 comment that "[t]o a large extent, the administration of criminal justice can be characterized as a series of important decisions from the time a crime is committed until the offender is finally released from supervision" (cited in Walker, 1992, p. 47). This seems obvious today, but at the time it was a novel observation. What is more, it ran quite counter to the progressive conception of a system removed from human faults and frailties. Remington was one of the lead researchers behind the American Bar Foundation's (ABF) Survey of the Administration of Criminal Justice (Remington, 1956; see also Dawson, 1969; LaFave, 1965; McIntyre, 1967; Miller, 1969; Newman 1966; Remington et al., 1969). Unlike the work of the crime commissions before it, the ABF survey included field observations of criminal justice agencies in action.

The ABF survey came at the request of Supreme Court Justice Robert H. Jackson in 1953. In a speech before the American Bar Association (ABA) he expressed alarm over the delay and ineffectiveness of the criminal justice system, but he also pointed out how little was known about its day-to-day operations. He urged the ABA to start researching criminal justice. Once funding for the research was secured, the ABA hired Wisconsin law professor Frank Remington to direct the field observation. Remington worked closely with Lloyd Ohlin, and both researchers shaped the survey and eventual research plan. The survey provided significant insight into real-world criminal justice operations. First, it highlighted the complexity of the criminal justice system. Whereas the progressive view was one of strict law enforcement, the ABF survey ". . . revealed a very different picture, in which the criminal process was used routinely to handle a broad range of social problems including alcohol abuse, mental illness, family difficulties, petty financial disputes, and other miscellaneous matters" (Walker, 1992, p. 67).

The survey also cleared up some misunderstandings concerning the police role. LaFave's (1965) study, which was based on the ABF survey, revealed that policing was more about peacekeeping than crime control. The researchers also discovered pervasive discretionary decision making, both in policing and beyond. In fact, some researchers (e.g., Walker, 1992) feel that the ABF survey's discovery of discretion is its most significant contribution. Decisions by police officers, prosecutors, and other officials appeared to be guided by anything but legal guidelines and organizational controls. Donald Newman's (1966) study on plea bargaining cast light on a phenomenon that progressive reformers totally ignored. The survey also revealed rampant lawlessness on the part of police at the time. The researchers ". . . were struck less by the illegality of so much police behavior than by the sheer fact that so much decision making had so little relationship to law on the books" (Walker, 1992, p. 68).

History Repeats Itself

The ABF survey painted an image of prosecution that was quite different from that envisioned by progressive reformers. For the first time prosecutors were seen as more than just blind enforcers of the law. They weighed the consequences of proceeding with criminal charges, considered alternatives to traditional adjudication, and plea-bargained extensively with the defense. This image was largely replaced, though, with a more contemporary version of the progressive ideal as a result of the 1967 President's Commission on Law Enforcement and the Administration of Justice (1967). The commission identified three prosecutorial functions: "[first] . . . to determine whether an alleged offender should be charged to obtain convictions through guilty plea negotiations . . . [second] the prosecutor has the responsibility of presenting [the] government's case in court . . . [and third] . . . the prosecutor is often an investigator and instigator of the criminal process (President's Commission, 1967, p. 72). In short, prosecutors were regarded as case processors, as enforcers of the law.

There was a measure of overlap between the ABF survey findings and the work of the President's Commission. Remington and his colleagues highlighted the "systemic" nature of criminal justice operations, just as the President's Commission did. Most readers are probably familiar with the commission's diagram depicting the flow of cases through the criminal process. Even so, prosecutors continued to be regarded as processors of criminal cases. The discretion they enjoyed and regularly exercised was played down to some extent as a result of the commission's work. It also is important to recall that the President's Commission was appointed during something of a national crisis over crime and justice. The 1960s saw a surge in crime and attention to it. The Law Enforcement Assistance Administration (LEAA) was formed, and for the first time significant federal funding was dispensed in the name of crime control. These developments added some fuel to the ABF survey fire (e.g., the survey revealed evidence of discrimination in criminal justice administration, which civil rights advocates of the 1960s picked up on), but the image of prosecution presented by the ABF was largely overshadowed by the politics of crime control in the 1960s.

The New Prosecution Paradigm

During the 1960s and 1970s the police came under significant public and legal scrutiny. Citizens were unhappy with the so-called "professional" model of policing, and the Supreme Court reigned in police investigative practices as a result of several important civil rights decisions. Also, policing research during the 1970s revealed that many traditional law enforcement strategies (e.g., reactive patrol) were largely ineffective. Together these developments encouraged the police to find a new strategy (Kelling & Moore, 1988). By the mid-1980s, police had honed in on a crime prevention and problem-solving focus. Decentralization became the word of the day, officers drew extensively on citizens for support and suggestions, and new patrol strategies were put into effect. Prior to the 1980s, police were in the throes of a crisis of legitimacy. The community-policing movement of the 1980s sought to restore a favorable police image.

One may conclude that prosecutors observed what police were up to and then followed suit. While certain prosecutors may have emulated police, there is more behind the emergence of a new prosecution paradigm. For one thing, prosecutors did not face the same threats to their legitimacy that police did; they were not compelled to "change their ways" just to appease the public. To some extent, though, as elected officials, prosecutors became familiar with voters' concerns over crime, especially the crack epidemic of the 1980s. Prosecutors—like the police—also began to learn that traditional case-processing strategies did not work well for all crime types; prosecutors were all too familiar with the "revolving door" concept and set out to identify effective strategies that would help them target seemingly intractable problems. Prosecutors also came to realize that getting tough on crime was not always the most effective approach, that problems were rarely solved by throwing the book at offenders.

Together these reforms signaled a shift toward "strategic" prosecution, emphasizing creative problem solving and collaboration not just with citizens but with other public agencies (an example is "community prosecution," touched upon in two chapters later in this book). Strategic prosecution occurs when the prosecutor views himself or herself as one piece in a larger crime control puzzle. It emphasizes awareness of crime trends, communication, creativity, and cooperation.

Whether the new prosecution paradigm will take hold remains to be seen. Most prosecutors remain case processors. Most aspiring prosecutors still want to litigate cases and send serious criminals to prison. Significantly fewer prosecutors have stepped out of this mold in favor of a new approach. There can be no denying, though, that prosecution is changing. The pressures that prosecutors face today are not necessarily the same as they have always been.

Novel crime problems also pose significant difficulty for prosecutors. Citizens are increasingly clamoring for prosecutors' attention. Organizational pressures, pressures from other governmental entities, and the like are ushering in a number of changes in American prosecution. These changes—more than just community prosecution and problem solving—are the focus of this book.

Prosecution in the International Context

This section offers a brief overview of how prosecution in the United States compares to prosecution abroad. It draws largely on the work of Minoru Shikita (Shikita, 1996), who presented on the subject at the ancillary meeting held at the Ninth United Nations Congress on the Prevention of Crime and the Treatment of Offenders, in Cairo, in 1995. We begin with the structure and organization of prosecution and then consider prosecutorial functions, the public-private prosecution distinction, and differences in prosecutorial discretion across the world.

Structure and Organization

In many countries, the chief prosecutor falls under the ministry of justice or the attorney general. In Thailand, however, the Prosecution Department of the Ministry of the Interior became independent from the attorney general in 1991. It is now directly under the prime minister. And just because a prosecutor's office falls under the ministry of justice does not mean it always answers to the office above it. In Japan, for example, the prosecutor's office comes under the Criminal Affairs Bureau of the ministry of justice, but prosecution is generally in the hands of the prosecutor-general, who leads the Supreme Public Prosecutor's Office, a Cabinet-level agency.

While district attorneys in the United States are elected, prosecutors in many countries are appointed. Throughout Europe and in most Asian countries, prosecutors usually are designated as such by the minister of justice or the president. Of course, the attorney general in the United States is appointed, but prosecutorial appointments are the exception in this country. Interestingly, some countries have started to move away from elections as a means of selecting prosecutors. Some East European countries have abandoned elections in favor of presidential or legislative prosecutorial appointments.

While elected prosecutors in the United States are to serve the constituents who put them there (or, at the least, the "public interest"), prosecutors in European countries most often serve the interests of the state. For example, the crown prosecution system in England and Wales falls under the director of public prosecutions yet operates at the local level with a measure of independence. There are also differences across countries in terms of education and legal qualification requirements for prosecutors. All prosecutors in the United States must be members of the bar in their respective states (or the federal bar), but Germany, England, and some Scandinavian countries permit prosecution by police or police-educated prosecutors, individuals with less than full legal credentials.

It also is important to note that while U.S. prosecutors have gained considerable power over the years, some countries have drastically restricted prosecutorial power. "This is the case particularly in Russia and other former CIS countries (including the Asian republics) where the Prokuratura played an all-powerful role under the Communist system. With its official passage (though bureaucratic vestiges persist)—the adoption of new constitutions, establishment of constitutional courts and major justice reforms—the authority of the Prokuratura has been considerably diminished and efforts are being made to curtail the virtual impunity it enjoyed" (Shikita, 1996, p. 55).

Prosecutorial Functions

The best way to grasp the prosecutorial function between various countries is to compare prosecutorial authority to police authority. In some countries, such as Germany and Korea, prosecutors exercise total control over criminal investigations. In others, such as Japan and the United States, prosecutors enjoy a prominent role in criminal investigation. In fact, district attorneys in the United States often have their own investigators. Still other countries completely separate prosecution from investigation. Examples include England, Indonesia, and Thailand. Police usually are responsible for making arrests, but in some countries prosecutors do so.

Rules of evidence and prosecutors' roles during trial also vary across the world. Prosecutors in the United States can of course subpoena and question witnesses. In other countries, they cannot. In some European systems, for example, written transcripts of testimony can replace oral interrogations. There also are significant differences between countries in terms of prosecutors' say during sentencing proceedings. In most countries, the United States included, prosecutors "advise" judges on sentences. In Japan, however, their recommendations almost always stand. There also are variations in terms of the prosecutor's role in sentence execution. In the United States prosecutors usually wash their hands of sentencing once a recommendation is made to the judge, but that is changing in some areas (as the chapter in this book on Brooklyn's DTAP program attests).

More on Public and Private Prosecution

We have already discussed the movement from private to public prosecution that has played out in this country. For the most part, private prosecution has given way to public prosecution across the globe, but there are exceptions. For example, public prosecutors may waive prosecution in certain cases, perhaps due to a lack of evidence, paving the way for private prosecution. Thailand permits private prosecutions, but only following an intense preliminary hearing on the matter. In other countries, when a prosecutor declines to pursue charges, victims, family members of victims, and other concerned citizens can lodge a complaint in court. Other jurisdictions maintain hybrid models of private and public prosecution. In Finland, for instance, the right to prosecute is shared by a prosecutor and the person harmed. Both individuals assume a prominent role in prosecution, quite opposite of what occurs in the United States.

Despite something of a move away from them, private prosecutions still occur in some European nations.

> In England, every citizen is entitled to initiate criminal proceedings, though it is rarely exercised in practice, and private prosecution occurs mostly in minor cases (e.g., shoplifting) where the police have declined to bring a charge. The French model restricts private prosecution to injured persons, and can combine an 'action civile' for damages with an 'action publique' that initiates criminal prosecution which the prosecutor is required to take over. In the majority of European countries, the injured party may not only initiate public prosecution but may also become a private prosecutor, who investigates a case, brings a charge and participates in the trial. In Sweden and Finland, the injured party may initiate private prosecution whenever the prosecutor declines to bring a charge, but in most others private prosecution is allowed only in the case of a petty offence [sic] affecting personal rather than pecuniary interest. (Shikita, 1996, p. 58)

Discretion

American prosecutors exercise enormous discretion in terms of who gets charged. This discretion, or something closely akin to it, is something prosecutors in many other countries enjoy. While in Japan, for instance, prosecutors cannot offer favorable treatment in return for guilty pleas, they can decide not to go forward with criminal charges. Their decisions are rarely challenged because they are signed off on by a superior. Japan also maintains legislation that can provide compensation for people wrongfully arrested and detained who, in the prosecutor's view, did not commit the crime. Other countries are more restrictive, however. In Korea, suspended prosecution with probation is only found in cases involving juveniles. Thailand and Indonesia have always limited prosecutorial discretion, but case overload and prison crowding have caused them to consider other alternatives. In short, prosecutors are increasingly moving from a "legality" principle of prosecution (charging all violators) to an "opportunity" or "expediency" principle, the latter of which addresses the realities of crime volume in the 21st century (Shikita, 2006).

The Changing Prosecutor

Earlier in this chapter we looked at the evolution of *prosecution*. That is, we examined how prosecution has begun a shift from case processing to problem solving and strategic thinking. We will continue to give attention to changing prosecution throughout this book, particularly in chapter 9. But *prosecutors* also are changing. Indeed, this book's title suggests a focus more on prosecutors than on the act of prosecution.

On one level, it is difficult to separate prosecutors from prosecution. Prosecution could not occur without prosecutors, and prosecutors certainly spend the bulk of their time involved in prosecution (or, more recently, trying to avoid it). At the same time, though, it is critical to view the prosecutor as more than a person who engages in prosecution. Elected district attorneys, for instance, worry about more mundane issues of securing funding and gaining reelection, each of which is only indirectly connected to the actual act of prosecution.

We have assembled a diverse collection of chapters for the reader. At a glance, some of the chapters may seem only remotely connected to each other. Upon closer examination, though, each tells a similar story. That story is the focus of this section. We argue that prosecutors have moved from running a largely "closed shop" to ensuring openness and accountability in their operations.

A Closed Shop

We mentioned that prosecution, in comparison to policing, has received little scholarly attention. This may be due to the visibility of policing vis-à-vis prosecution. It also may be due to an impression that prosecutors have traditionally run "closed shops." For example, there is a sentiment among at least some researchers that prosecutors have not been particularly receptive to sharing their records with members of the academic community. Even if this belief is wrong, it *is* safe to assume that prosecutors have historically isolated themselves from the environment around them. Up until recently, for example, there was little to no cooperation between police and prosecutors. If police brought prosecutors weak cases, then the cases were dismissed. Recent shifts toward community prosecution, however, reveal that prosecutors are learning about the benefits associated with outreach and cooperation.

To put the "closed shop" view in the context of organizational theory, prosecution has traditionally operated as a "closed system" (see, e.g., Katz &

Kahn, 1978, for an introduction to systems theory). This view of organizations regards a system as independent of external environmental influences (e.g., citizen preferences). Rather, closed systems concern themselves with internal operations and functioning, particularly with an eye toward reducing uncertainty. This view was expressed, for example, in Albonetti's (1986, 1987) work on prosecutors' charging decisions. Her argument was that prosecutors avoid uncertainty in their charging decisions by pursuing charges in cases where the odds of securing a conviction are favorable. Traditional performance measures in prosecution also reflect a concern over internal operations (e.g., conviction rates) rather than external pressures and influences.

Toward Openness and Accountability

The open systems view places organizations within a complex environment by which they are affected and with which they must interact. As Katz and Kahn (1978) observed:

> The open-system approach begins by identifying and mapping the repeated cycles of inputs, transformation, output and renewed inputs which comprise organizational patterns. Organizations as a special class of open systems have properties of their own, but they share other properties in common with all open systems. These include the *importation of energy from the environment* [italics added], the through-put or transformation of the imported energy into some product form . . . the exporting of that product into the environment, and the re-energizing of the systems from sources in the environment. (p. 33)

Of particular importance here is the "importation of energy," as well as the transformation and subsequent output of that energy. This is exactly what is happening in prosecution today, on a number of fronts. In the context of public organizations, environmental pressures often are construed to mean those emanating from citizens. Citizens clearly exert pressure on public organizations—and prosecutors' offices. Elected district attorneys, of course, must answer to the voters, but there are numerous other sources of environmental pressure and influence. Sentencing reforms have placed enormous discretionary power in the hands of prosecutors. The specter of terrorism has prompted prosecutors, at the urging of a number of sources, to get "creative" in targeting known and suspected offenders. Prosecutors' frustrations with seeing some of the same offenders (e.g., drug addicts) over and over again have prompted them to identify and implement creative solutions to problems. The pursuit of grants to fund various innovative programs has forced prosecutors to turn their attention outward (e.g., to financial support from community and corporate foundations). The list goes on, but the point is that these reforms would not be taking place but for the increased awareness on prosecutors' parts of what is transpiring *outside* of the courtroom and their office spaces.

Throughout criminal justice, there also is increasing concern with accountability. The move began, arguably, with policing. The civil rights era, coupled with police abuses and scandal, during the 1960s saw the emergence of citizen review commissions, law enforcement accreditation, a number of Supreme Court decisions providing due process protections for suspected criminals, and other reforms. Recently, prosecutors have followed suit, but not necessarily for the same reasons. Strained relations between the police and the public arguably prompted the former to change. Prosecutors have instead begun responding to a growing concern over accountability—particularly financial accountability—that has been evidenced *throughout* government. In an era of concern over runaway government spending and ensuring that tax-payers' dollars are well spent, prosecutors are taking heed. This move also is consistent with an open systems perspective, as it reflects concern with what outsiders prefer.

Connecting the Themes

This book began as a community prosecution book, but then it became apparent that the changing prosecutorial role is much more than a shift from case processing to problem solving and promoting accountability. Case processing remains perhaps the most significant prosecutorial function. Problem solving and accountability are important issues as well. Both must exist in tandem. But there is more. Prosecutors face numerous organizational, political, and legal pressures. They must continually adapt and respond to these. Add to that novel crime problems, collaboration, and stepping outside of the traditional mold of evaluating cases brought to them by the police and the picture becomes even more complex. Accordingly, this book contains several unique chapters providing a *comprehensive* overview of the changing face of prosecution in America. Moreover, in sticking with the closed- versus open-systems view of prosecution just laid out, each chapter provides an example of how environmental pressures are coming to shape the new prosecution.

The new prosecutorial environment. Part 2 introduces readers to what we call the "new prosecutorial environment." It begins with Kay Levine's chapter on the state's role in prosecutorial politics. Levine observes that two seemingly opposing movements have been afoot throughout criminal justice: federalization and community justice. The former is concerned with federal laws increasingly being used to target local criminal problems. Community justice, in contrast, is inherently at the local level and seeks to divorce crime control from sources other than local constituents and stakeholders. Levine, though, highlights another as yet largely ignored source of influence over local prosecution—state government. She concludes that the state, more than prosecutors' constituents or the federal government, shapes office priorities. Her chapter clearly highlights the influence of external factors on prosecutors' activities.

Brian Forst then calls attention to errors of justice, wrongful convictions and wrongful *nonconvictions*. He also discusses the effect that various case screening strategies can have on such errors. On the one hand, Forst couches errors of justice in performance measurement terms by arguing that they are something that should be of as much interest to prosecutors as conviction rates and case processing time. On the other hand, he also points out that egregious errors of justice are sensational, capture headlines, and cause people to cry for reform. This latter view is what prompts Forst to argue that prosecutors should not ignore the potential for justice errors in their pursuits to convict criminals; pressures to mitigate against wrongful convictions (and nonconvictions) emanate, for the most part, from the environment, from observers who regard them as miscarriages of justice.

Rodney L. Engen then takes up sentencing reform and its effects on prosecutorial discretion. Perhaps no other chapter in this book better calls attention to the environment of prosecution. He discusses how sentencing guidelines, mandatory minimums, and habitual offender statutes have removed sentencing discretion from judges and thereby enhanced prosecutors' *charging* discretion. Engen concludes, for example, that prosecutors often reduce the severity of charges in an effort to maintain the status quo. Whether prosecutors influence *sentencing* decisions any more or less than before sentencing reforms, however, remains unclear. In any case, the issues would be effectively moot but for the fact that external reforms have basically forced prosecutors to pick up where judges must now leave off.

M. Elaine Nugent-Borakove then discusses performance measurement, particularly the need for a broader conception of prosecutorial effectiveness. Her argument is that the traditional means of evaluating prosecution performance fails to adequately capture the nature of the prosecutorial role in the 21st century. She argues that prosecutors, besides securing convictions and dispensing justice, also must work toward promoting safe communities, maintaining their integrity, and improving their coordination with other criminal justice agencies. In short, prosecutors need to look beyond convictions. Nugent-Borakove calls for prosecutorial goals that probably would not be of much concern but for public pressure for prosecutors to reduce crime, act responsibly and professionally, run efficient and fiscally responsible offices, and coordinate their enforcement efforts.

Troublesome and emerging crime problems. The view of prosecutors' offices as open systems does not end in part 3 of this book, even though its title, "Prosecuting Troublesome and Emerging Crime Problems," suggests it does. It begins with Steven Belenko and his colleagues' chapter on Brooklyn's Drug Treatment Alternative-to-Prison (DTAP) program, a unique—and apparently effective—prosecutorial response to drug crime. The DTAP program represents a departure from traditional methods of dealing with drug offenders. Indeed, participants in the program are *screened* by prosecutors, thus setting it apart from the drug courts' approach. The chapter once again reflects increasing concern on prosecutors' part with what is happening *outside* of their offices. With respect to drug crime, prosecutors are realizing that they will see the same drug offenders time and again without an effective intervention that addresses the reasons these people offend in the first place.

Scott H. Decker and Jack McDevitt then provide an assessment of President Bush's Project Safe Neighborhoods (PSN) program. They examine PSN in the context of organizational change, noting that traditional prosecution (guided by what they call "legal thinking") stands in contrast to the problem-solving movement of late. Moreover, they show how problem solving is now occurring, due to PSN, in U.S. Attorneys' offices. They also discuss changes in the way particular cases (notably gun cases) are selected for prosecution in light of PSN. Whereas in the past the concern was with conviction rates, the new concern is with achieving the greatest deterrent effect, that is, stopping the problem that gives rise to such cases in the first place. This shift also is consistent with an increasing prosecutorial concern with environmental pressures and forces.

Finally, Robert Chesney discusses issues in the prosecution of terrorists, an important addition in light of recent terrorist attacks both in the United States and abroad. He argues that prosecutors are taking advantage of once largely dormant laws to prevent—rather than to respond to—terrorist attacks. Chesney's chapter is important, in part, because it calls attention to the influence of the U.S. government's antiterrorism policy on prosecution activities. Whereas a commonsense approach to targeting a suspected terrorist might entail surveilling the individual until concrete evidence develops, the Bush administration's approach is one of what Chesney calls "anticipatory prosecution," pursuing charges based on the *potential* for terrorist attacks. This "preventive paradigm," whether it represents the current administration's view, the public's, or both, has caused prosecutors to react. The troublesome problem of terrorism, then, is yet another source of influence in prosecutors' professional lives.

Community prosecution and problem solving. This book would not be complete without some significant attention to community prosecution and its parallels. Part 4 thus begins with Catherine M. Coles's assessment of the evolving strategy of the American prosecutor. The current chapter has already provided a brief overview of the new prosecution paradigm, but Coles explores it in much greater depth.

M. Elaine Nugent-Borakove and Patricia L. Fanflik then review the research on the extent to which community prosecution has gained a foothold across the country. They attempt to separate the rhetoric from the reality, and in so doing they find that prosecutors see themselves as having to fulfill two objectives: case processing and crime prevention. The extent to which one or the other of these goals is prioritized, however, varies between offices.

Both Coles's and Nugent-Borakove's and Fanlik's chapters further call attention to the "open" nature of prosecution of late. Prosecutors have come to realize, as the police have, that traditional, uncreative methods of crime control often fail to make dents in the problem. Prosecutors (and, again, the police) also have learned that private and public partnerships can assist significantly in this regard.

John L. Worrall then provides an assessment of prosecutors in problem-solving courts. The chapter is an important addition to the community prosecution part, because many community prosecution activities play out in specially designated community courts. A number of problem-solving courts operate in communities well removed from centralized courthouses. This close proximity to citizens also is consistent with many of the other developments we have touched upon thus far—and that will receive further attention in this book. Worrall goes on to argue that the broadened prosecutorial role in problem-solving courts is but one example of the "amalgamation of justice," combining several roles and strategies together in the name of crime control. His argument is consistent with the open systems view, too, in that prosecutors are increasingly opening their doors to collaboration and partnership. Domestic violence courts, for instance, often put prosecutors right alongside other criminal justice officials and service providers, a largely unprecedented development.

Part 5 of this book contains one chapter by Judith N. Phelan and Michael D. Schrunk. Phelan has retired from the Multnomah County (Portland, Oregon, area) district attorney's office, but Schrunk is—as of this writing—the elected DA of that jurisdiction. Schrunk is regarded by many as a visionary prosecutor. He was one of the first to adopt various strategies consistent with community prosecution. His office also has implemented a number of other novel prosecution strategies. Phelan and Schrunk's chapter provides a practitioner's assessment of what lies ahead for prosecutors. Toward the end, they point out that "in order for prosecutors to be successful in the problem solving and strategic investment roles they have had to leave the confines of their courthouse offices," further emphasizing that the role of the American prosecutor is indeed changing. "Openness" to partnership, collaboration, information sharing, and reform is indeed the buzzword of the day.

Uncharted Territory: Directions for Future Research

Readers can look between the lines throughout this book for some directions for additional research. Worrall's problem-solving courts chapter, for example, reviews some of the research on their effectiveness. But the literature review is relatively short due to the lack of research in this area—particularly beyond drug courts. Other chapters issue express calls for additional research. The latter part of Engen's chapter is illustrative; much remains to be learned concerning the influence of sentencing reform and its effects on prosecutors. Even so, we also feel it is important to offer up a call for more research at this juncture. Quite frankly, there is much we do not know about prosecutors, and there is even less we know about the changing role of the American prosecutor. A short—and far from an exhaustive—list of questions that researchers may hope to answer (some of which our contributors have asked, and some of which have been the object of at least some research) follows:

1. To what extent are prosecutors' offices changing—across the board—in response to state and federal priorities?
2. What are the social cost implications of errors of justice that are the product of prosecution decisions, including the costs of sanctions that err either on the side of being too lax or too punitive?
3. How might systems of accountability be designed to ensure that the prosecutor's responsibility for errors of justice is adequately monitored?
4. Which one is more influential in terms of judicial or prosecutorial discretion, mandatory sentencing or presumptive sentencing laws?
5. Are new strategies of performance measurement informing prosecutorial decision making with regard to priorities, policies, and practices, thereby making prosecutors more accountable to the public?
6. To what extent is deferred sentencing (and deferred prosecution) effective—particularly beyond the drugs context?
7. Has increased federal involvement in local crime control (e.g., PSN) effectively promoted crime control and prevention?
8. How effective can local prosecutors be with regard to the prevention and/or intervention of terrorism?
9. Is community prosecution continuing to catch on?
10. Is community prosecution effective?
11. Are community courts effective? Homeless courts? Domestic violence courts? Others?
12. Will prosecutors continue to cast a wider net to address public safety, assuming new roles beyond that of a case processor and focusing on issues such as offender reentry, alternatives to incarceration, and strategies for dealing with the mentally ill?

13. Can or will community prosecution and other efforts that move beyond the traditional purview of the prosecutor be sustained in the face of decreasing budgets? If so, how?
14. How will advancements in forensic science and the public's expectation for such science to be available as evidence impact the role of prosecutors?

References

Albonetti, C. (1986). Criminality, prosecutorial screening, and uncertainty: Toward a theory of discretionary decision making in felony case processings. *Criminology*, *24*, 623–644.

Albonetti, C. (1987). Prosecutorial discretion: The effects of uncertainty. *Law and Society Review*, *21*, 291–313.

Argersinger v. Hamlin, 407 U.S. 25 (1972).

Baker, N. (1932). The prosecuting attorney—provisions of organizing a law office. *Journal of Criminal Law and Criminology*, *23*, 926–959.

Cleveland Survey of Criminal Justice. (1922). *Criminal justice in Cleveland*. Cleveland, OH: The Cleveland Foundation.

Davidson, B. (1971). *Indict and convict*. New York: Harper and Row.

Dawson, R. O. (1969). *Sentencing: The decision as to type, length, and conditions of sentence*. Boston: Little, Brown.

Gideon v. Wainwright, 372 U.S. 335 (1963).

Illinois Association for Criminal Justice. (1929). *Illinois crime survey*. Montclair, NJ: Patterson Smith.

Jacoby, J. (1980). *The American prosecutor: A search for identity*. Lexington, MA: Lexington Books.

Katz, D., & Kahn, R. L. (1978). *The social psychology of organizations* (2nd ed.). New York: Wiley.

Kelling, G. L., & Moore, M. H. (1988, November). The evolving strategy of policing. *Perspectives on Policing*, 4. National Institute of Justice, U.S. Department of Justice, and the Program in Criminal Justice Policy and Management, John F. Kennedy School of Government, Harvard University. Retrieved from http://www.ksg.harvard.edu/criminaljustice/research/community_policing.htm.

Kress, J. M. (1976). Progress and prosecution. *Annals of the American Academy of Political and Social Sciences*, *423*, 99–116.

LaFave, W. R. (1965). *Arrest: The decision to take the suspect into custody*. Boston: Little, Brown.

Mallery v. Lane, 97 Conn. 132 (1921).

Mayers, L. (1964). *The American legal system*. New York: Harper and Row.

McIntyre, D. M. Jr. (1967). *Law enforcement in the metropolis*. Chicago: American Bar Foundation.

Miller, F. (1969). *Prosecution: The decision to charge a suspect with a crime*. Boston: Little, Brown.

Milliken v. Stone, 7 F.2d 397 (S.D. N.Y. 1925).

Miranda v. Arizona, 384 U.S. 436 (1966).

Missouri Crime Survey. (1926). *The Missouri crime survey*. New York: Macmillan.

National Association of Attorneys General. (1971). *Report on the office of the attorney general*. Raleigh, NC: The National Association of Attorneys General.

National Commission on Law Observance and Enforcement. (1931a). *Report on prosecution*. Washington, DC: U.S. Government Printing Office.

National Commission on Law Observance and Enforcement. (1931b). *Reports*. Washington, DC: U.S. Government Printing Office.

Newman, D. J. (1966). Conviction: The determination of guilt or innocence without trial. Boston: Little, Brown.

People v. Adams, 117 Cal. Rptr. 905 (1974).

People v. Berlin, 361 N.Y.S. 2d 114 (1974).

People v. Wabash, St. Louis and Pacific Railway, 12 Ill. App. 263 (1883).

Powell v. Alabama, 287 U.S. 45 (1932).

President's Commission on Law Enforcement and the Administration of Justice. (1967). *Task force report: The courts*. Washington, DC: U.S. Government Printing Office.

Remington, F. (1956). Survey of the administration of justice. *National Probation and Parole Association Journal, 2*, 260–265.

Remington, F., Newman, D. J., Kimball, E. L., Merci, M., & Goldstein, H. (1969). *Criminal justice administration: Materials and cases*. Indianapolis, IN: Bobbs-Merrill.

Shikita, M. (1996). The role of the public prosecutor in a changing world. In J. de Figueiredo Dias, G. Di. Federico, R. Ottenhof, J. F. Renucci, L. C. Henry, & M. Shikita (Eds.), *The role of the public prosecutor in criminal justice, according to different constitutional systems* (pp. 49–71). Bologna, Italy. Reports presented to the ancillary meeting held at the Ninth United Nations Congress on the Prevention of Crime and the Treatment of Offenders, Cairo, May 4, 1995.

Skogan, W. G. (1977). The changing distribution of big-city crime: A multi-city time-series analysis. *Urban Affairs Quarterly, 13*, 33–48.

State v. LeVien, 44 N.J. 323 (1965).

Surrency, E. (1967). The courts in the American colonies. *American Journal of Legal History, 11*, 253–276.

Van Alstyne, W. S. (1952). The district attorney—a historical puzzle. *Wisconsin Law Review, 11(3)*, 125–138.

Walker, S. (1980). *Popular justice: A history of American criminal justice.* New York: Oxford University Press.

Walker, S. (1992). Origins of the contemporary criminal justice paradigm: The American Bar Foundations survey, 1953–1969. *Justice Quarterly, 9,* 47–76.

Wilson v. County of Marshall, 257 Ill. App. 220 (1930).

PART II

The New
Prosecutorial Environment

Chapter Two

The State's Role in Prosecutorial Politics

KAY LEVINE

Introduction

Within the American federalist system of government, crime and crime control have long been regarded as quintessentially state concerns. State legislatures enact most of the criminal laws that govern our citizenry, and state penal institutions house most of the current population of incarcerated felons. Supplementing the myriad statewide penal codes and criminal statutes that identify the outer boundaries of the criminal law, counties and cities add texture through municipal ordinances, codes, and regulations. The provincial nature of the formal law mirrors that of crime itself, as well as the demographics of criminal court actors: most offenders commit crimes in their own backyards, their crimes produce the most direct effects on the communities in which they occur, and the prosecutors and judges who handle their cases are mostly public officials who answer to the local electorate (Jacoby, 1980; Baker, 1985, 1999). For these reasons, Americans have traditionally viewed the state as having primary jurisdiction over crime and criminal justice issues.

In the late 20th century two developments began to challenge this conventional allocation of power in the prosecution of crime. The first of these trends, federalization, refers to the increasing tendency of the federal government to enact and enforce criminal statutes that significantly duplicate existing state laws. The second phenomenon is the "community" approach to prosecution, which encourages local officials to prioritize local community issues rather than statewide criminal laws, in their interpretation of the prosecutor's role. Notably, these trends point in opposite directions in their respective assessments of which sovereign can best control crime—federalization suggests that the federal government is the proper site of criminal law and policy because crime is a national problem (Ashdown, 1996; Brickey, 1995), while community prosecutors emphasize that the neighborhood should be the primary source of authority for law enforcement, resource allocation, and innovation because crime is mostly a local issue (Thompson, 2002; Coles, 2002). In the wake of federalization and community prosecution, the intermediate jurisdiction—the state—seems to have become both too large and too small of a territory to control crime effectively.

In this chapter, I investigate whether the image of state weakness suggested by these developments comports with reality. I argue that while escalating drives for power at the federal and local levels certainly merit our attention, the state's ability in these changing times to maintain its position, and even to augment its authority, should not be underestimated. Despite (and alongside) federal and local initiatives, a sufficiently motivated state can continue to claim for itself an important role in dictating crime control priorities.[1]

Evidence of expanding state power can be found in the development of state-funded units in county prosecutors' offices. While such ventures exist in many states in the United States, I use California as my case study, as it has cultivated an advanced and a diverse system of state-funded prosecutorial programs over the past several decades. Furthermore, California has long been regarded as a trendsetter in the criminal justice arena, and its economy and justice system are among the largest in the nation (if not the world). Hence, an analysis of what California's government is doing offers insights into broader trends that are likely to emerge on a national scale in the near future.

In the standard model of crime control, the state is the source of formal penal legislation, but enforcement is determined exclusively by local prosecutors guided by community priorities and resources. State-funded prosecution units give the state government a much larger role in local enforcement than the standard model envisions. These programs provide state money to county prosecutors to prosecute aggressively, in their home districts, crimes that the state designates as high priority. But the money comes with strings attached; county prosecutors who receive grants must follow state-established rules for filing, court appearances, plea bargaining, and record keeping. A county that fails to comply with the rules of the program risks losing future monetary support from the state. Hence, in addition to enacting the formal criminal laws that county prosecutors enforce in their respective jurisdictions, a state using the grant-funded prosecution model can structure local enforcement in accordance with state mandates.

When state-funded enterprises emerge in response to grassroots organizing about salient local problems, they do not produce tension between state and community priorities and do not necessarily signal a power grab by the state. But where state initiatives arise without any urging from local officials, as was the case with California's Statutory Rape Vertical Prosecution Program, the state takes on a vastly different role vis-à-vis its municipal governments. When it seeks to increase prosecution of a crime that it *unilaterally* deems important, the state dangles funds as carrots in return for compliance with state mandates, knowing that counties are in no position to refuse. The state thereby assumes the lead in setting both statewide crime control priorities and local enforcement agendas.

The history of the state-funded prosecution unit, and of the statutory rape program in particular, signals the importance of including the state in any discussion of how crime policies form or why they succeed (or fail). The state can contribute to crime control by supporting local or federal initiatives, but it also can forcefully persuade localities to serve broader agendas. In either event, accounts of policy change that focus exclusively on the actions or rhetoric of one political entity (such as the federal government or the community) are sure to miss the contributions of other political actors (such as the state) and thereby paint an incomplete, imprecise, or improperly generalized portrait of how crime policies emerge and change over time.

The argument proceeds as follows. I first briefly explain the potential encroachments on state authority posed by federalization and community prosecution trends. I then introduce the state-funded vertical prosecution programs as signs of robust state involvement in criminal justice enterprises. I next discuss how the emergence and workings of the Statutory Rape Vertical Prosecution Program illustrate a state government's ability to usurp power from municipalities to serve state ends. I conclude by reflecting on the interplay between local, state, and federal crime policies for the local prosecutor in the 21st century.

Signs of a Weakening State:
Federalization and the Community Prosecution Movement

Prosecution scholar Joan Jacoby argues that the American prosecutor has had a distinctive history, serving as a "local represent[ative] applying local standards to the enforcement of essentially local laws" (Jacoby, 1980, p. 38). The American prosecutor's parochial nature sets him apart from his European precursors, who were likely to serve national authorities and to be organized along national ministries of justice (Jacoby, 1980, p. 20).[2] Today, the vast majority of American prosecutors are elected state-, county-, or city-level officials who possess the authority to prosecute state-designated crimes within specified geographical limits, and most criminal prosecutions are of state, rather than federal, origin (Misner, 1996).

Two recent trends have complicated the picture of predominantly state-designated but locally enforced crimes in American criminal justice: federalization and community prosecution. Federalization targets the balance of power between the state and the federal government with respect to crime control authority, while community prosecution challenges the boundary between the state and its municipalities. Each of these developments is explained later.

Federalization, the enactment of federal criminal legislation to address behaviors traditionally viewed as state violations, emerged as a hot-button issue when 20th-century legal scholars and practitioners observed increasingly frequent congressional activity in the criminal justice area. By the end of the century, the number of federal crimes had grown from a relative handful to several thousand, with more than 40% of those new laws enacted since 1970 (American Bar Association, 1998, p. 7; Maroney, 2000, p. 1327). For proponents of federalization, the impetus to federalize criminal conduct stems from the nature of crime itself. Crime transcends individual state borders because of the inherent mobility of criminals and the ease of moving the tools and spoils of crime vast distances in a short time (Ashdown, 1996, pp. 790–792; Brickey, 1995, pp. 1141–1142). As limited geographic jurisdictional units, states are ill suited to handle problems that extend beyond their borders; thus, proponents assert, crime control must follow a national approach in order to make headway. Moreover, by enacting federal legislation, Congress is simply responding to public clamor that *something* be done about crime (Baker, 1999, p. 679, 1985, p. 518).

Federalization has become controversial because much of the new federal legislation duplicates existing state laws. Federal prohibitions against carjacking, possession of firearms, drug manufacturing, failure to pay child support, and domestic violence are frequently cited as examples of this overlap (see, e.g., Ashdown, 1996, p. 793). As a result of this legislation, U.S. attorneys can prosecute traditionally "state" crimes in federal courts, which are presumably better equipped than state courts to obtain convictions and to impose lengthy sentences.[3] Yet opponents of federalization claim that the dual jurisdictional nature of most federal crimes and the heightened funding of federal agencies lead to widespread pilfering, or at least cherry-picking, by U.S. attorneys, leaving county prosecutors with the dregs of most caseloads (see, e.g., Baker, 1999, p. 681; American Bar Assocation, 1998, pp. 35, 40).[4] Federal prosecutions of crimes that otherwise belong in state courts thus raise concerns about preemption, discrimination, unwarranted competition, diminishing federalism, and inefficiency (Little, 1995; Kadish, 1995; Beale, 2005; Ashdown, 1996; Baker, 1999).[5]

In contrast to the "crime is national problem" perspective fostered by the federalization phenomenon, the community prosecution movement motivates prosecutors to think of criminal justice issues as, first and foremost, local concerns. While the contours of the term "community prosecution" remain somewhat unspecified (Thompson, 2002; Gramckow, 1997; Coles, 2002), at the very least it connotes "a decentralization of authority and accountability, with the ultimate aim of enabling an office to anticipate and respond to community problems" (Thompson, 2002, p. 323). County prosecutors following this model regard themselves primarily as members of the district in which they practice, rather than as agents of a large criminal justice bureaucracy. For example, Coles, in her study of community prosecution offices in various U.S. cities (2002, p. 4) observed that community prosecutors view and portray themselves "not [as] elected officials solely from an entire county or state; they are . . . accountable to citizens in specific neighborhoods or locales." Toward that end, they often establish neighborhood offices, forge partnerships with neighborhood service agencies, and host neighborhood meetings and events, all to increase their accessibility to the members of the community (Wolf, 2000a & 2000b; Thompson, 2002, p. 346; Coles, 2002, pp. 6–7; Wolf & Campbell, 2004, pp. 7–12). Moreover, although state penal codes and conventional adversarial techniques remain important components of the community prosecutor's arsenal, other tools and approaches may be used to address local issues (Coles, 2002, pp. 5–6; Wolf & Campbell, 2004, p. 14). For example, community prosecutors "place an emphasis on preventative measures for controlling crime instead of the reactive, case-driven approaches that characterize traditional prosecution efforts" (Thompson, 2002, pp. 323–324) and focus on quality-of-life offenses, not just serious felonies (Coles, 2002, p. 4). Community-based prosecution efforts thus can reverse the distancing tendency of the conventional American prosecutor (Thompson, 2002, p. 329), as they invite officials to substitute involvement for independence and to gain a deeper understanding of the crime problems that plague the regions they represent (Gramckow, 1997, p. 10; Alexander, 2000; Wolf, 2000a & 2000b).

A word of caution is in order. Despite the moniker, community prosecution does not signal the community gaining control over the prosecutor's office (beyond the ability to vote in the next election).[6] Virtually all of the community prosecution programs studied by scholars were implemented unilaterally by the chief prosecutor of the jurisdiction,[7] and therefore in all likelihood they could be eliminated if times and priorities change.

Both federalization and community prosecution, as conceived in the literature, stand to produce marked effects on a state's ability, and perceived ability, to handle crime within its borders. The threat to a state posed by federalization has been described thusly:

> Inappropriate federalization undermines the critical role of the states and
> their courts, which are constitutionally given the primary role of dealing
> with crime and which, after all, carry the overwhelming criminal case
> workload. This can lead to a notable diminution of the stature of state
> courts in the perception of citizens. . . . The unfortunate premise . . . is
> that the states are not capable of adequately handling important matters.
> (American Bar Assocation, 1998, p. 26)

Moreover, each new federal crime and concomitant federal prosecution
expands the power of the federal government vis-à-vis the states. Critics
charge that this usurpation of power, if unwarranted, undermines the federalist governmental system envisioned by the constitutional framers and ignores
long-standing public resistance to centralized police power in this country
(American Bar Association, 1998, pp. 27, 32; Baker, 1999). Federalization also
reduces the ability of the local citizenry to become involved in the setting of
criminal justice policies in their home regions. Because federal prosecutors are
appointed rather than elected, citizens of the state from which the prosecution
originates cannot hold them politically accountable. In comparison to county
prosecutors, then, U.S. Attorneys are likely to be less accessible, less involved
with, and less responsive to the populations of the states in which they work.
For all of these reasons, the increasing use of federal statutes and federal prosecutions to address state crime problems may lead the citizenry to underestimate a state's ability and willingness to manage its own criminal justice affairs.
    Community prosecution similarly downplays the contributions of the
state in the crime control arena. With its emphasis on neighborhood crime and
backyard conflicts, the community prosecution movement implicitly (and
sometimes explicitly) suggests that state authorities cannot respond to local
needs. Coles's observation (2002, p. 4), that community prosecutors actively
shape their public image as officials who are "accountable to citizens in specific
neighborhoods or locales," and *not* "elected officials . . . from an entire county
or state," aptly demonstrates this point. A prosecutor can only have one focus,
the state or the community; if her or his focus is the community, then the state
necessarily recedes in importance. The posited dichotomy between state and
community also suggests that prosecutors who concentrate on the state auto-
matically subordinate the community's interests, which likely accounts for at
least some dissatisfaction with the conventional model of prosecution.
    Both federalization and community prosecution appear to have taken
root, thereby signaling an increase in power for federal and municipal officials at the expense of the state. But this portrait of the new world order is
incomplete. Although these two trends call into question the ability of the
state as a criminal justice policy maker, they have not entirely kicked the state
out of the game.

Signs of a Robust State:
State-Funded Prosecution Programs

Despite predictions from the federalization and community prosecution literature, the states continue to be heavily engaged in crime control efforts. For example, the empirical data about dual jurisdictional crimes suggest that the pilfering claim raised by federalization opponents is vastly overstated. During recent decades of active federalization, states experienced a parallel increase in criminal case filings and enforcement activity for some of the federalized crimes (Brickey, 1995, p. 1160), and other crimes have remained exclusively state-prosecuted due to a complete lack of federal enforcement (Little, 1995, pp. 1040–1047; Maroney, 2000, pp. 1353–1359; American Bar Assocation, 1998, p. 20).[8] Community prosecution's claims about the state's neglect of local affairs are similarly exaggerated. Even in offices following the standard prosecution model, many prosecutors have devoted time and effort to developing community contacts and to working with community leaders (Gramckow, 1997, p. 11). Furthermore, community prosecution initiatives sometimes receive state or federal support (or funding), which signals enthusiasm at all stages of government for collaborative efforts to improve services to constituents at the local level (Coles, 2002, pp. 15, 23–27; Wolf, 2000a & 2000b, p. 2).

Yet the evidence of state activity extends beyond the antifederalization or cooperative community spheres. As citizens across the country have clamored for more responsive justice officials and have demanded that something be done about crime in their environment, states, like the federal government and many municipalities, have engineered new initiatives to help bring crime under control. While one might analyze this phenomenon in the context of newly enacted state sentencing schemes (see, e.g., Miethe, 1987–1988; Shepherd, in press), this chapter explores state involvement at a much earlier point on the crime control spectrum—the prosecution effort itself.

Scholars have long noted that state political institutions can drive social policies, particularly those used to maintain the social order (Yates & Fording, 2005, p. 1102). State-directed prosecutorial efforts are an example of this approach, as they encourage local district attorneys to prosecute crimes in their home districts using state money and in furtherance of state-identified priorities.[9] In the absence of this sort of program, typically 90% of local prosecution costs is funded exclusively with local money (Misner, 1996). In short, when jurisdictions are faced with huge numbers of crimes and political pressures to bring crime under control, state funds can make a big difference in local officials' ability to handle their caseloads.

While state-funded prosecution ventures have sprung up across the United States,[10] California has developed one of the most extensive networks of programs in the country. Since around 1980, it has initiated and funded units in county prosecution offices to address many kinds of criminal behavior and various forms of social harm. The list includes career criminals, gangs, rural crime, auto theft, narcotic sales, elder abuse, domestic violence, child abuse, and statutory rape. While the topics vary, the programs generally emerge from a common set of origins and follow a similar developmental path.

The establishment of a state-funded local prosecution program officially begins when the legislature or governor declares the target crime a high priority, which often includes identifying the target criminals as "a clear and present danger to the mental health and physical well-being" of California's citizenry (see, e.g., California Penal Code, section 999q, regarding the formation of the child abuser program, in California Penal Code, 2006). Following a declaration of this type, the legislature authorizes the disbursement of state funds for "enhanced prosecution efforts," which typically includes vertical representation, assignment of highly qualified investigators and prosecutors, significant caseload reduction, and resources for improved victim and witness services (see, e.g., California Penal Code, section 13826.2, establishing the gang unit program, in ???). The term "vertical prosecution" instructs specialized units, in contrast to conventional prosecution models, to prioritize consistency in personnel. While nonunit prosecutors pass case files around the office, the vertical prosecutor should handle a case himself or herself from filing through sentencing. This approach, along with the experience threshold for prosecutors assigned to vertical units, is meant to ensure that unit cases receive professional, sensitive treatment and to signal that the state now recognizes the crime as a high priority (Honomichi, Noble, & Bonnell, 2002).

Crimes that become subject to state-sponsored prosecution efforts are usually those whose enforcement the community (or some segment thereof) perceives is ineffective, despite preexisting legislation prohibiting the behavior. In 1998, for example, California started its Elder Abuse Program to invigorate prosecution of elder abuse crimes identified in legislation enacted more than a decade earlier (Santo, 2000, pp. 813–814; Greenwood, 2001). In the late 1990s, press reports of elder abuse became too frequent (and horrific) for legislatures to ignore, and commentators began to call for the state to fund its legislative aspirations (ibid.). After declaring that "crimes against elders and dependent adults are worthy of special consideration and protection" (California Penal Code, chapter 936, in ???), the legislature stiffened the penalties for crimes against elders, expanded reportable categories of abuse, and created and funded special prosecution units to augment enforcement efforts. While the elder abuse vertical prosecution concept began in one pilot county, state-funded units soon emerged in counties throughout California.

California's approach to funding local prosecution efforts is modeled on the plan that the federal Law Enforcement Assistance Administration

(LEAA) used several decades before to encourage state development in the crime control arena (Phillips & Cartwright, 1980; Feeley & Sarat, 1980).[11] Like the LEAA initiative, California does not typically fund every jurisdiction that applies for money; most of the grant programs are run on a competitive basis, with only a limited number of grants awarded in each funding cycle (see, e.g., Honomichi, Noble, & Bonnell, 2002; Phillips & Cartwright, 1980). Consequently, a county in pursuit of a grant has to articulate, cogently and persuasively, its particular need for the money; that is, the county district attorney has to convince Sacramento that the state-identified, high-priority crime is a particularly thorny problem in her or his region.

While counties can use grant funds to hire personnel, buy equipment, or restructure their case handling practices, they must agree to a series of terms and conditions in exchange for the money. The terms of agreement include, among other things, following the vertical prosecution model, prioritizing the categories of offenses identified by the grant, and keeping statistics on the facts and participants of crimes reported, cases filed, dispositions, victim services, costs, and general operations (ibid.; also see Couillard, 1998, p. 125). Attendance at annual or semi-annual statewide meetings and training sessions also may be required. Failure to comply with these terms and conditions may subject a derelict county to termination; at the very least, the county's chances for renewal in the next budget cycle will significantly drop, as many other counties are desperate for the money (Honomichi, Noble, & Bonnell, 2002).

While some variation in case-management practices exists in the pool of grant-funded counties (Phillips & Cartwright, 1980), the state officials who run these ventures strive to coordinate prosecution efforts on a statewide basis and to achieve some level of consistency in case handling (Levine, 2006). State-level bureaucrats who supervise the programs collect and review the county-level data, organize statewide meetings of grant recipients, and distribute literature to all involved counties informing them of acceptable and exceptional practices (ibid.). Moreover, continued press attention (often sponsored by the state) and the allocation of earmarked funds to accelerate enforcement virtually ensure that the number of arrests, complaints, and convictions will grow following the implementation of the new program; these increases in turn validate state officials' claims about the pervasiveness of the target crime and the inadequacy of previous enforcement efforts. Future requests for funding from the legislature thus become noncontroversial, as the programs appear to be absolute necessities in the state's war against crime.

When a state-funded program emerges in response to community concern about the criminal justice system's neglect of a salient local problem, the local DA is likely to regard the initiative as a welcome intervention. For example, the rural crime units in California's Central Valley originated after farmers voiced significant complaints about the impact of unprosecuted thefts of

State and local working together

farm equipment and inventories on the ability of their farms to succeed economically (Couillard, 1998). In 1996, a California assemblyman from this region, with help from the district attorney of Tulare County (one of California's predominantly agricultural counties), introduced a bill to establish the Rural Crime Prevention and Prosecution Model Program. The bill's preamble declared that "no law enforcement agency in the state had a program specially designed to detect or to monitor agricultural criminal activities," and that local law enforcement agencies lacked "the jurisdictional authority, investigative facilities [and] data systems to coordinate a comprehensive approach to the state's agricultural crime problem" (Couillard, 1998, pp. 124–125, quoting California Penal Code, section 14170, in ???). The sponsors contended that state funding could correct for these deficits by providing counties with rural crime prosecutors, training for law enforcement, and community education services.

Once this bill became law, the state sent approximately $1 million to the Tulare County District Attorney's Office to fund the program for three years. At the end of that period, the program was extended to seven other rural counties at a cost of more than $3.5 million; in 2002, it was renamed and refunded to the tune of $3 million annually (Central Valley Rural Crime Prevention Program, 2006). This program has been declared a stunning success, as the recovery rate for rural theft is more than double the rate for general property crimes in the state (SB 453, 2005). Moreover, the residents of California's Central Valley now receive from local law enforcement much-needed assistance with security and maintenance of their farm equipment, support that they had requested for years (Office of Justice Programs, 1999).

The state-funded vertical prosecution endeavor is, in short, evidence that the state remains an active player in the crime control enterprise. Typically these programs address an issue of widespread concern (such as career criminals, elder abuse, or drug sales), where local or regional enforcement efforts have fallen short. By funding county prosecutions of designated crimes, the legislature encourages vigorous local enforcement efforts and manifests its intent to make these crimes a statewide priority. State funding also ensures that more crimes will be uncovered and prosecuted throughout the state, which validates the state's claim that the target crimes are rampant and require aggressive prosecution to be brought under control. While there is a risk that the state will co-opt some of a county's decision-making authority through its mandated record-keeping procedures and grant applications, for many of these crimes the state priorities likely align with those of the counties. In that event, state funding allows the counties to accomplish state and local goals simultaneously. Finally, to the extent that many of the vertical prosecution defendants ultimately are incarcerated in state prison rather than county jail (a prediction consistent with the high priority status accorded to their crimes), cooperation between state and local authorities in their apprehension and prosecution makes sense.

Not all of California's state-funded ventures have followed this trajectory. The pages that follow describe the onset of the Statutory Rape Vertical Prosecution Program (SRVPP), which developed entirely at the state level and was imposed on county prosecutors who did not uniformly agree with its message and on communities who faced far more serious threats to security. The history of this program demonstrates that the state's role in crime policy is neither static nor consistent; like other sovereigns, its response to a given crime can swell or shrink in accordance with politics, personalities, and timing.

Signs of an Imperial State:
The Statutory Rape Vertical Prosecution Program

Following the sexual revolution of the 1960s and 1970s, the statutory rape law was a virtual dead letter throughout most U.S. jurisdictions, including California. But in 1995, former California governor Pete Wilson instigated a statewide campaign to turn statutory rape into a real and serious crime, a program that included creating state-funded prosecution units in every county. For most of California's cash-strapped counties, the offer of state money was too good to refuse, even for robust enforcement of a crime that most still regarded as insignificant. The development of the SRVPP thus merits a closer look, for it reveals a far more proactive and aggressive state than the prior sections of this chapter suggest, and it signals the importance of paying close attention to the precise combination of circumstances and actors driving any given policy change.

As I have explained in more detail elsewhere (Levine, 2003, 2005), policy makers in California and across the United States became concerned in the late 1980s about two alarming trends: the growing number of teenage mothers and the rising percentage of Aid to Families with Dependent Children (AFDC) recipients, especially teens, who appeared to remain on welfare for years. When several early 1990s' studies showed adult men to be the fathers of a significant percentage of the babies born to teens on welfare, the governor seized upon the preexisting statutory rape law as the answer to his state's woes. According to the governor, aggressive enforcement of the statutory rape law promised a trifecta of policy benefits: men would refrain from having intercourse with underage girls for fear of prosecution, the number of teenage girls becoming pregnant and seeking welfare would drop, and the state would be able to collect child support from those men foolish enough to sire children without marrying their mothers.

Throughout the spring and summer of 1995, the governor's office began releasing press statements to link lax enforcement of statutory rape with the teenage pregnancy/welfare crises (Levine, 2005, pp. 1134–1137). He then asked the legislature to appropriate $12 million to create the Partnership for Responsible Parenting, a comprehensive, statewide campaign incorporating both pregnancy prevention and male responsibility initiatives. Specialized vertical prosecution units, suggested by two high-level employees of the Governor's Office of Criminal Justice Planning as the key to transforming statutory rape from a low-priority crime to a high-priority crime (Levine, 2005, p. 1136, n. 24), soon became the centerpiece of the Partnership's male responsibility branch.

Yet when the governor announced in a radio address to the public, "[If you] get a teenager pregnant . . . we'll give you a year to think about it in county jail[,]" (see Gleick, 1996), most local prosecutors had to decide whether and how to operationalize this decree in their home districts. There had been no grassroots organizing at the county level for increased attention to this crime, and some prosecutors openly disagreed with the governor's plan to elevate statutory rape to high-priority status. Moreover, many local DAs were simply not prepared to incarcerate all statutory rapists for a year; they doubted that the county jails could handle this surge in population and did not believe that such a severe punishment was warranted in all cases (Levine, 2006).

Nonetheless, for almost all of California's counties, the offer of state money was too generous to ignore. Many county prosecutors' offices were operating on tight budgets and were in desperate need of additional resources. The grant funds would allow them to hire additional prosecutors, investigators, and/or victim advocates (Bonnell et al., 2001), some of whose time could be spent (unofficially) on other cases too. Some counties saw the funds as a way to buy cars or other office equipment to assist with investigations and prosecutions more generally (Levine, 2003). Even the record-keeping requirements, though a nuisance, did not amount to much of a deterrent.

For these reasons, even those prosecutors who personally and professionally regarded statutory rape as an insignificant crime in their jurisdictions accepted the program's money. Thus within one year the SRVPP grew from a pilot operation to a statewide venture, with the legislature authorizing more than $8 million annually to fund vertical prosecution units in any county that applied for a grant (ibid., 1138–1139; Bonnell et al., 2001).[12] All but two of California's 58 counties took the bait.

Through the SRVPP, the state transformed local enforcement strategies for age-of-consent crimes committed anywhere and everywhere in California. The program generated dramatic expansions in the numbers of arrests, prosecutions, and convictions of statutory rapists during the first few years of its operation, and the state experienced a fourfold increase in filing and conviction rates during the program's heydey (Bonnell et al., 2001; Levine, 2003,

2005). Within just a few years, statutory rape had gone from dead-letter status to a major crime, just as Wilson had planned.

While supporters sometimes claim that the program's success derives from its protection of community interests and response to community concerns, the SRVPP has always been a state-engineered and state-controlled enterprise. Its designers resided at the state level, and grant recipients must answer to state, rather than local, demands. For example, the state decides which cases, among the many crimes involving sexual activity with teenage victims, can be prosecuted with grant funds.[13] Under the original pregnancy/welfare rationale for the program, the state instructed that grant funds could only support prosecutions of adult males whose victims were female, and preferably females who were pregnant with or parenting the defendant's child (and among those, preferably teens who had applied for welfare because of that child) (Governor's Office of Criminal Justice Planning, 1997). Prosecutors soon became frustrated with the narrow conception of statutory rape embedded in this rationale, as they saw teens of both genders exploited by adults of both genders in ways that did not involve pregnancy and abandonment to welfare. Yet they were not allowed to use grant funds to address these cases (which generally meant the cases were not prosecuted) until Sacramento decided that the SRVPP should change its rationale to sexual exploitation, a concept that covers many forms of abuse and nontraditional gender dyads (Levine, 2003, 2006; Governor's Office of Criminal Justice Planning, 2001).

Moreover, the infrastructure of the program builds upon its state-level origins. In addition to collecting county-level data about cases and defendants, the state organizes annual conferences and distributes both informational and promotional literature to grant recipients to inform them of each other's practices, pitfalls, and successes. These activities suggest that the state is striving for a high level of consistency in county approaches to statutory rape, a strategy that leads to the valuation and promotion of the most aggressive enforcement techniques in order to suppress the remnants of statutory rape's dead-letter past. For example, many prosecutors reveal stories in private that they are not willing to share with their peers or with state representatives for fear of appearing too lenient or not committed to the program. Others consciously structure their quarterly and annual reports to highlight their most aggravated cases and most extreme sentencing outcomes, thereby making themselves appear to be overachievers in the program (Levine, 2003). Maintaining an image of unified vigor is critical to the success of the SRVPP, as a crime that was once universally disregarded cannot truly become a high priority unless change is consistently made. Independent or discretionary approaches at the county level, because they threaten the integrity of the state's message, must be sacrificed or downplayed.

The statutory rape program thus significantly differs from many of the other state-funded programs that were developed both before and after. It has a distinctly state, rather than local, flavor, both because it originated in Sacramento and because its longevity depends on the maintenance of a statewide image of the target crime. By its very nature, then, the SRVPP underscores the complex and highly contextual nature of criminal justice policy, causing us to reexamine the relationships between a state and its subdivisions and to play close attention to which entity actually controls policy changes.

Conclusion

I have attempted in this chapter to refocus attention on the contributions made by the state, as a jurisdictional entity, to crime policy. While the federalization and community prosecution literature suggests that the state may have lost strength in the crime control arena, state-funded prosecutorial programs contradict that image. States regularly identify and support local enforcement of high-priority crimes, while special efforts such as the SRVPP reveal that states have retained some activist tendencies as well. A state government that is sufficiently motivated and flush with available resources can design and deploy its own criminal justice policies to override individual community preferences. Faced with this evidence of state engagement, one cannot coherently discuss crime policy without recognizing that the state is an important political actor, capable of exercising its political will to accomplish its priorities.

The history of the statutory rape program tells another, larger story too. We cannot discern who is calling the shots on policy change just by looking at aggregate data on enforcement patterns. While some state-sponsored prosecution programs derive from local initiatives and ideas, some—such as the statutory rape program—have their roots in the governor's mansion or the state capitol; others may have been first conceived in Washington. While the end results (in terms of documented changes in conviction rates) might appear similar no matter which entity is at the helm, to truly understand how crime policies work we must investigate their origins; nuanced understanding of enforcement trends requires us to look for and to acknowledge the potential contributions made by governmental entities at *all* levels. Additionally, the particular combination of efforts, funding, and politics may differ depending on the crime, the jurisdiction, the personnel, and the time period at issue—who pushes for change and when (let alone why) are not inquiries susceptible to "one-size-fits-all" answers.

Looking more broadly, in an era where "get tough on crime" has become the rallying cry of every major U.S. political party, and funding for criminal justice programs remains steady, enthusiasm for approaches that promise stricter enforcement seems limitless. This is an environment in which any jurisdiction can get into the crime control game, and where initiatives at any level have the capacity to nurture and inspire, as well as to preempt and discourage, innovation by others. State-funded prosecutorial programs, community prosecution offices, and federal prosecutions of local crimes thus should be viewed as a web of social control techniques rather than as signs of an active rivalry between competitive sovereigns. Crime control is not a zero-sum game; in an era of ever-expanding resources for law and order institutions, there is more than enough power to go around.

Notes

1. In this chapter I make no normative claims about the proper allocation of power between sovereigns. My aim is simply to illustrate the ways in which the state appears to be holding its ground against federal and local initiatives, and to argue that states should not be left out of conversations about crime policy innovations.

2. Prosecution in many modern civil law countries remains organized along national lines, with tightly centralized bureaucracies and uniform training of prosecutors and judges (Levine & Feeley, 2001).

3. In 1997, for example, only 5% of federal prosecutions involved federal statutes that did not duplicate state statutes (American Bar Association, 1998, p. 23).

4. Ironically, the ABA Task Force (American Bar Association, 1998, pp. 18, 52–53) reports that federal criminal laws and prosecutions have been quite *ineffective* in combating crime, despite an overall decline in the national crime rate.

5. The Commerce Clause legally authorizes Congress to regulate criminal activities tied to interstate commerce; this threshold, with few exceptions, has proven quite low (see *Perez v. United States* [1971] for Supreme Court approval of congressional action; see *United States v. Morrison* [2000] and *United States v. Lopez* [1995] for the only two recent Supreme Court rejections of congressional action). However, two other features of the U.S. Constitution—the Tenth Amendment and the absence of a national police power—suggest that Congress should use this power sparingly, in order not to trample the rights of states to police and to protect their own populations (see, e.g., Beale, 2005, Ashdown, 1996, Kadish, 1995; for a contrasting opinion, see Maroney, 2000). The current federalization debate thus concerns the wisdom, rather than the legality, of federal intervention in conventional state criminal activity.

6. Members of the community can voice their support for, or concerns about, local and statewide prosecution policy through the electoral process: they can vote to reelect district attorneys whose policies they like and to oust those whose policies have failed. But often the ability of voters to influence policy is more theoretical than real, as the voting public has no say about the policies during the administration's tenure, and oftentimes the neighborhoods that experience the most crime have low voter turnout (Thompson, 2002, p. 353).

7. Others have made the same observation about the community policing movement (Sklansky, 2006, p. 90, citing Buerger, 1994, pp. 270–271, and Frug, 1998, p. 81).

8. For example, the federal laws prohibiting interstate stalking, interstate violation of a protective order, and interstate domestic violence were virtually unenforced even before the Supreme Court declared the federal Violence against Women Act unconstitutional (Maroney, 2000, p. 1355; American Bar Association, 1998, p. 20). The same is true of the federal carjacking statute. One former U.S. Attorney in New York State reports that during his 5-year tenure in that role, "no federal carjacking prosecution was ever sought or authorized" (Maroney, 2000, p. 1354).

9. In this respect, the dynamic between the state government and county prosecutors resembles that between the federal legislature and U.S. Attorneys; the U.S. Congress sometimes uses money to "encourage" local U.S. Attorneys' offices to adopt "particular priorities for investigation and prosecution" (Wright, 2005, p. 137, citing Richman, 1999, pp. 793–799).

10. For example, in the area of elder abuse, the state of Delaware created a full-time prosecutor position in its Attorney General's Office; federal grant money partially supported this program (Santo, 2000, pp. 819–820). In the area of domestic violence, prosecutors in Massachusetts, New York, and New Jersey have special grant-funded units, although much of the New York and New Jersey money comes from the federal Violence against Women Act (Nealon, 1992; Fava, 1998; Miller, 2003).

11. The federal government has recently used this approach with states in the area of sentencing reform. Pursuant to the Violent Offender Incarceration and Truth-in-Sentencing Incentives Grants Program in the 1994 Crime Act, codified at Pub. L. No. 103-322, 108 Stat. 1796 (1994), federal grants are awarded to states that can prove certain violent offenders serve at least 85% of their sentences. In the late 1990s, 28 states and the District of Columbia applied for these grants (Shepherd & Garoupa, 2006, p. 6). However, only a handful of such states reported that the federal program was a key factor in the decision to enact a statewide truth-in-sentencing law (Sabol et al., 2002, pp. 23–24, citing U.S. General Accounting Office, 1998; U.S. Department of Justice, 1999).

12. The SRVPP began in fiscal year 1995–96 as a pilot program with 16 counties. The next fiscal year it expanded statewide, and it remained at that level for 7 years. In fiscal year 2003–04, pursuant to the Budget Act of 2003, the funding structure changed. The SRVPP was consolidated with other grant-funded vertical prosecution programs into one master vertical prosecution grant program administered by the state. Counties now apply to the state for general vertical prosecution funds, but each county has the ability to determine which specific programs it wants to operate. Since this restructuring, approximately half of the counties have retained their SRVPP programs (Levine, 2005, p. 1139, n. 33).

13. The SRVPP has an advisory group consisting of state bureaucrats and six to eight prosecutors; this group generally sets policies and parameters for the programs (Levine, 2006). Consequently, at least a handful of local prosecutors have the ability to voice their concerns and ideas about the program's direction directly to the state employees who administer the program.

References

Alexander, A. (2000, March 9). Great Stories: Doing the Crime but Not the Time: Portland's Budget—4 Times Mecklenburg's—Buys Results. *Charlotte Observer.* Retrieved January 24, 2008 from http://web.archive.org/web/20060315224029 re_/www.knightridder.com/about/greatstories/charlotte/crime33.html.

American Bar Association. (1998). *The federalization of criminal law.* Washington, DC: American Bar Association, Task Force on Federalization of Criminal Law.

Ashdown, G. G. (1996). Federalism, federalization, and the politics of crime. *West Virginia Law Review, 98,* 789–813.

Baker, Jr., J. S. (1985). Nationalizing criminal law: Does organized crime make it necessary or proper? *Rutgers Law Journal, 16,* 495–588.

Baker, Jr., J. S. (1999). State police powers and the federalization of local crime. *Temple Law Review, 72,* 673–712.

Beale, S. S. (2005). The many faces of overcriminalization: From morals and mattress tags to overfederalization. *American University Law Review, 54,* 747–782.

Bonnell, R., Brannon-Patel, E., Tysoe, I., & Boyken, G. (2001). *An evaluation of the statutory rape vertical prosecution program.* Sacramento, CA: California Government Printing Office.

Brickey, K. F. (1995). Criminal mischief: The federalization of American criminal law. *Hastings Law Journal, 46,* 1135–1174.

Buerger, M. E. (1994). The limits of community. In D. P. Rosenbaum (Ed.), *The challenge of community policing: Testing the premises* (pp. 270–273). Thousand Oaks, CA: Sage Publications.

California Penal Code. (2006). Minneapolis, MN: West Publications.

Central Valley Rural Crime Prevention Program. (2006). Retrieved March 22, 2006, from http://www.oes.ca.gov/Operational/OESHome.nsf/Content/5873F58AAFOE4F 8E88256E22006F68FF?OpenDocument.

Coles, C. (2002). *Community prosecution: District attorneys, county prosecutors, and attorneys general* (Working Paper #02–02–07). Cambridge, MA: Program in Criminal Justice Policy and Management, Kennedy School of Government, Harvard University.

Couillard, K. M. (1998). Comment: California's war on agricultural crimes. *San Joaquin Agricultural Law Review, 8,* 119–138.

Dharmapala, D., Garoupa, N., & Shepherd, J. (2006). *Sentencing guidelines, TIS legislation, and bargaining power.* Retrieved ???, from http://works.bepress.com/nunogaroupa/5.

Fava, R. S. (1998). Passaic County expands unit for domestic violence victims. *Italian Voice, 67,* 1.

Feeley, M. M., & Sarat, A. D. (1980). *The policy dilemma: Federal crime policy and the law enforcement assistance administration, 1968–1978.* Minneapolis: University of Minnesota Press.

Frug, G. (1998). City services. *New York University Law Review, 73,* 23–96.

Gleick, E. (1996, January 29). Putting the jail in jailbait: To fight teen pregnancy, California will start to prosecute statutory rapists. *Time,* 33.

Governor's Office of Criminal Justice Planning. (1997). *Statutory rape vertical prosecution (SRVP) program guidelines.* Sacramento, CA: Office of Criminal Justice Planning.

Governor's Office of Criminal Justice Planning. (2001). *Statutory rape vertical prosecution (SRVP) program guidelines.* Sacramento, CA: Office of Criminal Justice Planning.

Gramckow, H. (1997). Community prosecution in the United States. *European Journal on Criminal Policy and Research, 5(4),* 9–26.

Greenwood, P. R. (2001). *Testimony before the special committee on aging, U.S. Senate.* Retrieved June 1, 2001, from http://www.aging.senate.gov/public_bak/events/hr69pg.htm.

Honomichi, R. D., Noble, A., & Bonnell, R. (2002). *An evaluation of the child abuser vertical prosecution program.* Sacramento, CA: Governor's Office of Criminal Justice Planning.

Jacoby, J. E. (1980). *The American prosecutor: A search for identity.* Lexington, MA: Lexington Books.

Kadish, S. H. (1995). The folly of overfederalization. *Hastings Law Journal, 46,* 1247–1251.

Levine, K., & Feeley, M. (2001). Prosecution. In N. J. Smelser & P. B. Baltes (Eds.), *International encyclopedia of the social and behavioral sciences* (pp. 12,224–12,229). Oxford: Elsevier.

Levine, K. L. (2003). *Prosecution, politics, and pregnancy: Enforcing statutory rape in California.* Unpublished doctoral dissertation, University of California, Berkeley.

Levine, K. L. (2005). The new prosecution. *Wake Forest Law Review, 40,* 1125–1214.

Levine, K. L. (2006). The intimacy discount: Prosecutorial discretion, privacy, and equality in the statutory rape caseload. *Emory Law Journal, 55,* 691–758.

Little, R. K. (1995). Myths and principles of federalization. *Hastings Law Journal, 46,* 1029–1085.

Maroney, T. J. (2000). Fifty years of federalization in criminal law: Sounding alarm or "crying wolf?" *Syracuse Law Review, 50,* 1317–1378.

Miethe, T. D. (1987–1988). Charges and plea bargaining practices under determinate sentencing: An investigation of the hydraulic displacement of discretion. *Journal of Criminal Law and Criminology, 78,* 155–176.

Miller, N. (2003). *Queens County, New York, arrest policies project: A process evaluation.* Retrieved March 13, 2006, from http://www.ncjrs.org/pdffiles1/nij/grants/201886.pdf.

Misner, R. (1996). Recasting prosecutorial discretion. *Journal of Criminal Law and Criminology, 86*, 717–724.

Nealon, P. (1992, November 2). With Mass. domestic violence up, DAs launch a raft of new programs. *Boston Globe, Metro/Region*, p. 23.

Office of Justice Programs. (1999). *Fiscal year 2000 program plan: Resources for the field, 162.* Washington, DC: U.S. Department of Justice. Retrieved January 24, 2008, from http://web.archive.org/web/20020215200157re_/www.ojp.usdoj.gov/00progplan.

Perez v. United States, 402 U.S. 1246 (1971).

Phillips, J., & Cartwright, C. (1980). The California career criminal prosecution program one year later. *Journal of Criminal Law and Criminology, 71*, 107–112.

Richman, D. C. (1999). Federal criminal law, congressional delegation, and enforcement discretion. *UCLA Law Review, 46*, 757–814.

Sabol, W. J., Rosich, K., Kane, K. M., Kirk, D. P., & Dubin, G. (2002). *The influences of truth-in-sentencing reforms on changes in states' sentencing practices and prison populations.* Washington, DC: National Institute of Justice.

Santo, N. (2000). Breaking the silence: Strategies for combating elder abuse in California. *McGeorge Law Review, 31*, 801–838.

SB 453 (Poochigian). (2005, May 11). Retrieved March 22, 2006, from http://www.info.sen.ca.gov/pub/bill/sen/sb_0451-0500/sb_453_cfa_20050620_103707_asm_comm.html.

Shepherd, J. (in press). *Blakely*'s silvery lining: Sentencing guidelines, judicial discretion, and crime. *Hastings Law Journal.*

Sklansky, D. A. (2006). Private police and democracy. *American Criminal Law Review, 43*, 89–105.

Thompson, A. C. (2002). It takes a community to prosecute. *Notre Dame Law Review, 77*, 321–372.

United States v. Lopez, 115 S.Ct. 1624 (1995).

United States v. Morrison, 120 S.Ct. 1740 (2000).

U.S. Department of Justice, Office of the Inspector General, Inspections Division. (1999). *The violent offender incarceration and truth-in-sentencing incentive grant program: Summary of inspection findings and recommendations, May 4, 1997–March 31, 1999.* Washington, DC: U.S. Department of Justice.

U.S. General Accounting Office. (1998). *Truth in sentencing: Availability of federal grants influenced laws in some states.* Washington, DC: U.S. General Accounting Office.

Wolf, R. V. (2000a). *Forging community links: Community prosecution in Denver, Colorado.* Washington, DC: Center for Court Innovation.

Wolf, R. V. (2000b). *Problem-solving prosecutors: Community prosecution in Portland, Oregon.* Washington, DC: Center for Court Innovation.

Wolf, R. V., & Campbell, N. (2004). *Beyond big cities: The problem-solving innovations of community prosecutors in smaller jurisdictions.* Washington, DC: Center for Court Innovation.

Wright, R. F. (2005). Trial distortion and the end of innocence in federal criminal justice. *University of Pennsylvania Law Review, 154,* 79–156.

Yates, J., & Fording, R. (2005). Politics and state punitiveness in black and white. *Journal of Politics, 67,* 1099–1121.

Chapter Three

Prosecution Policy and Errors of Justice

BRIAN FORST

Introduction

In 1940, former U.S. Attorney General and Supreme Court Justice Robert Jackson remarked famously on the extreme power of prosecutorial discretion, that the prosecutor has more influence than anyone else in America over the lives, liberties, and reputations of people suspected of violating the law. He might have noted that prosecutors also have more control than others over the risks that innocent people will be convicted and culpable offenders will not. They determine how carefully to screen arrests brought by the police and direct post-arrest investigations to resolve conflicting sources of evidence; how diligently to work with victims and witnesses to establish, precisely and accurately, pertinent events that preceded and followed the episode in question; and how carefully to direct the post-arrest processing of key items of physical evidence, to resolve ambiguities involving both exculpatory and incriminating evidence. While much of this work is initiated and managed by police departments, prosecutorial discretion and policy—determining what happens *after* arrest—serve as the filters through which all arrests must pass.

The decisions of the prosecutor are based largely on the standards of evidence used at each stage of prosecution—as low as probable cause at screening and as high as proof beyond a reasonable doubt in trial—and on plea bargaining policies. Should prosecutors screen arrests more carefully, or should more arrests be accepted using a lower standard and dropped later if the post-arrest investigation turns up weak? Should more cases be taken on and scarce prosecution time rationed by encouraging more pleas, or should more be rejected at screening so that attention might be paid instead to preparing more cases for trial? What effects do these decisions have on the rate at which errors of justice occur?

Prosecutors rarely articulate a rationale for determining how these choices are made. It is by no means clear that the decisions or policies that govern them in fact follow a coherent consideration of either the interrelationships among them or the overarching goals of prosecution: pursuit of justice, enforcement of the law, reduction in crime, evenhandedness, efficiency, celerity, and so on.

Traditional measures of prosecution performance—conviction rates, average case processing time, reelection success, and so on—shed little light on these questions, and they ignore justice errors. Research on prosecution tends also to ignore these issues. William Landes, among the first to study prosecutors using a formal theoretical and empirical research design, postulated that prosecutors aim to maximize the weighted number of convictions, where the weights are based on offense seriousness. Landes's model made no distinction between cases in which the defendant was factually guilty or innocent, tacitly assuming that all were culpable offenders of the crime for which they had been charged.[1]

The larger social returns to a primary focus on convictions and tough sanctions have by now been revealed as extremely dubious. Reflective people who have devoted themselves professionally to assessing the criminal justice system have concluded *both* that too many people in prison and jail do not belong there, and too many culpable offenders remain at large. Aiming to convict more persons arrested for felonies and put them away for long terms of incarceration has contributed to the overincarceration of marginally harmful offenders, and may even have accelerated the release from prison of more dangerous offenders, thus diminishing our ability to control crime in the name of ending it (Blumstein, 2002). Conventional performance measures of prosecutors overlook a valid concern that the interests of the community are not always served by incarcerating persons arrested for felonies. Some are, in fact, innocent. In capital cases, which one might expect are subject to greater due process protections than other felony cases, an astonishingly large number of persons sentenced to death have been subsequently exonerated of all charges, based largely on DNA evidence.[2] Liebman, Fagan, West, and Lloyd (2000) report prosecutor misconduct in 16% to 19% of appellate reversals of capital sentences.[3] And in many noncapital cases, the costs of incarceration appear clearly to exceed the alternative costs of intermediate sanctions that would permit those offenders to contribute to the productivity of the community and well-being of their families. While excessive punishments are not justice errors in the conventional sense, they are nonetheless errors imposed on the community that are largely a consequence of plea negotiations and sentencing recommendations by the prosecutor.

Managing errors of justice is a long-overlooked goal of prosecution, one that warrants serious consideration as a basis for assessing case processing policies and practices. Few would argue with the proposition that the prosecutor should work to ensure that culpable offenders are brought to justice and innocent people are not convicted. Failure to do either constitutes a fundamental lapse of justice. For all cases brought to the screening room, the prosecutor is responsible for both types of errors.

Prosecutorial Discretion and Errors of Justice

Prosecutors are known to exercise considerable discretion in deciding whether to prosecute individual cases and determining how much attention to assign to each case accepted. Justice Jackson (see this chapter's opening sentence) and others have called attention repeatedly to the dangers associated with this power. Independent prosecutor Kenneth Starr's impeachment investigation of President Bill Clinton is one of the more conspicuous recent examples of prosecutors exercising discretion in such a way as to damage the lives and reputations of the accused.[4]

Prosecutors are only occasionally overruled for engaging in such excesses. In the case of *Berger v. United States*, involving a federal prosecutor who grossly overstepped the bounds of proper behavior in order to win a conviction against a defendant, Supreme Court Justice George Sutherland wrote, "While (the prosecutor) may strike hard blows, he may not strike foul ones. It is as much his duty to refrain from improper methods calculated to produce a wrongful conviction as it is to use every legitimate means to bring about a just one" [295 U.S. 78 (1935)].

Sutherland's observation has gone unheeded by many a prosecutor in the decades since. Bedau and Radelet (1987) reported 35 cases of prosecutors suppressing exculpatory evidence in a sample of 350 potentially capital cases involving "wrong-person" conviction errors, and 15 other such errors attributable to "overzealous prosecution" (p. 57). Several other commentators have documented convictions of the innocent as a consequence of misconduct associated specifically with the prosecutor's withholding of exculpatory evidence from the defense (Gershman, 1999; Huff, Rattner, & Sagarin, 1996; Scheck, Neufeld, & Dwyer, 2001).

Prosecutorial misbehavior is sensational, and it sometimes leads to erroneous convictions, but a basic, innocuous aspect of prosecutorial discretion may be a far more profound source of errors of justice: the power of the prosecutor to determine the extent to which the courtroom standard of evidence—proof beyond a reasonable doubt—will be relaxed at any stage of prosecution, starting with the screening of arrests. In prosecutors' offices of all sizes, the exercise of discretion in screening arrests is not severely constrained by the U.S. Constitution or by case law. The decision to file an arrest in court depends on the threshold of evidence used by the prosecutor, which is largely a matter of office policy. In deciding whether to file a case in the court, the prosecutor is free to use any standard between "probable cause," the standard required for the police to make an arrest, and the beyond-a-reasonable-doubt standard used in trial. By lowering evidentiary standards at the pretrial stages of prosecution, the prosecutor raises the likelihood of winning convictions in cases involving innocent suspects, mostly by way of plea bargaining, and imposes potentially harmful costs on those defendants (and others) in the process. Others have noted that the controversy over plea bargaining has been misplaced. It is ostensibly a matter between pleas and trials, but more fundamentally a matter between case screening and plea bargaining (Wright & Miller, 2002).

This policy choice owes its existence to a tradition of loosely governed escalation in the legal standard of proof as felony cases proceed from arrest to indictment and adjudication in court. The level at which the chief prosecutor places the bar in the pretrial stages involves a trade-off between the certainty and severity of applicable sanctions. Lowering screening standards and getting more convictions by way of plea negotiations and fewer by guilty verdicts in trial are likely to be associated with shorter sentences. And as sentences of probation increase, such practices can be expected to lead to reduced incapacitation effects, but it comes with the substantially increased risk of convicting more innocent people, along with some compensation in convicting a larger share of culpable offenders. This trade-off will be considered in greater detail later in this chapter.

Improved Coordination with Police

In deciding what standard of evidence to use in screening arrests, the prosecutor sends a message to the police. If the prosecutor uses the probable cause standard, then case acceptance amounts to validating the police assessment that the evidence in the case was sufficient to make an arrest. In rejecting a case under this standard, the prosecutor ordinarily explains to the police officer either that the case was rejected "in the interest of justice," that the evidence met the probable cause standard but the nature of the case did not warrant prosecution (e.g., the arrest was needed only to prevent further harm, or the offense was trivial), or because the probable cause standard was not met, along with an explanation as to specific deficiencies in the case. If the prosecutor rejects the case using a higher standard than probable cause in screening cases, then she or he can tell the police officer what evidence would have merited case acceptance under the higher standard. Regardless of the evidence standard used by the prosecutor at the screening stage, this explanation provides useful feedback for the police, generally given informally and recorded routinely for the prosecutor's records, although not generally a matter of open public record.

This information is routinely given to the police as a matter of record only in a minority of jurisdictions, making it virtually impossible for police executives in most places to hold their officers systematically accountable for the quality of the arrests they make. The opportunity for improved coordination and reduced errors rests generally with systems of feedback that provide routine, nonaccusatory information as to how the police can strengthen cases legitimately with stronger tangible and testimonial evidence. Such systems appear to be the exception, not the rule.

The quality of coordination in individual cases depends largely on the underlying relationship between the police and the prosecutor. There is some strain in the relationship in most jurisdictions, if only because the cultures of both tend to be quite different (McDonald, 1982; Feeley & Lazerson, 1983; Coles, Kelling, & Moore, 1998). From the perspective of the police officer, the prosecutor's position often seems excessively sterile and formal, removed from the workaday reality of the cop on the street trying to fight crime against impossible odds. From the perspective of the prosecutor, the police often appear to be excessively zealous and insensitive to the prosecutor's case backlogs and the rigorous evidentiary standards of the court. The underlying tension occasionally escalates when the prosecutor goes public with criticism of police work in a particular case or series of cases, sometimes fueled by media inquiry. In other jurisdictions, the police and prosecutors enjoy a generally healthy, mutually supportive working relationship.

The quality of the police-prosecutor relationship in a jurisdiction is critical to the ability of the prosecutor to effectively monitor the problems discussed in the previous chapter: flawed lineups and other improper witness identification procedures, illicitly obtained confessions, improper use of informants, legally invalid searches, and faulty processing of physical and forensic evidence. The prosecutor cannot escape responsibility for failing to catch persistent policing problems, such as the fraudulent evidence technician. In some instances, prosecutors have been charged with conspiring with the police to make weak cases against innocent defendants appear stronger by withholding exculpatory evidence or overlooking flaws in police investigations (Scheck, Neufeld, & Dwyer, 2001, pp. 222–236). Police-prosecutor cooperation has not always been in the interest of justice.

Errors of Fact, Questions of Culpability, and Tactical Errors

Errors of due process and errors of failure to bring culpable offenders to justice are not the only kinds of errors influenced by the exercise of prosecutorial discretion.

Prosecutors err also when they give excessive concessions to offenders who testify against low-level, less culpable collaborators, and when they play the role of adversary aiming for a high conviction rate rather than fact finder in pretrial disclosure proceedings, to such an extent that legitimacy is lost through an ends-justify-the-means approach to justice. That defense lawyers may engage in similar practices on the other side is not an acceptable justification for such practices; it is the prosecutor who bears the burden of proof for all relevant facts in a case under our system of criminal justice,[5] unlike the continental European system of criminal law. Even when prosecutors engage in such practices that do not lead directly to the sort of errors that are the focus of this chapter, the practices are unseemly. Overly aggressive prosecution tends to repel the public and subvert our system of justice, undermining its legitimacy.

Another important type of error can result from the imprudent exercise of prosecutorial discretion: an error in the assessment of culpability. Questions about whether juveniles, or adults with serious mental impairments or emotional illness, are criminally liable are questions of law and culpability rather than questions of fact. So are questions about whether a defendant acted in self-defense in a case in which he or she is charged with assault. Similarly, violations of federal Racketeer Influenced and Corrupt Organizations (RICO) statutes and insider trading laws often are technically complicated and difficult to establish as criminal rather than civil matters. In all such cases, the question is not whether a defendant committed a particular act, but whether the act qualifies as criminal. Specific rulings may produce inconsistencies in the interpretation of the law or violations of ethical norms rather than errors about whether a particular person committed the act at issue. That the tools and frameworks for inquiry that are the staples of this book do not help resolve these questions does not mean that the questions are not important.

Even among the large class of cases that will qualify unambiguously as criminal rather than juvenile or civil, degrees of culpability are important to the prosecutor's decision to accept a case and determine the level of resources to allocate to it if accepted. To the extent that the degree of harm imposed on victims and the community at large is a measure of culpability, the prosecutor should allocate more resources to cases involving greater culpability, for any margin of cases in which the strength of the evidence and dangerousness of the offender to the community will be about equal. Prosecutors routinely exercise discretion in making such decisions, and occasionally use decision support tools to help guide this exercise, using such metrics as the sentence associated with the most serious charge as a measure of offense seriousness.

Prosecutors also may miscalculate in their tactical decision making, with the result that culpable offenders go free. The notorious error of Los Angeles Assistant District Attorney Christopher Darden's having defendant O. J. Simpson try on a pair of bloody, shrunken gloves in trial appears to be a case in point. Such miscalculations also are beyond the scope of the present inquiry, although the prospect of empirical analysis helping to establish prosecution approaches that are more or less effective in dealing with various classes of cases cannot be ignored. One might expect that these miscalculations are no more likely to occur in cases involving culpable offenders than in cases involving innocent defendants. Nonetheless, to the extent that they reduce the conviction rate, they will increase the number of culpable offenders set free and reduce the number of innocent people convicted. As with errors of culpability, I will leave the analysis of the effect of prosecutorial tactics in individual cases on errors of justice as a topic for future inquiry.

Should the Prosecutor Emphasize Conviction Quality or Quantity?

Determining the standard of evidence to use in screening arrests involves more than a trade-off between the certainty and severity of the eventual sanction in individual cases. It involves also a choice between the *number* of convictions and the *quality* of convictions. A prosecutor who uses a higher standard of proof in the screening room rejects arrests that would otherwise be accepted, freeing up resources to bring more cases to trial: a preference for quality of convictions over quantity. These options may have profound implications for justice errors. Emphasis on the quality of convictions includes greater attention to due process considerations and reduced risk of convicting innocent people; emphasis on the number of convictions reduces the rate at which culpable offenders are set free. Of course, higher-quality convictions need not come at the expense of the number of convictions. Additional resources can lead to a reduction of both the number of culpable offenders released and that of innocent persons convicted. For a given level of resources, however, the prosecutor often must choose between policies that tend to emphasize the minimization of one type of error or the other.

The choice of whether to focus on quality or quantity of convictions revolves around basic questions about the purpose of the criminal justice system, as well as consideration of the relative severity of sanctions that will apply under each option. An emphasis on quality of convictions over quantity may be justified on grounds of procedural justice and due process, based on the notion that the alternative may operate to undermine the defendant's fundamental Sixth Amendment right to an impartial trial. An emphasis on the number of convictions, in contrast, may be justified on grounds of the public's right to protection against crime and disorder, to ensure domestic tranquility by minimizing the number of culpable offenders escaping criminal sanction. It may be justified as well on grounds of just deserts, the notion that offenders deserve to be sanctioned for the crimes they commit,

assuming that the sanctions given to the margin of additional offenders convicted are not offset by the shorter sanctions given to offenders convicted
under an emphasis on quality.

But the choice over whether to emphasize quality or quantity of convictions involves more. In using a higher standard of evidence in screening
arrests, the prosecutor will be rejecting some cases at the margin that would
otherwise end up as convictions by pleas of guilt. Accordingly, the prosecutor
might do well to contemplate how many of those marginally acceptable cases
are likely to involve true offenders and how many are likely to involve innocent persons. If the prosecutor perceives those cases to have a high ratio of true
offenders to innocent persons, then he or she ought to be inclined to accept
more than otherwise; if the ratio is perceived to be low, the prosecutor should
reject more.

Of course, all arrestees do not fall neatly into the two categories of true
offenders and innocent persons. Many cases involve arrestees who in fact
committed crimes, but whose culpability is mitigated by factors such as trivi-
ality of offense, victim provocation, and a host of situational and personal factors. The social cost of pursuing convictions in such cases involving factually
guilty offenders may exceed that of rejecting these cases in the screening room
or dropping them (*nolle prosequi*, or "nol pros") after initial filing in court. This
is a substantial group of cases for which the prudent exercise of prosecutorial
discretion is required.

In other cases, the choice between the quality and number of convictions can involve a vexing trade-off between the two basic types of errors of
justice. The central question boils down to this: If a prosecutor were to shift
from an emphasis on quantity to an emphasis on quality of convictions—that
is, from a low arrest rejection rate and high ratio of pleas to trials to a high
rejection rate and a low ratio of pleas to trials—then what sort of shifts should
one expect between the number of offenders set free and the number of innocent persons convicted? How should these expectations change as the percentage of arrests involving true offenders grows larger?

Analyzing Data on Prosecution under a
Range of Assumptions About Factual Guilt

Prosecutors in fact vary widely as to the standard of evidentiary proof used in
the screening room, and this variation has been found to be related to the ratio
of pleas to trials from one jurisdiction to the next (Boland & Forst, 1985;
Wright & Miller, 2002). Some prosecutors are inclined to accept only trial-
worthy cases and obtain fewer convictions by plea, while others are inclined to
accept marginal cases and put greater effort into the task of negotiating pleas
and winning convictions in cases that would be rejected elsewhere.[6]

By incorporating available data on the court outcomes of felony arrests brought to the prosecutor in a cross section of jurisdictions in a computer template designed to accommodate a variety of assumptions about the mix of true offenders and innocent persons, we can assess the effect of a shift in strategy from quality to quantity, or vice versa, on errors of justice.[7] The scenarios presented next are based on cross-jurisdictional data on case acceptance rates, conviction and plea rates, and rates of acquittal in trial (Boland & Sones, 1986; DeFrances & Steadman, 1998; Forst, 2002). Two initial strategy scenarios are presented, one emphasizing conviction quantity and the other emphasizing quality, both making the following initial assumptions: 90% of all arrests involve true offenders,[8] 75% of all trials result in guilty verdicts, and prosecutors who are screening cases are able to distinguish between true offenders and others in such a way that produces higher case acceptance rates for true offenders than for innocent persons.[9] In Scenario A, the prosecutor opts for quantity over quality by rejecting relatively few (20% of all) arrests in the screening room and then engages extensively in plea bargaining and bringing few cases to trial. In Scenario B, the prosecutor screens more selectively (rejecting 40%) and then accepts fewer pleas and brings more cases to trial. Under Scenario B the differential in arrest acceptance rates for true offenders and innocent people is assumed to be larger than under a policy of emphasis on quantity, a product of the additional time spent at the screening stage.[10] And because fewer inducements to plead guilty are offered, the rate at which innocent people plead guilty is assumed to be lower.[11] Results are shown in Tables 3.1.a and 3.1.b.

These two scenarios were repeated under a range of assumptions about the percentage of all felony arrests involving true offenders (from a low of 75% to a high of 99%), the likelihood ratio of the case acceptance rate for true offenders to that for innocent persons (ranging from twice as likely to be prosecuted to five times as likely), the percentage of all trials resulting in guilty verdicts (ranging from 60% to 90%), and the percentage of pleas of guilt involving innocent persons (ranging from 1% to 5%).[12] The purpose here is not to suggest the accuracy of any particular assumption or set of assumptions but rather to examine the effect of *variation* in each assumption on justice errors, to see how sensitive the error rates and ratios are to changes in each. The true values are likely to vary from jurisdiction to jurisdiction, as do the documented values of known parameters such as case acceptance rates, plea-to-trial ratios, and conviction rates.

The findings are summarized in Table 3.2, showing how errors shift as the prosecutor shifts from one strategy to the other and as the percentage of innocents arrested increases. To put these numbers in perspective, recall Blackstone's (1765) dictum that it is better to free 10 offenders than to convict an innocent person. It must be noted that Blackstone's rule ignores the

TABLE 3.1.a
Prosecutor Accepts 80% of Arrests, Negotiates 15 Pleas for Each Trial*

	Committed Crime	Did Not Commit	Total	
Arrests Rejected	**129**	71	200	Offenders Freed per Innocent Convicted: 138.1/26.1=5.3
Guilty Pleas	727	**23**	750	
Guilty Verdicts	34	**4**	38	Percent of Cases
Acquittals	_10_	_2_	_12_	Decided in Error: 164.2/1,000=16.4%
Total Cases	900	100	1,000	

*Justice errors in boldface; cell entries are subject to rounding errors.

TABLE 3.1.b
Prosecutor Accepts 60% of Arrests, Negotiates 5 Pleas for Each Trial*

	Committed Crime	Did Not Commit	Total	
Arrests Rejected	**316**	84	400	Offenders Freed per Innocent Convicted: 337.4/12.4=27.2
Guilty Pleas	495	**5**	500	
Guilty Verdicts	68	**7**	75	Percent of Cases
Acquittals	_21_	_4_	_25_	Decided in Error: 349.8/1,000=35.0%
Total Cases	900	100	1,000	

*Justice errors in boldface; cell entries are subject to rounding errors.

substantial variation in social costs associated with each type of error across crime categories. Most communities are likely to prefer a larger number of shoplifters freed per innocent person convicted than serial rapists.

Two somewhat unexpected findings emerge consistently from these simulations. First, for all sets of assumptions tested, a shift to a prosecution strategy of more selective case screening and a greater emphasis on trials increases both the number of offenders set free per innocent person convicted and the total error rate. Second, as the percentage of felony arrestees who are innocent increases, both the number of offenders set free per innocent convicted and the total error rate tend to decrease under *both* strategies, making a more selective felony case screening strategy increasingly attractive as the quality of police arrests declines, and arguably essential at some arbitrary threshold. To oversimplify a bit, as the police become more accurate in iden-

TABLE 3.2

Error Ratios and Rates under Different Prosecution Strategies
and as Innocent Persons as a Percentage of Total Arrestees Increases*

Prosecution Strategy	Offenders Freed per Innocent Convicted			Errors as a Percent of Total Cases		
	True Offenders as a Percent of the Total			True Offenders as a Percent of the Total		
	95%	*85%*	*75%*	*95%*	*85%*	*75%*
Accept 80%, 15 Pleas/Trial	7	4	1	20%	13%	7%
Accept 60%, 5 Pleas/Trial	32	23	15	39%	31%	23%

*Values shown are based on the mid-range values of the following input parameters: True offenders are three times as likely to have their cases accepted as innocents under an emphasis on quantity and four times as likely under an emphasis on quality; 3% of all defendants who plead guilty are innocent under an emphasis on quantity, and 1% are innocent under an emphasis on quality; 75% of all defendants tried in court are found guilty.

tifying true offenders, the prosecutor need not spend as much time screening cases. As the percentage of true offenders falls below 85% of all arrests, the less selective screening strategy causes the number of innocent persons convicted to approximate the number of offenders freed.

The increases in both the ratio of offenders freed to innocents convicted and in the total error rate for the more selective, trial-oriented strategy can be understood by comparing the scenarios cell by cell. Reductions in the case acceptance rate tend to produce increases in the number of offenders set free at the screening stage and thus lower the rate at which arrests end in conviction. The increase in the number of trials associated with an emphasis on quality of convictions tends also to produce an increase in the number of true offenders acquitted, but in most scenarios these increases are offset by declines in the number of innocent persons convicted by plea or trial. The increases in the number of offenders set free under a more selective prosecution strategy may, of course, be offset by an incapacitative effect: longer terms of incarceration for convicted offenders.[13]

These findings suggest that prosecutors stand to gain substantially by being more conscious of the effects of their case screening standards on errors of justice. They suggest as well that prosecutors should be aware of the need to adapt their screening and plea bargaining policies to exogenous factors, such as changes in the quality of arrests brought by the police and shifts in the public's relative concerns over security and civil liberty. When the quality of arrests declines, as in the event of a crime wave or diversion of police resources to the press of other demands such as terrorism, more selective screening will be needed, not only to deal with the immediate need to correct the problem by checking the work of the police more carefully but also to manage the balance of errors of justice.

Analysis by Crime Category

The results just described are limited in several respects. They are based on aggregate statistics about felony cases, and felony cases are not homogeneous. As noted earlier, the social cost of an error of failure to convict a culpable offender, relative to that of convicting an innocent person, may be much higher for some crime and offender categories, such as stranger rape, than for others, such as shoplifting, because of the substantially greater harm if a dangerous offender is not incapacitated and more crimes result. For other categories, questions of culpability may be more important to prosecution strategy than questions of wrong-person error, as in the case of a 14- or 15-year-old child who commits homicide. Prosecutors must weigh the problem of wrong-person errors with other considerations.

Another limitation lends itself to further analysis: in any given jurisdiction, the underlying rates of actual innocence, case acceptance, jury trials, guilty verdicts, and so on are likely to vary from one offense category to another. Prosecutors should be less inclined to reject arrests for homicide than for less serious crimes and less likely to grant concessions for guilty pleas in such cases as well for reasons other than concerns about errors of justice. For some categories of crime, the likelihood of error in arrest may be greater—stranger-to-stranger crimes that are more susceptible to erroneous witness identification, crimes for which the quality of defense counsel tends to be weak, and crimes in which the police department is under intense pressure to solve the case. Given such variation, separate analyses should be conducted for each crime category based on the known parameter values of the respective crimes.

Consider, for example, two important felony offenses: homicide and burglary. Persons arrested for homicide are much more likely to be prosecuted and convicted and much less likely to plead rather than go to trial than persons arrested for burglary. Data from the National Judicial Reporting Program (NJRP) for 1996 reveal that for every 100 arrests for murder, 60 people are convicted and 57 are incarcerated, 55 to prison terms of at least a year (Brown, Langan, & Levin, 1999).[14] For burglary, the respective numbers are 26 convicted, 18 incarcerated, and 12 imprisoned.[15] Data from the Bureau of Justice Statistics survey of prosecutors for the 75 largest urban counties for the same year reveal that 85% of all murder trials end in guilty verdicts, and about one defendant pleads guilty for each who chooses to be judged in trial, while only 71% of all burglary trials end in guilty verdicts, with about eight pleas per trial overall (Hart & Reaves, 1999, p. 24). Given these differences, how are the prosecution policy options analyzed in the preceding section likely to influence the two types of justice errors in these two very different types of cases?

To assess the effect of a shift in strategy from quality to quantity (or vice versa) on errors of justice, we shall use the same approach as in the previous section but with different ranges of assumed values for each crime, based on the respective plea-to-trial ratios and conviction rates reported for these two crime categories, exclusive of juvenile cases. The mid-range assumptions for homicide used in this analysis are as follows: 90% of all arrests involve true offenders, 85% of all trials result in guilty verdicts (as reported), and the percentages of pleas involving innocent people are assumed to be 1% under the policy of emphasis on quantity and 0.5% under the policy of emphasis on quality, in which the incentives offered the defendant to plead guilty will tend to be less attractive. For burglary, the corresponding mid-range assumptions used are 90%, 71% (as reported), 3%, and 1%, respectively. As before, in Scenario A the prosecutor rejects relatively few arrests in the screening room (10% for homicides and 20% for burglaries),[16] then opts for quantity over quality by engaging extensively in plea bargaining and bringing few cases to trial (1.5 pleas per trial for homicide, 12 pleas per trial for burglary). In Scenario B, the prosecutor uses a more selective screening strategy (rejecting 20% of homicides and 40% of burglaries), with higher rejection rates for cases involving innocents than for cases involving true offenders, and then the prosecutor accepts fewer pleas and brings more cases to trial (one homicide plea per trial, four burglary pleas per trial). Results for homicide are shown in Tables 3.3.a and 3.3.b. Results for burglary are shown in Tables 3.4.a and 3.4.b.

Given existing patterns of case acceptance, pleas per trial and conviction rates for these two crime categories, the most striking difference that emerges is that the total error rates tend to be about twice as high for burglary than for homicide under either prosecution policy, and the ratio of offenders freed per innocent person convicted is slightly higher for burglary than for homicide under either policy. The general findings of the previous section hold up for both offense categories.

One might expect the prosecutor, a priori, to be more inclined to choose an emphasis on quality of convictions in homicide cases than in burglary. Our results are consistent with the wisdom of such a strategy. The more selective screening strategy for homicide cases produces the smallest number of innocent persons convicted of any of the four scenarios shown earlier. These patterns hold for all other scenarios considered, also described earlier.

TABLE 3.3.a
Prosecutor Accepts 90% of Homicide Arrests, Negotiates 1.5 Pleas per Trial*

	Committed Crime	Did Not Commit	Total	
Arrests Rejected	**32**	68	100	Offenders Freed per Innocent Convicted: 81.1/27.1=3.0
Guilty Pleas	535	**5**	540	
Guilty Verdicts	284	**22**	306	Percent of Cases
Acquittals	**49**	5	54	Decided in Error:
				108.3/1,000=10.8%
Total Cases	900	100	1,000	

*Justice errors in boldface; cell entries are subject to rounding errors.

TABLE 3.3.b
Prosecutor Accepts 80% of Homicide Arrests, Negotiates 1 Plea per Trial*

	Committed Crime	Did Not Commit	Total	
Arrests Rejected	**122**	78	200	Offenders Freed per Innocent Convicted: 177.7/17.7=10.1
Guilty Pleas	398	**2**	400	
Guilty Verdicts	324	**16**	340	Percent of Cases
Acquittals	**56**	4	60	Decided in Error:
				195.4/1,000=19.5%
Total Cases	900	100	1,000	

*Justice errors in boldface; cell entries are subject to rounding errors.

Conclusion

Much has been written about how prosecutors contribute to the convictions of innocent people through biased review of the evidence and breaches of ethical standards, such as failure to divulge important exculpatory evidence and fraudulent reporting of case processing practices (Scheck, Neufeld, & Dwyer, 2001; Huff, Rattner, & Sagarin, 1996; Radelet, Bedau, & Putnam, 1992). These sensational accounts are significant for calling attention to the importance of maintaining integrity in the practice of prosecution. They may have helped substantially to deter prosecutors from engaging in such unethical practices.

This approach to reform, however, may have considerably less impact on errors of justice than prosecution policies governing the routine prosecution decisions made in some 2 million or so felony cases annually, policies that

TABLE 3.4.a
Prosecutor Accepts 80% of Burglary Arrests, Negotiates 12 Pleas per Trial*

	Committed Crime	Did Not Commit	Total	Offenders Freed per Innocent Convicted:
Arrests Rejected	**129**	71	200	143.7/25.7=5.6
Guilty Pleas	716	**22**	738	
Guilty Verdicts	40	**4**	44	Percent of Cases
Acquittals	**15**	3	18	Decided in Error:
				169.4/1,000=16.9%
Total Cases	900	100	1,000	

*Justice errors in boldface; cell entries are subject to rounding errors.

TABLE 3.4.b
Prosecutor Accepts 60% of Burglary Arrests, Negotiates 4 Pleas per Trial*

	Committed Crime	Did Not Commit	Total	Offenders Freed per Innocent Convicted:
Arrests Rejected	**316**	84	400	346.9/11.9=29.2
Guilty Pleas	475	**5**	480	
Guilty Verdicts	78	**7**	85	Percent of Cases
Acquittals	**31**	4	35	Decided in Error:
				358.8/1,000=35.9%
Total Cases	900	100	1,000	

*Justice errors in boldface; cell entries are subject to rounding errors.

receive almost no attention at all. In determining whether to be more concerned about the quality of convictions, by rejecting more cases up front and then taking more cases to trial, or more about the number of convictions, by accepting more arrests and inducing more pleas and fewer trials, prosecutors can have a considerable impact on both the number of culpable offenders freed and the number of innocent persons convicted.

Although many of the findings reported here are robust with regard to a wide range of assumptions, such simplifying assumptions nonetheless tend to raise more questions than they answer. How do errors in the arrests brought to prosecutors *really* vary by jurisdiction and crime category? Could some of the scenarios in the real world be at rates outside of the ranges considered? What are the social cost implications of errors of justice that are the product of prosecution decisions, including the costs of sanctions that err either on the side of being too lax or too punitive? How might systems of accountability be designed to ensure that the prosecutor's responsibility for errors of justice is adequately monitored? Who should manage such systems? Are policies associated with high wrongful conviction rates and low wrongful nonconviction rates more common in jurisdictions in which prosecutors are elected than in jurisdictions where they are appointed?[17]

These are matters that researchers and prosecutors would do well to come to terms with in coming years. The public is not well served by having ready access only to media accounts of the prosecution of celebrity cases, with a paucity of data and research on what happens to the millions of felony arrests brought to prosecutors each year. Data and research on policing, sentencing, and corrections are far more plentiful than on prosecution, despite the central role played by the prosecutor in our system of justice.[18] This is a major blind spot, one that brings with it untold inefficiencies and injustices.

Some errors of justice are inevitable, but prosecutors could manage them more effectively and openly than they do and reduce both by being more aware of the relationship between their policies and justice errors. Sophisticated systems are in place to manage errors in scientific research and in production processes and to balance the risk of loss against yield in financial portfolios but not to manage errors that burden innocent people and victims of crime every day, errors that erode trust in our criminal justice system. The appeals process corrects some wrongful convictions, but on an episodic rather than on a systemic basis, and it ignores wrongful nonconvictions.

Errors of justice harm us all. They undermine the public's sense of criminal justice legitimacy, drain resources, create inequities, and restrict freedom. They also diminish the quality of our lives. They warrant more coherent, less adversarial treatment than we have given them. Prosecutors would do well to ensure that their policies and the systems of accountability that govern their practices deal honestly, comprehensively and effectively with the problem.

Notes

1. Landes was not the only researcher to ignore prosecution error. His model had been criticized by Forst and Brosi (1977) for failing to consider future crimes and the crime prevention goal of prosecution, not for failing to distinguish culpable offenders from innocent defendants. Forst and Brosi's model, like Landes's, assumes tacitly that the prosecutor always prefers a conviction to a nonconviction, as though all defendants are culpable offenders.

2. Some of these exonerations were based on procedural errors that do not necessarily imply factual innocence, and many of these may be connected to jurisdictions with serious lapses in due process controls, not typical of prosecution in most jurisdictions. Still, in most of the 80 cases forensic evidence implicated others, and in many capital cases DNA evidence is not available to exonerate the death row inmate; other

death row inmates sentenced during the period may be factually innocent too. The 1.3% figure is, by any reckoning, alarmingly high.

3. Liebman et al., text at note 42. Latzer and Cauthen (2000, p. 142) point out that most appellate reversals of capital sentences leave undisturbed the guilt of the murderer. Prosecutor misconduct is documented also by Bedau and Radelet (1987, pp. 57–60), Gershman (1999), Huff et al. (1996), and Scheck, Neufeld, and Dwyer (2001, pp. 222–236).

4. Benjamin Wittes has offered a charitable assessment of Starr's abuse of prosecutorial discretion, attributing it to his mistaken but good-faith belief that his mission was wide-ranging, to seek the truth of any and all presidential misconduct, rather than the conventional narrow one of investigating specific charges, in this case, the president's role in the Whitewater scandal. Starr's civil law perspective would substantially broaden the meaning of an error of justice. One might, in any case, question the ethics of the Starr team's threatening to jail Monica Lewinsky's mother for withholding information even under this more charitable view of Starr's role.

5. The prosecutor's responsibility for assembling and making available *all* relevant evidence, exculpatory as well as incriminating, was reinforced in a landmark 1963 ruling by the Supreme Court. Under *Brady v. Maryland*, a prosecutor's suppression of exculpatory evidence violates the defendant's right to due process (373 U.S. 83 [1963]).

6. Examples of jurisdictions in the former camp, with higher screening standards and fewer pleas per trial in the early 1980s, included New Orleans, Louisiana, Portland, Oregon, and Washington, D.C. Examples in the latter camp include Manhattan, New York, Geneva, Illinois, and Cobb County, Georgia (Boland & Forst, 1985, p. 11). Unfortunately, the data series on which this analysis was based was discontinued a few years after the study that used those data was conducted. Were data available to replicate the research reported here, the lists could well be different, although there is no compelling reason to expect that the essential findings on differences across district attorneys' offices would have changed.

7. All juvenile arrests are excluded, as are arrests accepted for prosecution and dropped later (*nolle prosequi*) following the successful completion of a treatment program. *Nolle prosequis* are regarded conceptually as a type of delayed rejection. The interests of justice may be served by filing a case and rejecting it later (e.g., because of successful completion of a drug treatment program), and a more elaborate model could be developed to account for such practices in the analysis of related issues.

8. The reader should not infer that the assumption shown here, that 90% of all arrestees are culpable offenders, is in fact closer to the truth than any other number. Police and prosecutors may see it as too low, and others may see it as too high. The values assigned to this assumption ranged from 75% to 99%. Although evidence on overturned convictions does not suggest any particular number, that evidence is not inconsistent with the range used here. But even that evidence misses the point of the analysis described here: to set an arbitrary point that has plausibility on its face and see how robust the findings are to *variation* around that point.

9. One can imagine a screening process that tends to bring cases involving innocent people to trial that are stronger than the ones involving culpable offenders, for
example, one that gives greater emphasis to the defendant's lack of jury appeal than to
valid evidence. It would be difficult, of course, to construct a valid test of such a
prospect.

10. For Scenario A, cases involving true offenders were assumed to be three
times more likely to be accepted than cases involving innocent arrestees; for Scenario
B, the acceptance rate multiple was assumed to be four. This parameter was varied from
lows of two to highs of five, subject to nonnegativity constraints for all cells and the
other constraints noted.

11. One might reasonably ask why an innocent person would *ever* plead guilty,
especially in Scenario B, in which the prosecutor offers less incentive to do so. There
are several plausible explanations. First, even when the incentives to plead are small,
defendants may be inclined to take advantage of them when the evidence against them
is strong. Second, some innocent defendants might plead guilty because they have got-
ten away with related crimes, perhaps more serious, that they fear might be unearthed
if they reject the plea offer and are subjected to further investigative scrutiny. Third,
judges show varying degrees of diligence to ensure that innocent people do not plead
guilty. Differences in the manner in which federal judges handle the fact-finding stage
of the review of a defendant's guilty plea have been documented by Jackman.

12. In addition, a constraint was imposed on all scenarios. Juries were assumed to
convict true offenders at a higher rate than they were innocent persons—that is, more
accurately than at random. Prosecutors could conceivably bring cases involving innocent
people to trial that tend to look stronger than the ones involving culpable offenders, but
one would expect that the better the pretrial screening process, the more likely trial cases
involving true offenders will be stronger than ones with innocent people.

13. Any such offsets are likely to be perceived as having both utilitarian and ret-
ributive value. The accumulated evidence on deterrence and incapacitation and on the
decline in criminal activity by age suggests stronger crime control effects from certainty
of punishment than from long sentences (Blumstein, Cohen, & Nagin, 1978). The
precise effects are likely to vary from one jurisdiction to the next.

14. These numbers are based on estimated totals in each category occurring
annually rather than the tracking of arrests over time. The Bureau of Justice Statistics
discontinued case-tracking statistics documenting the arrest-to-conviction process
after 1988, publishing instead numbers of convictions and incarcerations in selected
years in its *Felony Defendants in Large Urban Counties* (Hart & Reaves, 1999) and
Felony Sentences in State Courts (Brown, Langan, & Levin, 1999) series. Because many
convictions reported for any given year relate to arrests made in earlier years, some dis-
tortions result, especially when the aggregates change from year to year.

15. Conviction rates for burglary are much lower than for homicide, largely for
two reasons: (1) Juveniles constitute a larger share of burglary arrests than they do
homicide arrests, and they do not show up as convictions in either category; (2) Burglary arrests involving nonstrangers are much more likely to be dropped "in the inter-

est of justice" than are nonstranger homicides. It would make more sense for our purposes to restrict the analysis to stranger-to-stranger (adult) crimes, but the available data do not support such an analysis.

16. Case acceptance rates are generally higher for homicides than for burglaries (Boland & Sones, 1986). For both homicides and burglaries, cases involving offenders are assumed accepted at a higher rate than cases involving innocent persons.

17. Rainville (2002) has found systematic differences in several variables across the two settings, particularly ones related to community orientation. He concludes: "Elected prosecutors appear to be more interested in the political cachet associated with community prosecution than do appointed prosecutors" (p. 82).

18. The National Academy of Sciences highlighted this "paucity of research on the prosecutor's function" in a report by Heymann and Petrie (2001, p. 3). Their observation echoes a 1998 survey of over 500 research projects on crime prevention, sponsored by the National Institute of Justice and conducted by researchers from the University of Maryland, which found many innovative programs that were revealed to be effective, programs initiated by the police, social service agencies, schools, drug treatment specialists, and housing and correctional authorities. This report found just one program focusing on the prosecutor—an experiment designed to test the effect of alternative prosecution policies in domestic violence cases. The survey was conducted and documented by Sherman, Gottfredson, MacKenzie, Eck, Reuter, and Bushway (1999). The prosecution experiment, documented by Ford, tested three alternative domestic violence interventions in Indianapolis.

References

Bedau, H. A., & Radelet, M. L. (1987). Miscarriages of justice in potentially capital cases. *Stanford Law Review, 40*, 21–179.

Berger v. United States, 295 U.S. 78 (1935).

Blackstone, W. (1765). *Commentaries on the laws of England* (facsimile of 1765 edition). Chicago: University of Chicago Press

Blumstein, A. (2002). Prisons. In J.Q. Wilson & J. Petersilia (Eds.), *Crime: Public policies for crime control* (2nd ed.) (pp. 451–482). San Francisco: ICS Press.

Blumstein, A., Cohen, J., & Nagin, D. (Eds.). (1978). *Deterrence and incapacitation: Estimating the effects of criminal sanctions on crime rates.* Washington, DC: National Academy of Sciences.

Boland, B., & Forst, B. (1985). Prosecutors don't always aim to pleas. *Federal Probation, 49*, 10–15.

Boland, B., & Sones, R. (1986). *Prosecution of felony arrests.* Washington, DC: Bureau of Justice Statistics.

Brady v. Maryland, 373 U.S. 83 (1963).

Brown, J. M., Langan, P. A., & Levin, D. J. (1999). *Felony sentences in state courts, 1996.* Washington, DC: Bureau of Justice Statistics.

Coles, C. M., Kelling, G. M., & Moore, M. H. (1998). *Prosecution in the community: A study of emergent strategies—A cross site analysis.* Cambridge, MA: Harvard University Press.

DeFrances, C. J., & Steadman, G. W. (1998). *Prosecutors in state courts, 1996.* Washington, DC: Bureau of Justice Statistics.

Feeley, M. M., & Lazerson, M. H. (1983). Police-prosecutor relationships: An interorganizational perspective. In K.O. Boyum and L. Mather (Eds.), *Empirical theories about courts* (pp. 216–243). New York: Longman.

Ford, D. (1993). *Indianapolis domestic violence prosecution experiment.* Indianapolis: Indiana University Press.

Forst, B. (2002). Prosecution. In J.Q. Wilson & J. Petersilia (Eds.), *Crime: Public policies for crime control* (2nd ed.) (pp. 509–536). San Francisco: ICS Press.

Forst, B., & Brosi, K. (1977). A theoretical and empirical analysis of the prosecutor. *Journal of Legal Studies, 6,* 177–191.

Gershman, B. L. (1999). *Prosecutorial misconduct* (2nd ed.). St. Paul, MN: West.

Hart, T. C., & Reaves, B. A. (1999). *Felony defendants in large urban counties, 1996.* Washington, DC: Bureau of Justice Statistics.

Heymann, P., & Petrie, C. (Eds.). (2001). *What's changing in prosecution? Report of a workshop.* Washington, DC: National Academy Press.

Huff, C. R., Rattner, A., & Sagarin, E. (1996). *Convicted but innocent: Wrongful conviction and public policy.* Thousand Oaks, CA: Sage Publications.

Jackman, T. (2002, July 25). Judge seeks both sides' input on Moussaoui hearing. *Washington Post,* p. A14.

Jackson, R. H. (1940). The federal prosecutor. *Journal of the American Judicial Society, 24,* 18–19.

Landes, W. M. (1971). An economic analysis of the courts. *Journal of Law and Economics, 14,* 61–107.

Latzer, B., & Cauthen, J. (2000). The meaning of capital appeals: A rejoinder to Liebman, Fagan, and West. *Judicature, 84,* 142–143.

Liebman, J. S., Fagan, J., West, V., & Lloyd, J. (2000). Capital attrition: Error rates in capital cases, 1973–1995. *Texas Law Review, 78,* 1839–1865.

McDonald, W. F. (1982). *Police-prosecutor relations in the United States.* Washington, DC: National Institute of Justice.

Radelet, M. L., Bedau, H. A., & Putnam, C. E. (1992). *In spite of innocence: Erroneous convictions in capital cases.* Boston: Northeastern University Press.

Rainville, G. (2002). *Differing incentives of appointed and elected prosecutors and the relationship between prosecutor policy and votes in local elections.* Doctoral dissertation. Washington, DC: American University.

Scheck, B., Neufeld, P., & Dwyer, J. (2001). *Actual innocence: When justice goes wrong and how to make it right.* New York: Signet.

Sherman, L. W., Gottfredson, D., MacKenzie, D., Eck, J., Reuter, P., & Bushway, S. (1999). *Preventing crime: What works, what doesn't, what's promising*. Washington, DC: National Institute of Justice.

Wittes, B. (2002). *Starr: A reassessment*. New Haven, CT: Yale University Press.

Wright, R., & Miller, M. (2002). The screening/bargaining tradeoff. *Stanford Law Review, 55*, 29–118.

Chapter Four

Have Sentencing Reforms Displaced Discretion over Sentencing from Judges to Prosecutors?

RODNEY L. ENGEN

Introduction

Beginning in the mid-1970s, state and federal lawmakers in the United States have enacted a diverse array of laws designed to regulate criminal sentencing by reducing or eliminating discretion on the part of judges and correctional officials. These include the enactment of *mandatory minimum* sentencing laws for some crimes in every state, most often drug and weapon offenses; *habitual offender* laws, including "three strikes and you're out" in a majority of states; and various forms of *sentencing guidelines* in roughly 18 states (Austin, Jones, Kramer, & Renninger, 1996; Zimring, Hawkins, & Kamin, 2001). These reforms vary substantially in their scope, in the limitations they place on judicial discretion, and in the severity of the sanctions they specify, but they all attempt to increase uniformity (and reduce unwarranted racial disparity) in sentencing, and ensure that sentencing is determined by the conviction offense and/or the offenders' criminal history. Often they also seek to increase both the likelihood of incarceration and the duration of sentences for certain crimes, particularly for violent crimes and drug offenses, and for repeat offenders.[1]

One potential consequence of these reforms, however, is that they "displace" discretion over sentencing from judges to prosecutors, potentially undermining both the philosophical and practical aims of the reforms. Perhaps most famously, Alschuler (1978) argued:

In my view, fixed and presumptive sentencing schemes . . . are unlikely to achieve their objectives so long as they leave the prosecutors' power unchecked. Indeed, this sort of reform is likely to produce its antithesis— a system every bit as lawless as the current sentencing regime, in which discretion is concentrated in an inappropriate agency, and in which the benefits of this discretion are made available only to defendants who sacrifice their constitutional rights. (p. 551)

Tonry (1996) is equally critical of mandatory sentencing laws:

Evaluated in terms of their stated substantive objectives, mandatory penalties do not work. The record is clear from research in the 1950s, the 1970s, the 1980s, and the 1990s that mandatory penalty laws shift power from judges to prosecutors, meet with widespread circumvention, produce dislocations in case processing, and too often result in imposition of penalties that everyone involved believes to be unduly harsh. (p. 135)

How can this happen? As Cohen and Tonry (1983) argue, "Prosecutors can always and everywhere elect whether to file charges bearing mandatory minimum sentences or some other charge, and whether to dismiss charges" (p. 340). Qualitative studies find that prosecutors frequently engage in plea bargaining over the seriousness of charges (charge bargaining) and over facts that can affect sentences (fact bargaining), such as whether a weapon was used, the quantity of drugs, or the existence of prior "strikes" in a defendant's record (Schulhofer & Nagel, 1997; Ulmer, 2005). Even if legislation directs prosecutors to file all relevant information (e.g., all "strikes"), they often are able to dismiss them on grounds of insufficient evidence or, as in California, for the "furtherance of justice" (Harris & Jesilow, 2000; Zimring, Hawkins, & Kamin, 2001). Likewise, under presumptive sentencing guidelines, prosecutors can reduce a defendant's sentence by reducing the primary charge to a less serious one (Alschuler, 1978; Miethe, 1987).

While researchers might do this is a separate issue, and largely beyond the present discussion, but researchers typically argue that prosecutors and other court actors circumvent sentencing reforms either because the laws conflict with local norms or "going rates" for punishment, because court actors perceive the laws to be unjust in some cases, or simply because reducing the charges gives prosecutors a powerful means of enticing (or coercing) defendants to plead guilty (Bynum, 1982; Coffee & Tonry, 1983; Heumann & Loftin, 1979; Schulhofer & Nagel, 1997).

While it is clear that the potential exists for these laws to enhance prosecutors' control over sentencing, many questions remain. The displacement hypothesis actually contains several related predictions. Mandatory and presumptive sentencing laws transfer control over sentences from judges to prosecutors, prosecutors will adapt their charging practices in response to changes in the laws, and these adaptations will work to mitigate the effects of sentencing reforms. Undoubtedly, "circumvention" of the laws happens, but how often and in what kinds of cases? Prosecutors probably can affect sentences under these laws, but have these laws really shifted control over sentencing to prosecutors, and to what degree? Have prosecutors undermined the goals of these reforms, such as increasing uniformity and reducing unwarranted disparities?

I contend that the empirical record on these questions is quite limited. This chapter reviews empirical research on prosecutorial decision making in the application of mandatory minimum sentences, including habitual offender/three-strikes statutes, and under presumptive sentencing guidelines, with an emphasis on research in the past 10 years. The question of whether sentencing laws displace discretion is complex, and no study provides a comprehensive assessment. Therefore, I organize the empirical findings around three issues: (1) How do prosecutors exercise their discretion under mandatory or presumptive sentencing laws? (2) Do sentencing reforms increase prosecutorial discretion in sentencing? (3) Do prosecutorial adaptations to sentencing laws undermine uniformity in punishment? I conclude by outlining a research agenda with an explicit focus on the exercise of prosecutorial discretion.

Prosecutorial Discretion under Mandatory and Presumptive Sentencing: Do Prosecutors Circumvent Mandatory Sentencing Laws?

Several well-known studies evaluating mandatory minimum sentencing laws enacted in the 1970s (New York's 1973 "Rockefeller Drug Laws," Massachusetts's 1975 Bartley-Fox Amendment, and Michigan's 1977 "Gun Law") found that prosecutors, and in some instances police and judges, effectively neutralized these laws through charge reductions and outright dismissals or acquittals. Offenders convicted of the targeted offenses generally received the mandated sanctions, but the number of offenders arrested, charged, and convicted of these crimes decreased (see reviews by Cohen & Tonry, 1983; Tonry, 1996). Although these studies implicated prosecutors in circumventing "get tough" laws, their focus was largely on assessing whether the laws increased sentence severity for the targeted crimes, which they did not.

A few studies, however, examine prosecutors' application of mandatory sentencing laws explicitly. For instance, Bynum (1982) found that prosecutors in Michigan charged the Gun Law enhancement in 65% of the eligible cases statewide. More recent research on mandatory minimums for firearm and drug offenses finds that prosecutors apply them even less often in some other states. Farrell (2003) found that Maryland prosecutors applied a mandatory 5-year firearm enhancement in only 37% of the eligible cases. Likewise, Ulmer, Kurlychek, and Kramer (2003) found that Pennsylvania prosecutors imposed mandatory minimum sentences in only 8% of eligible drug trafficking cases in 1997. Each of these studies also found substantial variation between counties in prosecutors' decisions to apply mandatory minimum sentences.

Research under the U.S. Sentencing Guidelines finds that U.S. attorneys also circumvent mandatory minimums in a substantial minority of cases. The U.S. Sentencing Commission (USSC, 1991) found that among drug and firearm cases eligible for mandatory minimum sentences, federal prosecutors initially charged 74% with the highest applicable charge, but reduced many of them prior to conviction. Ultimately, only 59% were convicted of crimes requiring the most severe mandatory sentence applicable, and 25% were convicted of crimes that did not carry mandatory sentences. Prosecutors also granted "substantial assistance" departure motions in one third of cases convicted under a mandatory minimum provision, negating the mandatory sentence. Other evaluations estimate that from one third (U.S. General Accounting Office, 1993) to half (Meierhoefer, 1992) of offenders eligible for mandatory minimums in U.S. courts avoided them. Likewise, Schulhofer and Nagel (1997) estimated that federal prosecutors circumvented the guidelines in 20% to 35% of cases, most often in cases involving mandatory minimums. Even more striking, the USSC found that federal prosecutors filed firearm enhancements in only 20% of qualified cases in 2000, down from 45% in 1991 and 35% in 1995 (USSC, 2004).

Prosecutorial circumvention of mandatory sentences for habitual offenders, including "three-strikes" laws, may be even more common. The best evidence of this is the simple fact that most states convict very few offenders under these laws, with the notable exception of California (Campaign for an Effective Crime Policy, 1996). Unfortunately, very few studies examine the rate at which prosecutors charge eligible offenders under three-strikes or habitual offender laws, but the studies that do have found that prosecutors reduce the charges or simply do not file "strikes" in the majority of cases. Ulmer et al. (2003) found that Pennsylvania prosecutors filed "strikes" in 29% of second and third strike cases. In Florida, Crawford, Chiricos, and Kleck (1998) and Crawford (2000) found that only 20% of eligible males (21% of Blacks and 17% of Whites) and only 6% of eligible females were charged and sentenced as habitual offenders. Even in California, where tens of thousands have been sentenced under the three-strikes law, the law has been applied selectively (Greenwood et al., 1998; Austin, Clark, Hardyman, & Henry, 2000). Zimring et al. (2001) estimated that in roughly one third of second-strike cases, and in the vast majority of third-strike cases, prosecutors simply did not prosecute them as second and third strikes. Also, when they did prosecute two-strike cases, prosecutors often negotiated guilty pleas by reducing the second strike to a less serious offense, which in turn reduces the mandatory sentence in California.

To summarize, the evidence is unequivocal with respect to mandatory minimums for drugs and weapons and habitual offender/three-strikes laws— prosecutors frequently circumvent these laws by dismissing, reducing, or simply not filing the charges that would trigger the mandatory sentences. However, the frequency of circumvention varies tremendously. Some studies find that prosecutors apply these laws in a substantial majority of cases. Others find that they apply them in only a minority of cases. Also, every study that examined multiple jurisdictions (federal districts or counties) found substantial variation in charging practices across jurisdictions (Bynum, 1982; Crawford et al., 1998; Crawford, 2000; Zimring et al., 2001; Harris & Jesilow, 2000; Ulmer et al., 2003; Farrell, 2003; Nagel & Schulhofer, 1992; Schulhofer & Nagel, 1997).

The few studies that included multivariate analyses reveal that several offender and case characteristics predict the likelihood that prosecutors will charge mandatory minimums. Prosecutors were more likely to charge weapon enhancements for Black offenders in Michigan (Bynum, 1982) and Maryland (Farrell, 2003), and mandatory minimum drug charges for Hispanic offenders in Pennsylvania (Ulmer et al., 2003). Habitual offender statutes were applied more often to Black than White offenders in Florida (Crawford et al., 1998; Crawford, 2000). Males are also more likely to be charged with mandatory minimums (Farrell, 2003; Ulmer et al., 2003; Crawford et al., 1998; Crawford, 2000). Legal and case processing factors matter as well. Offense seriousness, criminal history, and trial convictions significantly increase the probability of being charged with mandatory minimums (Bynum, 1982; Farrell, 2003; Ulmer et al., 2003; Crawford et al., 1998; Crawford, 2000). Bynum in particular concluded that Michigan prosecutors used the Gun Law like a habitual offender statute (1982, p. 58). Also, Ulmer et al. found that prosecutors charged mandatory minimum offenses in drug cases less often as the distance increased between the mandatory sentence and the guidelines range that would apply if the mandatory were not charged. In other words, the more severe the increase in sentence that would result from the mandatory minimum, the less likely prosecutors were to use it.

Do Prosecutors Circumvent Sentencing Guidelines? Yes,

The most extensive research on the displacement of discretion under sentencing guidelines was conducted 20 years ago in Minnesota, which adopted presumptive sentencing in 1980. Miethe and Moore (1985) and Miethe (1987) each found that charge reductions were common both pre- and post-guidelines in Minnesota, and there was little change in their frequency. Furthermore, in each period, sentence bargaining was more common than charge bargaining, and reductions in the *number* of charges (i.e., dismissals) were more common than reductions in the *seriousness* of the primary charge. For example, Miethe (1987) showed that in 1978, 2 years prior to the guidelines, 33% of cases received a charge dismissal as part of a negotiated plea, while only 13% received a reduction in the primary charge. In 1982, 2 years after the adoption of the guidelines, 39% received dismissals and 8% received reductions in the primary charge. The authors assert that this contradicts the displacement hypotheses, in that the frequency of charge reductions, especially in seriousness, did not increase. Finally, Miethe (1987) also found that charge bargaining (i.e., reduction in seriousness) was more likely when the original charge carried a presumptive prison sentence. Among less serious cases, sentence bargaining was more common, even post-guidelines.

Other research, however, concludes that prosecutors mitigated the impact of the Minnesota guidelines. Frase (2004) reports that "Resistance by judges and attorneys to one of the commission's most significant 'prescriptive' choices—to imprison more 'person' offenders with low criminal histories— was immediate" (p. 174), and that the rates of charge reductions in these cases were "much higher in 1981 through 1983 than they were in 1978" (p. 175) (see also Frase, 1993; Knapp, 1984). This was especially true for child sex abuse cases, in which charge reductions increased from 50% of cases to 80% following implementation of the guidelines.

Unfortunately, pre- and post-guideline analyses like those done in Minnesota have not been performed in other states with sentencing guidelines, or in the federal courts. However, one report in Washington State, which implemented presumptive guidelines in 1984, shows a 40% decrease in the number of cases convicted for crimes carrying a presumptive prison sentence, and a corresponding increase in convictions for less serious offenses (Washington State Sentencing Guidelines Commission, 1985). Thus prosecutors may have increased charge bargaining especially in cases where the guidelines required a prison sentence for the original charge, as happened in Minnesota.

More recently, Engen and Steen (2000) examined several changes to the sentencing guidelines for drug offenders in Washington and found that prosecutors adapted in each instance, but with very different consequences. When the legislature attempted, in 1988, to require prison sentences for all first-time drug dealers, prosecutors responded by reducing a substantial portion of drug delivery cases to simple possession, effectively neutralizing the law. The rate of imprisonment and the average sentence length for drug offenders did not change. However, when the legislature doubled the prison sentence for drug delivery in 1990 (to about 2 years), prosecutors adapted quite differently. The percentage of offenders convicted of delivery versus possession returned to their previous levels, and overall sentence severity increased sharply. Engen and Steen concluded that, in each instance, prosecutors used the available charging options not to maintain "going rates" but to maintain a high rate of guilty pleas.

In a follow-up to this study, Steen, Gainey, and I collected case-level data on charging decisions in drug cases in three counties in Washington State (Steen, Engen, & Gainey, 1999). Engen, Steen, and Gainey (2000), focusing on offenders who were arrested for drug delivery, found that prosecutors charged 81% with drug delivery, but more than half of these were later reduced. In the end, only 39% were convicted of drug delivery and faced prison. The remainder pled guilty to lesser offenses, resulting in much shorter jail sentences. Younger offenders and offenders who played a minimal role in the offense were more likely to receive charge reductions, but White offenders were no more likely to receive charge reductions than Black or Hispanic offenders.

Finally, researchers have begun to examine charging decisions in North Carolina, which adopted "mandatory" sentencing guidelines known as "Structured Sentencing" in 1994 (see Wright, 1998). The North Carolina Sentencing Policy and Advisory Commission (NCSPAC) examined charging decisions for 42,000 felony cases sentenced in the period 1999–2000 and found that *nearly half* (49%) were convicted of less serious crimes than were initially charged, with 36% reduced to misdemeanors (NCSPAC, 2002). As in Minnesota, crimes carrying presumptive prison sentences are reduced at higher rates than cases charged with less serious felonies. Wright and Engen (2006) reexamined the NCSPAC data for a variety of crime types and found that for each offense type examined, charge reductions parallel the overall findings reported by the commission. Charges were reduced in 80% of serious assaults, 59% of robberies, 66% of kidnappings, 43% of burglaries, and 43% of cocaine sale/deliveries. Moreover, within each crime category, charge reductions were most common for the most serious degree of charge.

Multivariate analyses of the North Carolina data found that, in addition to the effects of offense class, charge reductions were less likely for offenders with more criminal history, less likely for males than females, more likely for offenders who pled guilty, and varied significantly between districts (NCSPAC, 2002). No significant race effects were revealed in the commission's analysis, but in a re-analysis of the NCSPAC data, Engen, Rikard, Parrotta, and Antonaccio (2004) found a surprising race-by-sex interaction. African American females were significantly more likely to receive charge reductions than any other race-sex combination, followed by White females.

In summary, the evidence in guideline jurisdictions is limited but indicates that charge reductions are common, especially for crimes carrying presumptive prison sentences (serious crimes against persons) in Minnesota and

North Carolina, and for narcotic deliveries in Washington. Charge reductions in cases not involving mandatory minimums may be less common in the federal courts, but evidence is scant. Charge reductions also may be related to race and sex, although the findings are inconsistent. Finally, as was the case with mandatory sentences, research on charge reductions under guidelines consistently finds significant differences between counties in the likelihood of charge reductions in Minnesota (Miethe & Moore, 1985; Miethe, 1987), Washington (Engen, Steen, & Gainey, 2000), and North Carolina (NCSPAC, 2002), and between federal court districts (Nagel & Schulhofer, 1992; Schulhofer & Nagel, 1997).

Do Sentencing Reforms Increase Prosecutorial Discretion in Sentencing?

It not enough to show that prosecutors often bargain around guidelines or mandatory sentencing laws. They may apply these laws selectively, but do they usurp sentencing authority from judges? Perhaps, but not necessarily. For example, Heumann and Loftin (1979) found that despite the Wayne County (Detroit) prosecutor's policy of no plea bargaining over the Gun Law, sentences changed very little overall. *Judges* mitigated the impact of the law. They dismissed gun charges in some cases, reduced sentences for the underlying offenses in order to offset the enhancements in others, or found defendants guilty of misdemeanors rather than felonies. Consequently, although prosecutors controlled the charging decision, they did not control sentencing.

Similarly, Schulhofer and Nagel (1997) conclude that "In the vast majority (approximately 65–80%) of cases . . . plea negotiations are not used as a vehicle to circumvent the intent of the [federal] Guidelines. Contrary to the claims of many judges, *the Guidelines have not transferred sentencing discretion from the court to the prosecutor*" (pp. 1284–1285, italics added). In this, as in their earlier research (Nagel & Schulhofer, 1992), they conclude that when guideline circumvention occurs, in most cases the resulting sentence is similar to what a judge likely would have ordered otherwise, or "perhaps 10–25% below the "proper" guideline sentence" (1997, p. 1291). However, they also report "huge discounts" in some jurisdictions and, equally important to the present discussion, they acknowledge that when prosecutors bargain around the guidelines "the sentencing decision is not being made by the judge, as the guidelines contemplated. It is being made exclusively by the parties" (Nagel & Schulhofer, 1992, p. 551).

This reveals the crux of the matter. *Who really controls sentencing?* This is the critical test of the displacement hypothesis: *Under these sentencing laws, for a given population of offenders, do prosecutors exert more control over sentencing than judges do* (or, in a more moderate form, *does their control over sentencing increase relative to that of judges*)? In order to answer this question, research must address several closely related and more specific questions: (1) What effect do discretionary charging and plea bargaining decisions have on sentence severity? (2) How does the effect of these decisions on sentences compare to the effect of judicial discretion? And, perhaps most importantly, (3) Is the relative effect of charging decisions versus judicial discretion greater under mandatory or presumptive sentencing laws than it would be if those laws were not in place? To date, no such study has been published, but a few address the first two questions and illustrate some potential avenues for future research.

One innovative analysis (Miller & Sloan, 1994) comparing the effects of prosecutorial and judicial discretion on sentencing measured prosecutorial discretion (i.e., the magnitude of charge reductions) by computing the difference, in months, between the midpoint of the sentence range for the primary charge initially filed by the prosecutor and the midpoint of the sentencing range for the primary charge for which the defendant was convicted or pled guilty. They measured judicial discretion as the difference in months between the actual sentence ordered and the midpoint of the guideline range for the primary conviction charge. Miller and Sloan found that charge reductions had a substantial effect on sentence severity, but judges had an even bigger effect. For offenders sentenced to prison, prosecutors reduced the presumptive sentence by an average of 46 months (210 to 164 months) but, in addition, judges reduced sentences on average by more than 100 months. They concluded, contrary to the prediction that prosecutors wield greater control over sentencing than do judges, "The amount of judicial discretion was significantly greater than the amount of prosecutorial discretion" (1994, p. 113). This finding may reflect the fact that the guidelines in this jurisidiction were voluntary. Research under presumptive guidelines may reach a different conclusion.

In a series of analyses of the North Carolina charging and sentencing data, my colleagues and I adopted Miller and Sloan's approach to measure the effects of charge reductions on presumptive sentences (Engen et al., 2004; Wright & Engen, 2006). We found that nearly half (47%) of the cases facing presumptive prison sentences, based on the initial charges, were convicted of less serious crimes, making them eligible for intermediate or community-based sanctions (Engen et al., 2004). Charge reductions reduced presumptive sentence durations by an average of 18 months for the defendants who received charge reductions. As a result, the average presumptive sentence among *all* felony cases was reduced roughly in half, from 19.4 months based on the original charges to 10.5 months based on the conviction charge. The magnitude of the reductions also is greater for more serious than less serious crimes.

The effect that charge reductions have on actual sentences is complex, however. One analysis (Engen, 2006) found that charge reductions explain 47% of the total variance in the duration of sentences ordered and account for

85% of the variance that is not attributable to the original charge and the defendant's criminal history. However, charge reductions did poorly in predicting whether or not offenders received prison sentences (improving the predictive accuracy of the model by only 3%). In comparison, judicial discretion accounted for the bulk of the in/out decisions (over 80%) but explained less than 10% of the variance in sentence duration. Thus judges continue to control the in/out decision in North Carolina, but prosecutors exert much more control over sentence duration. This likely is due to the structure of North Carolina's guidelines. The sentencing grid has a disposition line above which a prison sentence is essentially mandatory, but even if prosecutors reduce a serious crime to one that falls below the line, judges may still order a prison term in most cases, albeit a shorter one. Also, most felony cases are not the serious violent ones that carry a presumptive prison sentence. Consequently, a charge reduction often does not change the disposition options available to the judge, but it always changes the presumptive duration.

Together these analyses suggest several important conclusions. Charge reductions have a substantial impact on the severity of punishment that can (or must) be imposed at sentencing, especially sentence duration, but this does not necessarily translate to prosecutorial control. Under voluntary guidelines (which were not the object of Alschuler's and others criticisms), prosecutors can have a substantial effect on the recommended sentence but still have less influence than judges. In one presumptive guideline state, however, sentence duration is almost entirely determined by the charges filed. What may be more surprising is that even in a state that virtually mandates prison (i.e., judges cannot depart) for whole classes of offenses and for offenders with extensive records, judges still have more control over imprisonment than prosecutors do. Unfortunately, similar analyses under other sentencing systems are not available for comparison. No studies have attempted to quantify the relative impact of judges' versus prosecutors' decisions in cases eligible for mandatory sentencing, and no studies have addressed our earlier question number 3—is the impact of prosecutorial discretion relative to judicial discretion greater under sentencing guidelines or mandatory minimums than it would be otherwise?

Does Prosecutorial Adaptation Undermine Uniformity and Produce Disparity?

Does the exercise of discretion in charging and plea bargaining by prosecutors undermine uniformity in punishment for offenders who have committed similar crimes? Undoubtedly, the fact that some offenders who qualify for mandatory sentences receive them, while many do not, results in disparate punishments (Tonry, 1996). As Zimring et al. (2001) observe with respect to three strikes in California, "The same criminal record and current crime could result in a short stay in a parole return center or a 25–year-to-life prison term" (p. 84). Likewise, if half of all offenders charged with felonies in North Carolina and a majority of offenders charged with delivering narcotics in Washington State pled guilty to less serious crimes, then "uniformity" in the punishment of similar offenders in these states, and potentially in other states with presumptive sentencing guidelines, may be an illusion. As a result, the potential for racial-ethnic and gender disparity in punishment is great as well. Thus these laws, which were intended to ensure uniform punishment and to increase the severity of punishment of certain targeted offenders, may have had exactly the opposite effects—failing to increase or possibly even decreasing the severity of punishment, while potentially making punishments less consistent.

However, in general, *the impact of mandatory minimums and sentencing guidelines on uniformity in punishment is unknown.* To be sure, there are many examples of individual injustice, where mandatory sentences result in what may be unduly harsh punishments for undeserving offenders (Tonry, 1996), and it is possible that sentences are more disparate under mandatory sentencing than they were prior to the enactment of these laws. Conversely, the evidence under sentencing guidelines seems to suggest that guidelines have reduced unwarranted disparities (Tonry, 1996), but this is only for offenders *convicted* of similar crimes with similar criminal histories. To my knowledge, no published research to date has shown or, tested, whether sentences for offenders who have *committed* similar crimes are more or less uniform under mandatory or presumptive sentencing laws than they would be otherwise.

Again, though, the best available evidence comes from Minnesota. Miethe's and Moore's research (Miethe & Moore, 1985; also see Miethe, 1987) is composed of two of the few studies that present quantitative multivariate analyses of charging decisions under sentencing guidelines, and theirs are the only analyses of plea bargaining pre- and post-guidelines. These authors reasoned that if the displacement hypotheses is correct, then prosecutors would increase the emphasis placed on status characteristics in plea bargaining. However, they concluded, unequivocally, that the introduction of guidelines did *not* increase discrimination at the charging stage. They observed some changes, but "charging and plea bargaining practices remained fairly stable across pre- and post-guideline periods" (Miethe, 1987, p. 165). Contrary to displacement predictions, the importance of legal factors (alleged severity, criminal history, and weapon use) diminished post-guidelines, and there was no change in the effects of race, marital status, or education, which were not significant in either time period.

Other research on the factors that affect prosecutors' decisions under mandatory or presumptive sentencing also is relevant to the question of whether disparities in punishment are likely. Several studies cited earlier find that race, ethnicity, and sex affect the application of mandatory sentences (Bynum, 1982; Farrell, 2003; Ulmer et al., 2003; Crawford et al., 1998; Crawford, 2000). If we assume that charging decisions affect actual sentences, then any bias in a charging decision is likely to contribute to disparities in punishment. It is unclear, though, whether these disparities are any larger or smaller than they were prior to mandatory sentencing. The evidence under presumptive guidelines is mixed. Studies in Minnesota and Washington find that race and sex have no effect on the likelihood of charge reductions (race-sex interactions were not tested) (Miethe & Moore, 1985; Miethe, 1987; Engen, Steen, & Gainey, 2000). In North Carolina, women are more likely to receive charge reductions, and they received larger reductions in the presumptive sentence than men, especially African American women (NCSPAC, 2002; Engen et al., 2004). However, charge reductions in North Carolina do *not* appear to explain the effects of race and sex on actual sentencing decisions (Engen, 2006). It may be that these indirect effects are so small that they become unimportant, net of other factors such as offense seriousness.

Summary and Directions for Future Research: Moving beyond the Displacement Hypothesis

The research reviewed here shows that prosecutors exercise substantial discretion in deciding whether or not to charge crimes that require mandatory minimum sentences and in deciding the severity of charges under presumptive sentencing guidelines. In both contexts, the research shows that prosecutors frequently reduce the severity of charges, probably in exchange for guilty pleas in most cases, but how often they do this varies tremendously, not only between states with different laws but between jurisdictions under the same laws. Multivariate studies find that these decisions are related to individual offense and offender characteristics as well. With respect to mandatory minimums, we can conclude that the exercise of prosecutorial discretion has probably mitigated the impact of these laws on sentencing to some extent, and probably has undermined to some extent the goals of ensuring uniformity and reducing racial-ethnic and gender disparities in the punishment of offenders who have committed similar crimes, and who have similar criminal histories. With respect to sentencing guidelines, uniformity in punishment has probably not been achieved, but the evidence available does not indicate that charging decisions contribute significantly to unwarranted disparities.

It is difficult to draw conclusions beyond these, however. It is not clear to what extent mandatory or presumptive sentencing laws have shifted control over sentencing to prosecutors, nor is it clear whether punishment is more or less uniform under these laws than it would be otherwise. The evidence simply is incomplete. In the past 20 years, very few studies have examined charging decisions regarding mandatory minimums with individual-level data, and even fewer have examined charging decisions in states with presumptive sentencing guidelines. Most importantly, very few studies have estimated the effect of charging decisions in these cases on either the likelihood of imprisonment or the length of sentences ordered, net of other factors.

This last point requires clarification. Several studies found that offenders charged with mandatory minimum offenses received more severe sentences than those who were not. This is a start, but it is not sufficient to answer the question. These same studies find that prosecutors are more likely to apply mandatory minimums in more serious cases, for offenders with more criminal history, for males, and for offenders who did not plead guilty. These are the same characteristics that predict sentence severity generally. Therefore it is possible, perhaps even likely, that the application of a mandatory minimum makes little difference in whether an offender is sentenced to prison (i.e., it might be applied mainly to cases that would be sentenced to prison anyway). Indeed, the one study that estimated the effect of charge reductions on sentences under presumptive guidelines found that charging decisions made little difference in predicting in/out decisions. In both cases (mandatory minimums and sentencing guidelines), charging decisions might have a greater effect on the length of sentences, but how much? These are empirical questions that currently are not answered. In fact, I submit that these are the critical questions upon which any conclusions regarding the displacement of discretion rest. Without first establishing the effect that charging decisions have on the severity of sentences—among offenders who have committed similar crimes—conclusions about the effects of prosecutorial discretion on disparity in sentencing and conclusions about whether these laws shift control over sentencing to prosecutors are premature.

By now one thing should be clear. Much more research is needed in examining the questions posed here: How do prosecutors exercise their discretion in charging under mandatory and presumptive sentencing laws? What effect do these decisions have on sentences and on sentence uniformity or disparity? How do the effects of charging decisions on sentences compare to the effects of judicial discretion? And, the ultimate test of the displacement hypothesis—*Is the relative importance of charging versus judicial discretion greater under mandatory or presumptive sentencing laws than it is in the absence of those laws?*

At this point I would like to shift the focus of this discussion and propose a more comprehensive research question that subsumes these questions and may organize a long-term research agenda. *To what extent is the distribution and exercise of prosecutorial versus judicial control over sentencing related to the structure of sentencing laws?* Several legal analysts have offered useful ideas that can inform this question and move research beyond the narrow focus on whether prosecutors circumvent specific reforms. For example, Reitz (1998) argues that sentencing structures (mandatory minimums, sentencing guidelines, etc.) differentially allocate sentencing authority among legislators, correctional officials, and various court actors in different ways. Knapp (1993) argues that the specificity of criminal laws influences the allocation of discretion under guidelines; the more narrowly crimes are defined, the more control prosecutors have. Ronald Wright and I, in our description of charge reductions in North Carolina, suggest that the "depth" (variety) of charging options available to prosecutors and the "distance" (change in sentence severity) between those options are likely to affect the probability that prosecutors will reduce charges and affect the impact that these choices have on the sentence. Other dimensions of sentencing guidelines also are likely to be important, such as the width of sentence ranges, the ability of judges to depart from them, and whether the guidelines have a "hard" disposition (in/out) line (e.g., Minnesota and Washington) or one that judges can cross readily, at least in some cases (e.g., North Carolina and Pennsylvania).

A number of findings reported here also suggest that the likelihood of charge reductions, and their effect on sentences (and thus prosecutorial control over punishment), depends on structural features of the sentencing laws that are in place. Research on mandatory minimums, and research on charging under sentencing guidelines in Minnesota, North Carolina, and Washington, suggests that charge bargaining is likely in more serious cases, especially when laws prescribe a prison sentence for the original charge. This may mean that charge bargaining has more value in cases where a prison sentence is at stake, or simply because a reduction has a larger effect on the sentence duration. Among less serious cases, a reduction in charge severity has less impact on the sentence, so negotiations may more often revolve around other factors.

Shifting the focus from the displacement hypothesis to the broader question of the relationship between sentencing laws and discretion also opens up many opportunities for research. While pre- and post-reform analyses such as Miethe's and Moore's would be ideal, opportunities for such research are rare (a situation that is unlikely to change any time soon). However, other avenues can offer important insights. For example, I have found no studies in the past 20 years that examine the application of mandatory minimums in jurisdictions that did not also have sentencing guidelines (I apologize in advance for any oversights). Would such research find, like Heumann and Loftin (1979), that mandatory minimums do not increase prosecutors' control over sentencing? Also, many states have multiple mandatory minimum sentencing laws. Are these all applied similarly, or does their application depend on the severity of the sentences mandated and the distance between charging options (Zimring et al., 2001; Ulmer et al., 2003)? Comparative research among states with different sentencing structures also would be beneficial, as it poses many methodological challenges but could prove exceptionally valuable in lieu of pre-post designs. Finally, research on adaptations to changes in existing sentencing guidelines could generate important insights into prosecutors' use of guidelines (Engen & Steen, 2000). Moreover, research on adaptations to existing guidelines may have greater practical value given that the movement toward guidelines has slowed (Tonry, 1999), but states where guidelines have endured continue amending them (Dailey, 1998; Steiger, 1998). Researchers also can take advantage of the fact that sentencing commissions have been systematically collecting sentencing data for years prior to and following changes in their sentencing laws.

In closing, I also would like to issue a call for theory and theoretically grounded research. Theoretical understanding of prosecutorial discretion, generally, and particularly regarding adaptations to changes in sentencing laws, is severely limited. As I noted in the Introduction to this chapter researchers typically attribute prosecutorial adaptations either to local norms, concerns about equity and justice, or administrative expedience in obtaining guilty pleas. Sometimes empirical evidence supports these explanations, but often these explanations are merely invoked as plausible interpretations. We need better theoretical models that can predict if, and when, either of these explanations is likely to affect prosecutors' choices and empirical research testing these predictions. Until we have a better grasp of what motivates prosecutors in using their discretion, our understanding of and ability to predict the consequences of efforts to reform the criminal justice process will be incomplete.

Note

1. For detailed discussions of "three-strikes" laws, see Schicor and Sechrest (1996) and Greenwood, Everingham, Chen, Abrahamse, Merritt, and Chiesa (1998). For a comprehensive survey of sentencing reforms, including sentencing guidelines, see von Hirsch, Knapp, and Tonry (1987), Austin et al. (1996), and Tonry (1996). A few states also enacted "determinate sentencing laws" in the 1970s. Given that these are less common than the mandatory sentences and sentencing guidelines discussed here, I refer interested readers to Cohen and Tonry (1983).

References

Alschuler, A. (1978). Sentencing reform and prosecutorial power: A critique of recent proposals for fixed and presumptive sentencing. In *University of Pennsylvania Law Review, 126,* 550–577.

Austin, J., Clark, J., Hardyman, P., & Henry, D. A. (2000). *Three strikes and you're out: The implementation and impact of strike laws.* Washington, DC: National Institute of Justice.

Austin, J., Jones, C., Kramer, J., & Renninger, P. (1996). *National assessment of structured sentencing.* Washington, DC: U.S. Department of Justice, Bureau of Justice Assistance.

Bynum, T. (1982). Prosecutorial discretion and the implementation of a legislative mandate. In M. Morash (Ed.), *Implementing criminal justice policies* (pp. 47–59). Beverly Hills, CA: Sage Publications.

Campaign for an Effective Crime Policy. (1996). *The impact of "three strikes and you're out" laws: What have we learned?* Washington, DC: Campaign for an Effective Crime Policy.

Coffee, J. Jr., & Tonry, M. (1983). Hard choices: Critical trade-offs in the implementation of sentencing reform through guidelines. In M. Tonry & F. E. Zimring (Eds.), *Reform and punishment: Essays on criminal sentencing* (pp. 155–203). Chicago: University of Chicago Press.

Cohen, J., & Tonry, M. (1983). Sentencing reforms and their impacts. In A. Blumstein, J. Cohen, S. Martin, & M. H. Tonry (Eds.), *Research on sentencing: The search for reform* (pp. 305–459). Washington, DC: National Academy Press.

Crawford, C. (2000). Gender, race, and habitual offender sentencing in Florida. *Criminology, 38*, 263–280.

Crawford, C., Chiricos, T., & Kleck, G. (1998). Race, racial threat, and sentencing of habitual offenders. *Criminology, 36*, 481–511.

Dailey, Debra L. (1998). Minnesota sentencing guidelines: A structure for change. *Law & Policy, 20(3)*, 311–332.

Engen, R. (2006, March). *The indirect effects of prosecutors' charging decisions on punishment under sentencing guidelines.* Paper presented at the annual meeting of the Academy of Criminal Justice Sciences, Baltimore, MD.

Engen, R., Rikard, R., Parrotta, K., & Antonaccio, O. (2004, April). *Prosecutorial discretion under structured sentencing.* Paper presented at the annual meeting of the Southern Sociological Society, Atlanta, GA.

Engen, R., & Steen, S. (2000). The power to punish: Discretion and sentencing reform in the war on drugs. *American Journal of Sociology, 105(5)*, 1357–1395.

Engen, R., Steen, S., & Gainey, R. (2000, November). *The impact of race and ethnicity on charging decisions for drug offenders.* Paper presented at the annual meeting of the American Society of Criminology, San Francisco, CA.

Farrell, J. (2003). Mandatory minimum firearm penalties: A source of sentencing disparity. *Justice Research and Policy, 5(1)*, 95–115.

Frase, R. S. (1993). Implementing commission-based sentencing guidelines: The lessons of the first ten years in Minnesota. *Cornell Journal of Law and Public Policy, 2*, 278–337.

Frase, R. S. (2004). Sentencing guidelines in Minnesota, 1978–2003. In M. Tonry (Ed.), *Crime and justice: A review of research, 32* (pp. 131–220). Chicago: University of Chicago Press.

Greenwood, P. W., Everingham, S. S., Chen, E., Abrahamse, A., Merritt, N., & Chiesa, J. (1998). *Three strikes revisited: An early assessment of implementation and effects.* Santa Monica, CA: Rand Corporation.

Harris, J. C., & Jesilow, P. (2000). It's not the old ball game: Three-strikes and the courtroom workgroup. *Justice Quarterly, 17(1),* 185–203.

Heumann, M., & Loftin, C. (1979). Mandatory sentencing and the abolition of plea bargaining: The Michigan felony firearm statute. *Law & Society Review, 13,* 393–430.

Knapp, K. A. (1984). *The impact of the Minnesota sentencing guidelines: Three-year evaluation.* St. Paul, MN: Minnesota Sentencing Guidelines Commission.

Knapp, K. A. (1993). Allocation of discretion and accountability within sentencing structures. *University of Colorado Law Review, 64,* 679–705.

Meierhoefer, B. S. (1992). *The general effect of mandatory minimum prison terms: A longitudinal study of federal sentences imposed.* Washington, DC: Federal Judicial Center.

Miethe, T. D. (1987). Charging and plea bargaining practices under determinate sentencing: An investigation of the hydraulic displacement of discretion. *Journal of Criminal Law & Criminology, 78,* 155–176.

Miethe, T. D., & Moore, C. A. (1985). Socioeconomic disparities under determinate sentencing system: A comparison of pre guideline and post guideline practices in Minnesota. *Criminology, 23,* 337–363.

Miller, J. L., & Sloan, J. J. III. (1994). A study of criminal justice discretion. *Journal of Criminal Law and Criminology, 22,* 107–123.

Morris, N., & Tonry. M. (1990). *Between prison and probation.* New York: Oxford University Press.

Nagel, I. H., & Schulhofer, S. J. (1992). A tale of three cities: An empirical study of charging and bargaining practices under the federal sentencing guidelines. *Southern California Law Review, 66,* 501–561.

North Carolina Sentencing and Policy Advisory Commission (NCSPAC). (2002). *Sentencing practices under North Carolina's structured sentencing laws.* Raleigh, NC: North Carolina Sentencing and Policy Advisory Commission.

Reitz, K. (1998). Modeling discretion in American sentencing systems. *Law & Policy, 20,* 389–428.

Schicor, D., & Sechrest, D. (Eds.). (1996). *Three strikes and you're out: Vengeance as public policy.* Thousand Oaks, CA: Sage Publications.

Schulhofer, S. J., & Nagel, I. H. (1997). Plea negotiations under the federal sentencing guidelines: Guideline circumvention and its dynamics in the post-Mistretta period. *Northwestern University Law Review, 91,* 1284–1316.

Steen, S., Engen, R., & Gainey, R. (1999). *The impact of race and ethnicity on charging and sentencing processes for drug offenders in Washington State.* Olympia, WA: State of Washington Minority and Justice Commission.

Steiger, John C. (1998). Taking the law into our own hands: Structured sentencing, fear of violence, and citizen initiatives in Washington State. *Law & Policy, 20(3)*, 333–356.

Tonry, M. H. (1996). *Sentencing matters*. New York: Oxford University Press.

Tonry, M. H. (1999). *Reconsidering indeterminate and structured sentencing*. Washington, DC: U.S. Department of Justice, National Institute of Justice.

Ulmer, J. T. (2005). The localized uses of federal sentencing guidelines in four U.S. district courts: Evidence of processual order. *Symbolic Interaction, 28*, 255–279.

Ulmer, J. T., Kurlychek, M., & Kramer, J. (2003, November). *Prosecutorial discretion and the imposition of mandatory minimum sentences*. Paper presented at the annual meeting of the American Society of Criminology, Denver, CO.

von Hirsch, A., Knapp, K., & Tonry, M. (Eds.). (1987). *The sentencing commission and its guidelines*. Boston: Northeastern University Press.

U.S. General Accounting Office. (1993). *Mandatory minimum sentences: Are they being imposed and who is receiving them?* Washington, DC: U.S. General Accounting Office.

U.S. Sentencing Commission (USSC). (1991). *Special report to Congress: Mandatory minimum penalties in the federal criminal justice system*. Washington, DC: U.S. Sentencing Commission.

U.S. Sentencing Commission (USSC). (2004). *Fifteen years of guidelines sentencing: An assessment of how well the federal criminal justice system is achieving the goals of sentencing reform*. Washington, DC: U.S. Sentencing Commission.

Washington State Sentencing Guidelines Commission. (1985). *Sentencing practices under the Sentencing Reform Act*. Olympia, WA: Washington State Sentencing Guidelines Commission.

Wright, R. F. (1998). *Managing prison growth in North Carolina through structured sentencing*. Washington, DC: U.S. Department of Justice, National Institute of Justice.

Wright, R. F., & Engen, R.L. (2006). The effects of depth and distance in a criminal code on charging, sentencing, and prosecutorial power. *North Carolina Law Review, 84*, 1935–1982.

Zimring, F. E., Hawkins, G., & Kamin, S. (2001). *Punishment and democracy: Three strikes and you're out in California*. New York: Oxford University Press.

Chapter Five

Performance Measures and Accountability

M. ELAINE NUGENT-BORAKOVE

Introduction

Since its inception, the public's expectations for the justice system have vacil-lated from a punitive system to a rehabilitative system to a deterrent system (DiIulio, 1992). These contradictory and ever-changing expectations for the system as a whole have ultimately shaped public expectation of prosecutors. More-over, the effectiveness of prosecutors has largely been judged on the basis of the public's expectations of justice, too often shaped by a few high-profile cases (Forst, 1990) rather than an empirically based set of performance measures.

Throughout its history, the American prosecutorial function has shifted from a relatively minor actor in the colonial justice system to one of the most powerful actors in the modern-day criminal justice system (Jacoby, 1997). Despite the changes in prosecutorial function, the purpose has largely remained the same for the past 100 years:

1. to represent the interests of the state in criminal matters
2. to seek justice
3. to hold offenders accountable for their actions
4. to protect communities from criminal offending (Anderson, 2001; Hey-mann & Petrie, 2001)

More recently, the prosecutorial role definition has been expanded to protect the rights of victims. In addition, Misner (1996) notes that a secondary role of the prosecutor is to establish policy that is designed to impact crime in the local jurisdiction. The most robust articulation of the prosecutorial function is offered by Jacoby (1978) as "representing the interests of the state and the interests of the public in creating and maintaining a lawful and orderly society" (p. 76). Such is the view held by the National District Attorneys Association, as promulgated in its *National Prosecution Standards* (1991):

> . . . the standard—indeed all of the standards—recognizes that the prosecutor has a client not shared with other members of the bar, i.e., society as a whole. . . . The prosecutor must seek justice. In doing so, there is a need to balance the interests of *all* members of society, but when the balance cannot be struck in an individual case, the interest of society is *paramount* for the prosecutor. (Standards 1.1 and 1.3, p. 11)

As the state's representative in criminal matters, and more importantly as the people's attorney, the prosecutor has tremendous power over life and liberty. For this reason, much of the interest in prosecution focuses on the use of power, examining the appropriateness of the prosecutor's use of his or her discretion, charging decisions, and plea negotiations or plea bargaining (Fisher, 1989; Griffin, 2001; Misner, 1996; Wright & Miller, 2002). Unfortunately, with a few notable exceptions, a significant portion of the research conducted on prosecutors does little to shed light on the prosecutorial process as a whole (Heymann & Petrie, 2001). Part of the difficulty with a more in-depth study of prosecution in its totality is a lack of clearly defined outcomes. Performance measures specifically linked to prosecution goals and objectives will provide a framework for a more empirical and rigorous examination of the prosecution function. In addition, the implementation of a comprehensive and regular performance measurement can increase transparency in prosecution, allowing for a more systematic assessment of prosecutorial operations and innovations (Forst, 1990). Moreover, performance measures can help shape the political environment as it relates to public safety through the collection of data for strategic and legislative planning, and such measures, if articulated precisely, can help the public make more informed decisions about its prosecutors' performance.

The idea of performance measures in the justice system and for prosecutors is not new (Cole, 1993; Jacoby, 1982). In fact, a number of researchers and professional organizations such as the National District Attorneys Association have struggled with performance measurement, ultimately focusing in on the prosecutorial process and such indicators as conviction and dismissal rates (Cole, 1993; Jacoby, 1982). Jacoby's model (1982) of performance measurement focused on measuring whether the prosecutor's office was adequately performing the functions that fall under its authority and describing the structure and activities for the overall prosecutorial process. However, this effort falls short on two fronts.

First, performance measures based on the decision points in the life of a case do not necessarily provide meaningful information about the quality of justice and what prosecution means for victims and communities (Cole, 1993; Forst, 2001; Garner, 2005). Second, prosecutors are increasingly involved in a variety of activities that fall outside of the "traditional" notion of prosecution, such as crime prevention, problem solving, and the use of alternative sanctions, which are more difficult to quantify in terms of outcomes and do not necessarily result in criminal cases or convictions (Cole, 1993; Dillingham, Nugent, & Whitcomb, 2004; Nugent, Fanflik, & Bromirski, 2004).

A central problem in the attempt to define performance measures in prosecution is the lack of a clear definition of prosecutorial goals and objectives. For performance to be gauged against outcomes rather than just process, it is critical that prosecutorial activities be placed in a framework with clear links to goals and objectives.

Prosecution Goals and Objectives

There is a remarkable paucity of literature focusing on prosecution, as well as the goals of prosecution. Until the 1960s, goal definition was limited to a description of prosecutorial roles (i.e., to enforce laws or to prosecute criminals). The first effort to define prosecutorial goals was undertaken by Herbert Packer, who articulated two distinct models of prosecution: (1) the due process model, and (2) the crime control model.

Under the due process model, the local prosecutor focuses on the structure and operations of law and the criminal process—essentially supporting a goal related to the administration of justice. The crime control model, on the other hand, focuses on repressing criminal conduct through enforcement, arrest, conviction, and punishment. Both general deterrence and specific deterrence are emphasized, suggesting a goal of public safety.

These two models were later criticized by Roach and others. Of particular concern was the fact that the due process model necessarily creates crime control, and that the two models are too limited in scope—failing to take into consideration victims of crime (Roach, 1999).

Subsequent efforts to define models of prosecution, including Roach's victim-centered models, have fallen short in terms of describing the totality of the prosecutor's role. Moreover, the role of the local prosecutor has evolved substantially. As such, so too must the goals of prosecution. In the late 1990s, an examination of prosecution roles was conducted by the Kennedy School of Government at Harvard University through its Executive Session on State and Local Prosecution. This endeavor identified and described five types of prosecutors:

1. the pure jurist (case processor), whose goal is efficient and equitable case processing
2. the sanction setter, whose goals are rehabilitation, retribution, and deterrence
3. the problem solver, whose goal is to prevent and control crime
4. the strategic investor, whose goal is to bolster the efficacy of prosecution by adding capacities
5. the institution builder, whose goal is to restore the social institutions that help control crime (Tumin, 1990)

Although the most comprehensive attempt, to date, to articulate prosecution goals, the Kennedy School models were descriptive in nature and did not operationalize goals in a manner that allowed for strategic planning, accountability, or performance measurement. Moreover, while these roles captured a broad range of prosecution activities, they did not adequately identify measures and outcomes in prosecution. Finally, the roles were not mutually exclusive—a single prosecutor's office may take on one or more of these roles based on the overall goal of the office. By 2001, it had become clear that local prosecutors were again undergoing a role change, and these changes have been largely undocumented, suggesting a need to revisit how best to conceptualize justice and measure practices in prosecution (Heymann & Petrie, 2001).

Much of the challenge in trying to define performance measures in prosecution has been in the lack of concrete goal definition; however, other challenges loom large. The performance of justice organizations often is measured in simple, practical terms: crime rates, conviction rates, and recidivism rates. Without question, the actions of law enforcement, prosecutors, courts, and corrections must have some impact on crime rates. Otherwise, as James Q. Wilson so eloquently noted, if justice organizations had no impact on crime, then "we could abolish arrests and prisons with no adverse effects on society" (as quoted in DiIulio, 1992, p. 3). However, prosecutors operate as part of the criminal justice system, and each entity within that system has some impact on crime and justice. As such, isolating the contribution of prosecutors to the reduction of crime, for example, would not necessarily produce meaningful information. Moreover, any attempt to define goals for prosecution must be tied specifically to the activities carried out by prosecutors and must be mindful of the external influences on the prosecution function.

External Influences Affecting
Performance Measurement in Prosecution

Because prosecutors operate within the context of a larger system, a number of external factors outside of the control of the prosecutor's office impact the number of cases entering the system and set the parameters for the administration of justice. There are two primary categories of external factors: (1) legislative and operational, and (2) the criminal justice system.

Public opinion, special interests, and politics influence the nature and substantive content of legislation adopted in the United States, particularly legislation related to public safety issues and how the criminal justice system operates. For prosecutors, two types of legislation are most likely to impact how they do business, in turn, affecting performance: (1) statutory and (2) operational. Statutory legislation that is most likely to affect prosecutors includes the following:

1. mandatory sentencing legislation, which may impact plea and trial rates (Parent, Dunworth, McDonald, & Rhodes, 1997; Tonry, 1987)
2. mandatory charging of serious and violent juvenile offenders as adults
3. changes in offense classification and/or penalties, such as stricter penalties for crimes committed with a firearm (both of which may impact trial rates)
4. changes in punishable crime based on emerging and new offending patterns, for example, gang crimes that require more investigative and research time (Johnson, Webster, & Connors, 1995)

Operational policies and procedures govern how the criminal justice system operates. Legislation that mandates specific operational policies and procedures generally affects resources allocated to the criminal justice system and prosecutors' offices, the administration of justice, and the justice process in general. Examples of statutory-based operational policies and procedures that can impact prosecutors' performance include:

1. restricted use of plea negotiations (Nugent & McEwen, 1988)
2. criminal procedural rules and evidentiary rules
3. non-case specific administrative responsibilities of the prosecutor, such as the preparation of the trial court docket (Dorer, 1997)
4. organization of the courts, including the case track, number of courts available, number of judges, and existence of specialty courts, such as drug, domestic violence, or mental health

In addition to the court organizational structure, the local legal culture in which it operates can have a significant impact on the performance of the courts and prosecutors in particular (Church, 1985). This culture is based on the local customs that have evolved and become accepted practice in the adjudication process and largely encompass the way the various actors in the system behave (e.g., the practice of regularly filing motions or asking for continuances) and case handling procedures.

By nature, component parts of a system are interrelated and dependent upon each other in order for the system to operate. As a result, factors that influence parts of the criminal justice system will have an effect on the performance of the adjacent entity in the system as well as the system as a whole. Thus factors that affect the police will affect prosecutors, which in turn will affect the courts, and so forth. These factors may include:

1. police policies and procedures (e.g., enforcement of previously nonenforced laws, search and seizure rules, police stops) (Nugent & McEwen, 1988)
2. court delays (Nugent & McEwen, 1988)
3. availability of pretrial diversion and alternative sanctions in the jurisdiction

Any attempt to establish performance measures in prosecution must be cognizant of the various external influences on the prosecutor's office. Moreover, the actions of the prosecutor's office can change the dynamics of the system and the relative impact of the various external factors on the operations of the office, which also must be considered in shaping a framework for performance measurement.

A Measurement Framework for Prosecution

Public accountability has become paramount in a world of competing social interests for limited public resources. Public safety has remained at the forefront of funding priorities but is increasingly pressed to justify huge expenditures of taxpayers' dollars with evidence that the dollars are being used in a way that makes communities safer. Yet other than the option to elect or not elect a prosecutor,[1] the public lacks a tool to hold prosecutors (and others in the criminal justice system) accountable for their performance.

In 1990, the Bureau of Justice Statistics and Princeton University undertook the first major effort to define performance measures for the criminal justice system. In doing so, the endeavor produced four goals for the system as a whole:

1. doing justice
2. promoting secure communities
3. restoring crime victims
4. promoting noncriminal options

Although these are appropriate goals for the criminal justice system as a whole, they are too broad to be applied to any one component of the system, such as prosecutors. As part of this effort, performance measures for the trial courts as a whole were proposed, focusing on five performance areas: access to justice; timeliness of justice; equality, fairness, and integrity; independence and accountability; and public trust and confidence (Cole, 1993). As with the goals articulated earlier, the performance areas for the trial courts were not operationalized in a manner that allowed for the measurement of prosecution performance.

As noted earlier, Jacoby (1982) focused on the functions of the office and the process. Among the measures found to be important in her framework were the following:

1. criminal justice system characteristics, including volume of cases referred for prosecution, size of the office, jurisdiction of the prosecutor and the courts, and the number of criminal courts
2. prosecution characteristics, including experience level of assistant prosecutors, existence of intake procedures, charging unit, charging decisions reviewed and accepted, disposition set, disposition frequency, time from arrest to charging and to arraignment and disposition, type of accusatory used and frequency, type of preliminary hearing, disposition decisions reviewed and approved, case assignment type, court docketing procedures, docket control, type of plea bargaining used, type of negotiation, continuance policy, trial policy, sentencing recommendations, and use of habitual or multiple offender acts (Jacoby, 1982)

None of the measures articulated in this framework takes into consideration the quality of justice for victims, the leadership role of the prosecutor, or the non-case processing activities of the prosecutor. Moreover, the measures are not linked to clearly defined goals and objectives, which are critical for measuring performance.

Performance measures are meaningless if they do not support goals and objectives and if they are not tied to specific strategies and practices. Good performance measures must be meaningful and relevant, that is, they should make sense and be logically related to prosecutors' goals and objectives. They also should quantify achievement and be supported by empirical evidence. Finally, they must be precise, easy to understand, and able to be measured against a baseline or a standard.

The measurement framework, shown in Figure 5.1, outlines critical objectives (outcomes) associated with three primary prosecution goals, which in turn are operationalized into a menu of performance measures associated with the various practices of a prosecutor's office. The framework is intended to provide a guide for performance measurement in prosecution that is tailorable to the unique situations of individual prosecutors' offices but also broad enough to suggest appropriate measures for more large-scale research on prosecution.

The local prosecutor's goals, as defined by an expert working group of prosecutors, are as follows:

Objectives/Outcomes

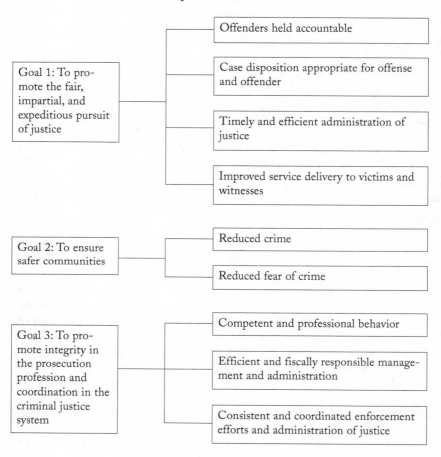

FIGURE 5.1
Prosecution Goals and Objectives

1. to promote the fair, impartial, and expeditious pursuit of justice
2. to ensure safer communities
3. to promote integrity in the prosecution profession and effective coordination in the criminal justice system (Dillingham, Nugent, & Whitcomb, 2004)

The three goals are defined in a manner to capture the intended results of all of the various functions of the local prosecutor—case processing, crime prevention and intervention, and the overall administration of justice—respecting the unique role of the prosecutor and accounting for the continual evolution of the prosecutorial function. Related to each of these goals is a series of objectives from which performance measures can be generated.

Goal 1: Promotion of the Fair, Impartial, and Expeditious Pursuit of Justice

The promotion of the fair, impartial, and expeditious pursuit of justice captures the intended impact of more "traditional" prosecutorial roles. As the chief law enforcement executive in the community, it is clearly established that a primary function of the local prosecutor is to enforce the laws and prosecute offenders. With this role comes the responsibility to ensure that the laws are enforced equally and without bias, and that prosecutorial discretion in charging decisions be exercised uniformly and with the interests of justice in mind. Specifically, this first goal involves holding offenders accountable, ensuring that case dispositions are appropriate for both the offense and the offender, administering justice in a timely and an efficient manner, and improving service delivery to victims and witnesses.

Offenders held accountable. Holding offenders accountable is intrinsic to the prosecutor's mission. Several of the more "traditional" performance measures can be associated with this objective: convictions, dismissals, prison sentences, placements in treatment or alternative dispositions, and restitution ordered and completed. As noted earlier, prosecutors are only one part of a system, and although it is difficult to isolate the impact of prosecutors alone on these traditional measures, many prosecutorial policies and practices may influence the measures in important ways.

For example, prosecutor screening and charging polices may have significant implications for case outcomes (Wright & Miller, 2002). Prosecutorial screening, the first decision point in the system where the prosecutor exercises his or her discretion, determines which cases enter the system, which are diverted, and which are refused for prosecution. Likewise, the decision of which charges to file and ultimately whether or not pleas will be negotiated often is a matter of prosecutorial policy, which can affect case outcomes. As such, examining the prosecutor's decision making at these critical points is essential and will ultimately impact on how offenders are held accountable, how quickly justice is administered, and that case dispositions are appropriate for both the offense and the offender. In addition, as research has shown, more intensive screening can lead to a greater likelihood that a defendant will plead guilty as charged—avoiding a costly trial (which in turn will affect another performance measure related to the fiscally responsible administration of justice discussed later in this chapter) (Wright & Miller, 2002).

Prosecutorial practices in negotiating pleas and dismissing lesser included offenses also influence measurements of outcomes. It is important to take into consideration that cases can be counted in different ways, and these different calculations will affect the performance measurement. Offices that count individual charges against a defendant will show very different outcomes from offices that count cases by defendant (i.e., all charges against a defendant are "bundled").

Case disposition appropriate for offense and offender. The discretionary power of the prosecutor is among the most significant in the criminal justice system. The local prosecutor has the authority to decide whether or not to file charges and what charges to file, and to make sentencing recommendations. As a result, a significant amount of attention is paid to the prosecutor's use of discretion (Barry & Greer, 1981; Forst, 1990; Mulkey, 1974; Schoenfeld, 2005).

No plea policies, written charging guidelines, and the use of experienced prosecutors are all prosecutorial practices designed to ensure that the appropriate charges are considered uniformly. Although a variety of case specific factors can influence the charging process (such as quality of evidence, availability of witnesses, willingness of the victim to cooperate with the prosecution, etc.), performance measures that help judge the extent to which prosecutors are seeking dispositions that are appropriate for both the offense and the offender are critical. Thus one measure of performance takes into account the consistency of dispositions for like offenders and offenses and pleas to original charges.

Like prosecutorial discretion, much attention is paid to the prosecutor's practice of plea negotiations. Pleas are negotiated for many different reasons and can serve in the interest of the community in that a plea negotiation may result in a conviction for a lesser offense, incapacitating the offender for at least a short period, whereas justice may not have been served by pursuing the original charge. On the other hand, the prosecutorial practice of "overcharging" in order to be in a better position to negotiate a plea needs to be accounted for in a performance measurement framework. The number of pleas to the original charge can serve as an important performance measure to help ensure that prosecutors are using plea negotiations in the best interests of their communities.

Timely and efficient administration of justice. The criminal justice system is predicated on the notion of swift and certain justice. However, over the past several decades, court dockets have been overcrowded, continuances on the part of the prosecutor and the defense bar have become the norm, and caseloads are burgeoning as resources dwindle. Nonetheless, most states require that defendants receive their arraignment or preliminary hearing within a certain amount of time from their arrest. While timely charging and arraignment are important, simply using this as a benchmark would only tell us how well prosecutors are doing meeting a statutory mandate. What is not currently measured, and should be, is the amount of calendar time that elapses from the initial review to the final disposition to ensure that justice is being meted out in a timely and an efficient manner.

In addition, many states require offenders to pay restitution, and some prosecutors' offices are responsible for tracking restitution orders. An important measure of the timely administration of justice is the average amount of time taken to complete restitution. The ratio of restitution ordered to restitution paid also can be a useful measure of performance.

Improved service delivery to victims and witnesses. The victims' right movement in the 1980s brought to the forefront the importance of victims in the criminal justice system and the pivotal role that prosecutors play in meeting victims' needs. It is not enough for a prosecutor to pursue a case; victims must feel that justice is being served. As such, victim and witness attitudes about personal safety during the prosecution, their satisfaction with their criminal justice system experience, and the actions taken on their behalf are critical for measuring how well prosecutors are supporting victims. In addition, prosecutors are statutorily mandated to notify victims of case events, thus prosecutors should be held accountable for the number of notifications sent to victims.

Goal 2: Ensuring Safer Communities

Clearly, prosecuting offenders and enforcing the laws create both specific and general deterrence and help make communities safer. However, with the advent of community prosecution and involvement in treatment efforts, prosecutors are taking a more preventive approach to crime. Using varied enforcement methods and problem-solving techniques, prosecutors are educating their constituents about crime prevention and attempting to address the underlying causes of crime, such as neighborhood disorder, drug addiction, mental health issues, and more. Thus ensuring safer communities takes on a dual purpose as a goal for prosecutors.

The two primary objectives for prosecutors in ensuring safer communities are a reduction in crime and, equally important, a reduction in the fear of crime. Although it can be argued that prosecutors alone cannot reduce crime, as noted earlier, prosecuting offenders, holding them accountable for their actions, and sending a general deterrent message to would-be offenders are all important functions that ultimately can have some, if even a marginal, impact on felony, misdemeanor, and juvenile crime rates. It is important, however, that these measures be placed in context with other performance measures and the specific prosecutorial practices aimed at reducing crime in order for crime rates to be a useful measurement of performance.

The vast majority of the public will never come into direct contact with the criminal justice system (Surette, 1997). However, community members have strong opinions about crime and particularly how safe they feel in their homes, places of work, and communities in general. Too often, these opinions are shaped by media attention to high-profile crimes, and they can be misleading.

Prosecutors are increasingly called to task to help explain the true prevalence of crime in the community. Conversely, residents are increasingly working with prosecutors to identify their crime priorities through such efforts as community prosecution. The prosecutor's role in helping shape public opinion about crime is new and evolving, and the intent is to help reduce the fear of crime by changing community attitudes about crime and safety and to increase public awareness of prosecution and prosecution outcomes. In addition, as prosecutors work in closer partnership with community members to address crime and the fear of crime, citizens gain a greater understanding of the prosecutor's role and his or her limitations and perhaps, more importantly, become engaged in the process and more knowledgeable of the criminal justice system.

Goal 3: Promotion of Integrity in the Prosecution Profession and Coordination in the Justice System

The third and final goal—to promote integrity in the prosecution profession and coordination in the criminal justice system—takes into account the leadership role of the prosecutor. Unlike the other goals, this one focuses on the prosecutor's role in the system and as a public agency in an attempt to lend some transparency to the role. Prosecutors are accountable to their constituents, and the public should have the tools to measure a prosecutor's performance in terms of his or her conduct. It must be ethical and professional. Moreover, as a publicly funded agency, prosecutors' offices must be fiscally responsible.

Competent and professional behavior. The American criminal justice system is based on an understanding of full discovery and by having an adversarial system for the trial, the guilt or innocence of the accused will be revealed. Under this system, the burden of proof lies with prosecutors, who are charged with proving defendants' guilt, but not at all costs—prosecutors also must seek the truth. The discretionary power of the prosecutor's office, if left unchecked, can create the potential for prosecutorial misconduct (Heymann & Petrie, 2001). Moreover, prosecutors are bound by an ethical code, which is frequently challenged by any number of ethical dilemmas. In addition, as prosecutors move out of the courtroom into more community-based activities, the issue of ethical conduct becomes increasingly complex (Kuykendall, 2004). Important measures of professional and competent behavior include the number of meritorious ethics violations, prosecutor error, and disciplinary actions taken for ethics violations or errors.

Established ethical codes of conduct and ethical standards are one practice to ensure that prosecutors are carrying out their duties in a competent and professional manner. Another practice is the provision for ongoing professional training on a variety of topics, including ethics, trial advocacy, and office policies and practices. Whether provided in-house or received through professional organizations such as the National District Attorneys Association, the amount of professional and legal training completed is an important measure of how well prepared and trained prosecutors are.

Efficient and fiscally responsible management and administration. Prosecutors' offices are publicly funded agencies. As such, they are charged with managing taxpayer monies in a fiscally responsible way and ensuring that their offices are operating as efficiently as possible. The following three measures capture the efficient and fiscally responsible management and administration:

1. staffing levels and composition
2. staff workloads
3. costs and revenues

For an office to operate efficiently, it must be staffed adequately and appropriately. Although the work of attorneys in a prosecutor's office is generally the focus—the roles of investigators, victim and witness personnel, and clerical support staff are critical. The ratio of attorneys to these other staff should be representative of the workload and should eliminate duplication of effort, or worse, the practice of more highly paid attorneys performing the work of other support staff instead of or in addition to their own work.

A related measure is the workload of staff. Offices cannot operate and are not operating efficiently if the amount of work per staff member is so great that cases are not handled in a timely manner. Traditionally, the public and the media focus on the number of cases per attorney. However, there is an important distinction between caseload and workload. The American Prosecutors Research Institute, in its study of prosecutorial resources, defines caseload as the number and array of cases per staff member, whereas workload represents caseload plus non-case-related activity, such as office management, community outreach, and professional development (Nugent, Rainville, Finkey, & Fanflik, 2002). This distinction is important in performance measurement, because the intent is to measure performance in its totality, not just the case processing functions.

A likely performance measure would focus on a comparison of an office's workload per staff member to a national standard, however, no such standards exist (Nugent et al., 2002). Therefore, prosecutors must measure their own office caseload and, more importantly, workload not only for the attorneys in the office but also for other staff. In addition, prosecutors must take into consideration the impact of their chosen managerial and operational policies and practices on workload. Little is known about the impact of different organizational structures (i.e., vertical vs. horizontal prosecution, offense-based units vs. function-based units, etc.) on office efficiency. Likewise, different operational processes, such as no plea policies, can impact on the workload.

Consistent and coordinated enforcement efforts and administration of justice. One of the roles largely ignored in the literature is that of a leader in the justice system. The power of the prosecutor's office has grown tremendously over time, and prosecutors are increasingly exercising that power to fill voids in the system to increase capacity for responding to both victims' and offenders' needs. Even though this function has been paid little attention to, it is an important aspect of the prosecutorial function for which performance should be measured. Among the possible performance measures are joint policy and legislative actions between prosecutors and allied professionals, the formation and institutionalizing of partnerships within the justice system and with less traditional partners, such as faith-based groups, to increase the system's ability to address crime, the cross-designation of attorneys as U.S. Attorneys to aid in the prosecution of cases at both the federal and the state and local levels, and the provision of training to law enforcement and others.

Conclusion

The performance measurement framework presented in this chapter is an important first step in lending transparency to the prosecution function and establishing a foundation for a more rigorous study of local prosecutors. There is, however, much work to be accomplished to facilitate the implementation of performance measures in local prosecutors' offices.

The adversarial nature of the justice system creates a tendency to resist the disclosure of information about cases, and this tendency spills over into the disclosure of performance measures (Forst, 1990). Moreover, prosecutors feel that their work is not easily captured by statistics (Heymann & Petrie, 2001). They may view performance measures as missing the level of effort required to administer justice. This view, however, creates a self-fulfilling prophecy, in that without measurement, prosecution outcomes and effectiveness toward goal attainment cannot be captured, which in turn will render any measurement of level of effort meaningless because it cannot be linked to outcomes.

Prosecutors' offices are notoriously lacking in data collection efforts. Information systems used by their offices generally serve as case management systems and require extensive programming to extract data and run reports needed to support many of the performance measures, such as convictions, dismissals, pleas, length of sentence, restitution, calendar days between case initiation and final disposition, and so on. Many offices, particularly in smaller, more rural jurisdictions, do not even have case management systems. Thus much of what needs to be collected on the most basic of the performance measures (i.e., the more traditional measures of convictions, pleas, and dismissals) may be the only information readily available. Data on other measures, such as restitution, length of sentence, and elapsed time between case initiation and disposition, must be collected and tabulated manually. Moreover, to ensure uniformity in the collection of these data to allow for more rigorous research, a national data collection system is needed.

The less traditional measures related to victim and witness attitudes and satisfaction, community attitudes about crime and safety, and public awareness of prosecution and outcomes require a method of collection that does not exist in prosecutors' offices. The American Prosecutors Research Institute has developed surveys to help facilitate the collection of these data, but prosecutors lack the necessary resources or skills to administer the surveys or to do anything but the most basic analysis.

Measures related to competent and professional behavior and consistent and coordinated enforcement efforts and the administration of justice are less complicated in terms of collection but nonetheless require manual tabulations. Prosecutors are perhaps most likely to have available information regarding their staffing levels, workload, and costs versus revenues.

Clearly the challenge of performance measurement in prosecution is only partially solved with the development of concrete, measurable goals and objectives. Accessing the data for the performance measures remains largely unaddressed. Furthermore, as prosecutors struggle to maintain their budgets and recruit and retain qualified staff to manage the workload, the dedication of resources to collect performance measurement data will remain a hurdle, despite the fact that performance measures can help justify budget requests. Prosecutors need to be educated about the benefits of performance measurement, its utility for planning and budgeting, and the methods for collecting performance measurement data.

Finally, each local prosecutor's office is unique and operates within a distinctive political environment. The context of the environment in which a prosecutor's office operates will have an impact on various policies and practical decisions within the office, such as how it is organized based on the resources available (e.g., units to handle specific offenses, units to handle specific functions, or no specialized units) or which case processing policies should be put into place (e.g., no plea policies, fast track dockets, referrals to treatment programs, etc.). These factors must be taken into account when selecting and using performance measures for research purposes.

The implementation of performance measures in an office also can influence the political environment in which the office operates. Performance measures will yield empirical data that ultimately will inform policy and practice, thereby establishing a dynamic relationship in which performance data can be used to influence political decisions in terms of resource allocation, legislative changes, and public support for prosecutorial candidates.

The political environment also can have negative effects with regard to performance measurement. As publicly elected officials, prosecutors are wary of the potential for the misuse of performance measurement data by opponents, the media, the defense bar, and policy makers. These concerns should not influence decisions about which performance measures are appropriate for an office, but they may. Precise, easy-to-understand measures minimize the risk of misinterpretation. Moreover, uniform and consistent reporting of performance will enable prosecutors to monitor their progress and take proactive steps to make policy and practice changes if the data show they are not meeting their goals.

Clearly there are a number of challenges to overcome with regard to institutionalizing performance measurement for prosecutors. Nevertheless, the articulation of a variety of performance measures is a critical first step toward lending transparency to the prosecutorial function and developing a more in-depth understanding of prosecutors as a whole.

Notes

The information in the section "A Measurement Framework for Prosecution" is based on the work of the author and her colleagues at the American Prosecutors Research Institute under a grant from the U.S. Department of Justice, Office of Justice Programs, National Institute of Justice, and the Charles G. Koch Charitable Foundation. The performance measurement framework was published initially in 2004 (see Dillingham, Nugent, & Whitcomb, 2004).

1. Prosecutors are elected in 47 states. The local prosecutor is appointed by the governor in New Jersey and Connecticut, by the attorney general in Alaska, and by the U.S. president in the District of Columbia, where the local prosecution function falls under the jurisdiction of the U.S. Attorney.

References

Anderson, S. (2001). The changing role of the prosecutor. In *The prosecutor's deskbook: Ethical issues and emerging roles for 21st century prosecutors* (3rd ed., pp. 3–23). Alexandria, VA: American Prosecutors Research Institute.

Barry, D., & Greer, A. (1981). Sentencing versus prosecutorial discretion: The application of new disparity measure. *Journal of Research in Crime & Delinquency, 18*, 254–271.

Church, T. (1985). Examining local legal culture. *American Bar Foundation Research Journal, 3*, 449–518.

Cole, G. F. (1993). Performance measures for the trial courts, prosecution, and public defense. In *Performance measures for the justice system* (pp. 86–107). Washington, DC: U.S. Department of Justice, Office of Justice Programs, National Institute of Justice.

DiIulio, J., Jr. (1992). *Rethinking the criminal justice system: Toward a new paradigm.* Washington, DC: U.S. Department of Justice, Office of Justice Programs, Bureau of Justice Statistics-Princeton Project.

Dillingham, S., Nugent, M. E., & Whitcomb, D. (2004). *Prosecution in the 21st century: Goals, objectives, and performance measures.* Alexandria, VA: American Prosecutors Research Institute.

Dorer, P. (1997, January–February). North Carolina's response to burgeoning prosecution needs. *The Prosecutor, 31*, 38–41.

Fisher, S. Z. (1989, Winter). Zealousness and "overzealousness": Making sense of the prosecutor's duty to seek justice. *The Prosecutor, 22*, 9–28.

Forst, B. (1990). Prosecution's coming of age. *Justice Research and Policy Journal, 2*, 21–46.

Forst, B. (2001). *Measuring what matters in prosecution.* Alexandria, VA: American Prosecutors Research Institute.

Garner, J. (2005). What does the "prosecution" of domestic violence mean? *Criminology & Public Policy, 4*, 567–574.

Griffin, L. C. (2001). The prudent prosecutor. *Georgetown Journal of Legal Ethics, 14*, 259–308.

Heymann, P., & Petrie, C. (2001). *What's changing in prosecution? Results of a workshop.* Washington, DC: National Academy Press.

Jacoby, J. (1978). *The charging policies of prosecutors: From "The Prosecutor," 1979, by William McDonald.* Washington, DC: U.S. Department of Justice, Office of Justice Programs, National Institute of Justice. In W. McDonald (Ed.), *The prosecutor* (pp. 75–97). Beverly Hills, CA: Sage Publications.

Jacoby, J. (1982). *Basic issues in prosecution and public defender performance.* Washington, DC: National Institute of Justice.

Jacoby, J. (1997). The American prosecutor's discretionary power. *The Prosecutor, 31*, 25–27, 38–39.

Johnson, C., Webster, B., & Connors, E. (1995). *Prosecuting gangs: A national assessment.* Washington, DC: U.S. Department of Justice, Office of Justice Programs, National Institute of Justice.

Kuykendall, M. (2004). *From the courtroom to the community: Ethics and liability issues for the community prosecutor*. Alexandria, VA: American Prosecutors Research Institute.

Misner, R. L. (1996). Recasting prosecutorial discretion. *Journal of Criminal Law & Criminology, 86,* 717–778.

Mulkey, M. (1974). The role of prosecution and defense in plea bargaining. *Policy Studies Journal, 3,* 54–60.

National District Attorneys Association. (1991). *National prosecution standards* (2nd ed.). Alexandria, VA: National District Attorneys Association.

Nugent, H., & McEwen, J. T. (1988). *Prosecutors' national assessment of needs*. Washington, DC: National Institute of Justice.

Nugent, M. E., Fanflik, P. L., & Bromirski, D. (2004). *The changing nature of prosecution: Community prosecution vs. traditional prosecution approaches*. Alexandria, VA: American Prosecutors Research Institute.

Nugent, M. E., Rainville, G., Finkey, R., & Fanflik, P. L. (2002). *How many cases can a prosecutor handle? Results of the national workload assessment project*. Alexandria, VA: American Prosecutors Research Institute.

Parent, D., Dunworth, T., McDonald, D., & Rhodes, W. (1997). *Key legislative issues in criminal justice: Mandatory sentencing*. Washington, DC: National Institute of Justice.

Roach, K. (1999). Four models of the criminal process. *Journal of Criminal Law and Criminology, 89,* 671–717.

Schoenfeld, H. (2005). Violated trust: Conceptualizing prosecutorial misconduct. *Journal of Contemporary Criminal Justice, 21,* 250–271.

Surette, R. (1997). *Media, crime, and criminal justice: Images and realities* (2nd ed.). Belmont, CA: Wadsworth.

Tonry, M. (1987). *Sentencing reform impacts*. Washington, DC: National Institute of Justice.

Tumin, Z. (1990). *Summary of proceedings: Findings and discoveries of the Harvard University executive session for state and local prosecutors at the John F. Kennedy School of Government, 1986–1990*. Cambridge, MA: Harvard University Press.

Wright, R., & Miller, M. (2002). The screening/bargaining trade-off. *Stanford Law Review, 55,* 29–118.

PART III

Prosecuting Troublesome and Emerging Crime Problems

Chapter Six

Prosecutors and Treatment Diversion

The Brooklyn (NY) Drug Treatment Alternative to Prison Program

STEVEN BELENKO,
HUNG-EN SUNG, ANNE J. SWERN,
and CAROLINE R. DONHAUSER

Introduction

The quadrupling in the number of inmates over the past 20 years (Harrison & Beck, 2005) has been fueled mainly by drug and other offenses directly related to substance abuse (Blumstein & Beck, 1999), and more arrests, convictions, and prison sentences for drug offenses (Blumstein & Beck, 1999). The connections between illegal drug use and crime include high rates of drug use and dependence among arrestees (Zhang, 2004) and other offenders: 69% of state prison inmates report regular lifetime illicit drug use, and more than 80% have indications of serious drug or alcohol involvement (Belenko & Peugh, 2005). Recidivism rates are higher for inmates with substance abuse histories, and absent treatment interventions, the likelihood of relapse to drug use and rearrest is high (Belenko, Foltz, Lang, & Sung, 2004; Inciardi, Martin, & Butzin, 2004). Within three years of release from prison, 68% of released state inmates are rearrested, 47% reconvicted, and 25% sentenced to prison for a new crime (Langan & Levin, 2002).

In response, new interest has emerged over the past 15 years in alternative prosecution and adjudication strategies to reduce drug-related crime and incarceration. Research on drug courts (Belenko, 2001; U.S. GAO, 2005),

111

Treatment Alternatives for Safer Communities (TASC) programs (Anglin, Longshore, & Turner, 1999), and residential prison treatment with aftercare (Inciardi et al., 2004; Prendergast, Hall, Wexler, Melnick, & Cao, 2004) finds reductions in recidivism and relapse. However, methodological problems and inconsistent findings raise questions about their effectiveness (Belenko, 2001, 2002; U.S. GAO, 2005). Also, legal and political considerations may affect the adoption of different treatment models, and existing interventions have not gained sufficient funding or political support to serve more than relatively small proportions of drug-involved offenders[1] (Belenko, 2002).

Prosecutors' ability to impact drug-related crime has been described as "spotty and uneven" (Jacoby & Gramckow, 1994, p. 165), due in part to large caseloads and the need to efficiently prosecute cases (Goerdt & Martin, 1989). Prosecutorial goals have never routinely included solving health or social problems (Hora, Schma, & Rosenthal, 1999). Thus it is not surprising that the cycling of drug-involved offenders through the criminal justice system (CJS) with limited drug treatment access (Belenko & Peugh, 2005; Mumola, 1999) has had little impact on recidivism and relapse (Zimring & Hawkins, 1992).

There are several limitations of current prosecutorial treatment diversion models. First, most programs target only drug possession cases, or first-time offenders. Fears about the political ramifications of offering treatment to drug sellers *in lieu* of incarceration or releasing offenders with prior criminal records into community-based treatment lead many prosecutors to play it safe by limiting diversion to less risky offenders with low incarceration likelihood. Of course, legal restrictions (e.g., mandatory sentencing laws) may limit prosecutorial discretion to offer treatment alternatives to drug sellers or repeat offenders. However, drug sellers typically seen in state criminal courts also have high rates of drug abuse and thus could benefit from treatment.

Second, most existing programs (e.g., drug courts, diversion programs) emphasize outpatient rather than residential treatment. However, due to the many social and health problems of drug-involved offenders, as well as their often lengthy addiction histories and previous treatment failures, the type of low-intensity treatment usually offered may not be sufficient to effectively address the drug abuse and related problems of many offenders (Belenko & Peugh, 2005; Hammett, Roberts, & Kennedy, 2001).

Considering the multiple risks and service needs of drug-involved offenders, risk-responsivity" theory (Andrews & Bonta, 1998; Marlowe, 2003; Thanner & Taxman, 2003) offers a useful framework for understanding targeting and treatment intensity issues. Key elements of this theory are (1) outcomes are improved by identifying risk levels and targeting services specific to those risks, and (2) higher-risk offenders need a greater intensity of services than moderate- or low-risk offenders (Festinger, Marlowe, Lee, Kirby,

Bovasso, & McLellan, 2002; Thanner & Taxman, 2003). Thus treatment diversion or alternative-to-incarceration programs serving the high-risk end of the continuum could have a larger impact on economic benefits and recidivism (Griffith, Hiller, Knight, & Simpson, 1999). Conversely, programs targeting lower-risk offenders can inefficiently place them in high-cost, high-control programs, without sufficient treatment effects to counteract these costs.

Previous Treatment Diversion Models

Many prosecutors have developed and implemented, or participated in, new approaches for addressing drug-related crime. These include diverting drug-involved offenders from prosecution or incarceration into treatment, or using alternative processing techniques to reduce the resource impacts and backlogs created by large drug caseloads (Goerdt & Martin, 1989). Although some of these innovations, such as drug courts, have achieved widespread popularity, many have failed to achieve their original goals or have been modified substantially. In addition, they have tended to remain outside of mainstream prosecutorial practice (Belenko, 2002; Sung & Belenko, 2006). In the pages that follow we briefly describe these types of treatment diversion models.

Pretrial Diversion Programs

Formal diversion programs originated in the late 1960s (Hillsman, 1982) and still exist in many jurisdictions. Here arrestees are offered an opportunity to have their cases held in abeyance while they attend a court-monitored treatment program. Successful completion results in the original criminal charges being dismissed (for pre-plea models), the withdrawal of the guilty plea and dismissal of the charges or plea to lower charges (post-plea model), or a reduction in the sentence from incarceration to probation (in the post-plea, post-sentencing model). Diversion programs are nearly always operated and controlled by the district attorney, who has the overall responsibility for determining eligibility, screening the cases, and monitoring treatment progress.

One problem with pretrial treatment diversion is the briefness of the pretrial period relative to the optimal length of treatment needed by many drug-involved offenders. Once the prosecutor's legal leverage ends after case disposition, the offender's incentive to remain in treatment diminishes. Drug relapse may mean a violation of release conditions and possible sanctions, including incarceration. Thus the offender could receive harsher sanctions than if he or she had not participated in a treatment program, with a net effect of increasing jail overcrowding and clogging court calendars.

Prosecutor control has been criticized, particularly with regard to the issue of "net-widening" (Hillsman, 1982). One example is the Court Employment Project (CEP), created in Manhattan in 1967 and the first formal pretrial diversion program for juvenile offenders in the United States (Feeley, 1983). The CEP staff advocated prosecutors and judges to send eligible juveniles to a 90–day intervention, which included counseling, job training, and employment. If the participant met all program obligations, the CEP would recommend that the charges be dropped. In one of the first empirical documentations of "net-widening," Baker and Sadd (1981) found that most of the diverted cases would have been dismissed by prosecutors had the program not existed. This research, and the subsequent loss of city funds, nearly eliminated the CEP. Rather than a solution, the prosecutors' tight control over the program became a problem (Feeley, 1983).

Despite their long history, diversion programs are still relatively uncommon and serve a small percentage of drug-involved offenders. First, many prosecutors, not wanting to be viewed as "soft on crime," are hesitant to offer treatment, except for misdemeanants or first offenders. This population is more politically acceptable, with fewer restrictions placed on case processing alternatives by mandatory sentencing laws or plea bargaining restrictions. However, diverting more serious offenders may save more resources and may have a greater impact on crime.

Second, diversion programs require additional screening, assessment, and monitoring resources that many prosecutors' offices lack. Third, treatment resource constraints or reluctance by providers to accept criminal justice clients can impact treatment availability. Fourth, by placing release conditions on defendants that may be difficult to fully adhere to (such as abstention from drugs for an addict or a heavy user), there becomes a high probability of failure and the subsequent revocation of release or the imposition of additional sanctions.

Fifth, these earlier efforts often were fragmented, with several agencies responsible for treatment supervision; this made it difficult to monitor treatment progress or compliance with court-imposed conditions. Treatment services might be applied inconsistently or inappropriately, resulting in high rates of treatment failure. Finally, organizational problems have been common: Funding streams were not always consistent, rendering it difficult to maintain treatment or staff continuity. Program interventions were not always well planned or coordinated among the various criminal justice agencies involved, and poor information flow between criminal justice and treatment agencies made it difficult to monitor treatment progress.

Drug Courts

Beginning in the mid-1980s, some state courts began experimenting with dedicated courtrooms for drug cases in an effort to ameliorate the effects of large numbers of drug cases (Belenko & Dumanovsky, 1993; Cooper & Trotter,

1994). These early efforts made it clear that absent treatment interventions, many offenders would simply recycle through the CJS, albeit more quickly. The first drug court began in Miami, Florida, in 1989 (Goldkamp & Weiland, 1993); by March 2005, there were 1,320 drug courts operating in all 50 states (Drug Court Clearinghouse, 2005). The key components of drug courts typically include: (1) judicial supervision of long-term structured treatment with regular urine monitoring; (2) timely assessment and treatment placement; (3) assessment and case management; (4) use of graduated sanctions and rewards; and (5) case dismissal or sentence reduction upon graduation.

Drug courts engage in long-term treatment and other services offenders who have had limited past treatment and provide closer supervision than received under other forms of criminal justice community supervision (Belenko, 2001). Drug use and criminal activity are comparatively reduced during program participation. Average treatment retention is substantially longer than found in community-based treatment overall, or in other criminal justice treatment (Simpson, Joe, Broome, Hiller, Knight, & Rowan-Szal, 1997). Studies of drug courts that included a comparison group have generally found that post-program re-arrest rates for drug court participants are significantly lower 1 year post-program than for offenders adjudicated through standard courts (Belenko, 2001; U.S. GAO, 2005).

The popularity of drug courts has meant growing scrutiny. Critics are concerned that their nonadversarial structure leads to poor adjudication decisions, that drug courts are too coercive and that defendants' rights can be compromised, that they use sanctions too freely, or that many judges are forced into a role, such as problem solver or "social worker," that makes them uncomfortable (Boldt, 1998; Hora et al., 1999; Nolan, 2003).

TASC Programs

The federally funded Treatment Alternatives to Street Crime (TASC) program began in 1972.[2] The basic goal of TASC is to identify offenders in need of drug treatment early in the criminal justice process and, under close supervision, to provide community-based treatment as an alternative or a supplement to more traditional criminal justice sanctions. The assumption is that the threat of criminal sanctions for violating conditions of the treatment program or TASC supervision requirements increases the likelihood of successful treatment completion. The range of possible processing under TASC supervision now includes deferred prosecution, community sentencing, diversion, pretrial intervention, and probation or parole supervision.

Several TASC evaluations have concluded that these programs generally have been effective in reducing drug abuse and criminal activity, identifying previously untreated drug-dependent offenders, and establishing links between the CJS and treatment programs (Bureau of Justice Assistance, 1997). Offenders mandated to treatment through TASC and other criminal justice referrals tend to remain in treatment longer and thus have higher rates of treatment success, although the independent effects of TASC have not been determined (Anglin et al., 1999; Hubbard, Marsden, Rachal, Harwood, Cavenaugh, & Ginzburg, 1989).

Alternative Sentencing Programs

Although not as systematically defined or structured as other treatment delivery models, offenders also may be given nonincarcerative sentences requiring treatment participation. Such treatment orders are generally given by the judge in a sentencing order in conjunction with a probation sentence, usually with approval by the prosecutor. More recently, models such as California's Proposition 36 have allowed rapid placement on probation for some drug offenders provided they attend treatment (Farabee, Itser, Anglin, & Huang, 2004). These models have had mixed success: relapse often results in a probation violation rather than changes in treatment intensity, high probation officer caseloads make monitoring and supervision difficult or inconsistent, and little attention is given to proper clinical assessment and placement in the appropriate level of treatment (Belenko & Peugh, 2005; Farabee et al., 2004; Marlowe, 2003).

The Creation and Implementation of the DTAP Program

Charles J. Hynes was elected Kings County (Brooklyn, NY) district attorney in November 1989, amidst record numbers of felony drug arrests and indictments, reflecting changes in enforcement practice (Kleiman & Smith, 1990), the crack "epidemic" (Belenko, 1993), and a general shift toward more punitive law enforcement and sentencing policies (Zimring & Hawkins, 1992). Concerned about the limited effectiveness of punitive drug sentencing policies, Hynes envisioned a strategy that would incorporate treatment diversion to reduce incarceration and to mobilize community resources to address problems of drug-related crime.

Although evidence was beginning to emerge by the late 1980s about the effectiveness of prison treatment programs (Inciardi et al., 2004; Prendergast et al., 2004) and drug courts (Belenko & Dumanovsky, 1993), the highly publicized article by Martinson (1974), that "nothing works" in correctional programming, still produced skepticism about treatment alternatives. At the time of Hynes's election, research findings of the efficacy of mandatory treatment programs were emerging (e.g., National Institute on Drug Abuse [NIDA], 1988). In January 1990, he announced a plan to offer a treatment alternative to incarceration "to eliminate dependency and inculcate life and job skills to enable offenders to resist return to drug-related crime" (Powers & Dynia, 1992a, p. 2).

Hynes and his team at the Kings County District Attorney's (KCDA) office initially focused on securing funding, establishing procedures and protocols, and garnering the support of the judiciary, defense bar, probation, and parole. Planning sessions were regularly attended by representatives of the New York State Division of Alcohol and Substance Abuse Services, the Legal Aid Society, the Legal Action Center,[3] the Assigned Counsel Panel, and two large treatment providers. Each agency made unique and important contributions to the new diversion program concept by raising its concerns and enabling brainstorming about potential problems and solutions. For example, the Legal Aid Society and the Assigned Counsel Panel, which handle most New York City criminal cases, were concerned about "net widening" and insisted on ensuring meaningful prison displacement by targeting only prison-bound offenders.

The two treatment providers expressed a need for additional resources and were concerned that the prosecutor's office might make demands that interfered with clinical services delivery. They were already overwhelmed by noncriminal justice clients and thus had little incentive to allocate additional treatment slots for mandated criminal justice clients. The KCDA office responded by working with providers to attract external funding, providing guarantees that participants would receive the same treatment as other clients and treatment providers would determine the clinical suitability for treatment and would be allowed to expel program participants for breaking the rules.

It also was recognized that many repeat felons eligible for the program would already be on probation or parole, thus the new arrest could lead to incarceration due to probation or parole revocation, making community-based treatment impossible. It was decided to hold revocation proceedings in abeyance to allow arrestees under their supervision to receive treatment via the new program. The involvement of multiple agencies in the screening of cases raised the concern of the judges that the program could slow case disposition and increase pretrial detention. The KCDA office agreed to complete the screening process within 5 days of the defendant's first court appearance.

The Drug Treatment Alternative-to-Prison (DTAP) program began operating as a deferred prosecution program on October 15, 1990. The Robert Wood Johnson Foundation funded a study of the pilot phase of the program, which was instrumental in the formation of a permanent research unit that has enabled the DTAP program to develop an internal monitoring, data collection, and evaluation component and work on research efforts with external evaluators. Establishing a permanent in-house research unit, uncommon among prosecutors, turned the DTAP program into an information-driven innovation. Hynes and his program administrators explained the program's operations, analyzed impacts, and justified program changes backed by research data.

Accepted into the DTAP program during its first operating year were 138 participants (Powers & Dynia, 1992b). Preliminary findings were encouraging: participants had a 1-year treatment retention of 58%, substantially higher than the 13% to 29% retention reported in other national and local studies of community-based residential treatment (Hubbard et al., 1989; Simpson et al., 1997). The first DTAP program graduate completed treatment in May 1992, 17 months after the program began, and by 1994 the program had graduated more than 50 participants.

The DTAP program's initial achievement rapidly attracted public and research attention (e.g., Clines, 1993) and kept it in the public spotlight through the sometimes heated debate over U.S. drug policy in the early 1990s (Belenko, 2000; Zimring & Hawkins, 1992). This helped the KCDA office to secure more permanent budget support from New York State. In 1993, the National Institute of Justice awarded a grant to the Vera Institute of Justice to study the way in which the DTAP program's legal coercion affected its high retention rate (Young, 1996).

The initial positive response to the DTAP program precipitated widespread interest in establishing similar programs in other counties. In 1992, New York State Governor Mario Cuomo announced an effort to assist other district attorneys to implement the DTAP model. The New York State Office of Alcohol and Substance Abuse Services provided funding for 350 new residential treatment beds for DTAP programs. During the period 1992–1993, the New York State Division of Criminal Justice Services allocated $700,000 in Federal Anti-Drug Abuse Act monies to support the Brooklyn DTAP program and to enable its replication by other prosecutors in New York City. By June 2000, 11 prosecutors' offices in New York State had replicated the DTAP program (New York State Commission on Drugs and the Courts, 2000). An evaluation of the program's expansion noted retention rates at least 1.5 times higher than for comparable treatment programs (Young, Cocoros, & Ireland, 1995).

Enhancement and Expansion

Many innovations demonstrate an initial positive impact during a period when there is enthusiasm for the project and high visibility. Over time, however, the institutionalization of programs can lead to the dilution of effects as staff members change, program operations become routinized, and special funding and oversight end. The DTAP program has largely avoided these problems. The number of contracted treatment providers grew from two in 1990 to seven in 1996, and some began offering services to special-needs participants (e.g., Spanish-speaking clients, those with HIV/AIDS, and individuals under 24 years of age).

Based on data from an internal evaluation indicating that employment was tied to lower recidivism (Sung, 2000), a job developer was added in 1994 to provide job counseling and placement services to DTAP program graduates. The Business Advisory Council, comprised of dozens of large and medium businesses in Manhattan and Brooklyn, was established to identify employment opportunities for these graduates. In 1999, the DTAP Alumni Association was founded by a group of graduates to provide a formal framework for continued peer support. In collaboration with the DTAP program job developer, alumni are referred to KCDA resources in case of unemployment or to assist in career changes.

In 1994, the National Institute on Drug Abuse (NIDA) awarded a 5-year grant to the National Center on Addiction and Substance Abuse at Columbia University to evaluate the DTAP program. This large-scale study assessed the impact of treatment on participants on recidivism, drug use, and social adjustment, examined relative economic costs and benefits, and analyzed the role of legal pressure on retention. Key results from this research are summarized later. In December 1997, the U.S. Department of Justice selected the DTAP program as one of the six most effective programs among the 500 programs that had received funding from the Edward Byrne Memorial Law Enforcement Assistance Formula Grant Program, and it urged other states and localities to replicate it (Bureau of Justice Assistance, 1997).

Four program changes were introduced in January 1998, designed to improve retention and expand the eligibility pool. These modifications were informed by recent research and experiences of DTAP programs implemented by other New York City prosecutors that differed from the Brooklyn DTAP program in using a deferred sentencing model and allowing treatment readmission (Young et al., 1995).

The first key change was from a deferred prosecution to deferred sentencing program. Instead of holding the indictment in abeyance, new participants were now required to plead guilty to a felony with a specific deferred prison sentence. Upon program completion, the sentence would not be executed, the guilty plea withdrawn, and the charges dismissed. The sentence was imposed if the participant dropped out of or was dismissed from the DTAP program. This increased certainty of punishment was expected to deter participants from dropping out of treatment, thus increasing retention (Young, 1996).

Second, the DTAP program adopted a more flexible readmission policy: participants who relapsed to drug use were now considered for readmission into the same or different treatment facility. Previously, the DTAP program rarely placed treatment failures into another program. This change acknowledged recovery as a process in which relapse problems are part of successful rehabilitation.

The third modification was to offer treatment to all nonviolent defendants who committed crimes to support their drug abuse. Although most DTAP program participants continue to be charged with felony drug sales, the percentage has been decreasing. During the period 1998–2005, the average yearly percentage of drug cases out of all accepted cases was 85%. For the most recent period, from January 2005–January 2006, that percentage decreased to 74%.

Finally, the TASC program, a nonprofit case management agency, was contracted to perform clinical assessments and screening, treatment placement and monitoring, and case management. This new collaboration added the TASC program's expertise in treatment assessment, placement, and case management. For every candidate, the TASC program now performs a psychosocial assessment and verifies substance abuse history. Once accepted into the DTAP program, the TASC program places the participant in the most appropriate treatment facility. Case management functions include both site visits and monthly reports to the court, prosecutor, and defense counsel regarding the defendant's progress. Following successful completion of the residential portion of treatment, the TASC program monitors the defendant's aftercare and reentry process, including employment, housing, and abstinence until final graduation from the DTAP program.

The enhanced and expanded DTAP program has resulted in important changes in operations and retention. Since 1998, its average active treatment population has grown from less than 120 to more than 330 (Hynes & Swern, 2006, p. 21). One-year treatment retention has increased from 64% under the deferred prosecution model to 75% under the deferred sentencing model (Hynes & Swern, 2006). The number of graduates has increased to an average of 83 per year between 2001 and 2005, up from 53.

As a consequence of the growth of the DTAP program and positive research findings from external evaluations (see text that follows) the U.S. Congress has periodically drafted and considered legislation over the past few years to promote the DTAP model nationally. Existing versions of this DTAP legislation encourage and authorize funding state and local prosecutors to set up and oversee drug treatment options for nonviolent offenders, although future passage remains uncertain.

The DTAP Model

The DTAP program originally targeted defendants arrested for undercover "buy-and-bust"[4] felony drug sales, with one or more prior nonviolent felony convictions. The focus on "buy-and-bust" cases (that usually rest on strong material evidence and witnesses) helped ensure targeting those facing incarceration upon treatment failure. An extensive screening process weeded out weak cases to reduce the possibility of diverting defendants not facing incarceration. If convicted of a drug felony sale, second felony offenders receive a mandatory prison sentence (typically a minimum of 2–3 years and a maximum of 4–6 years) under New York State law. The DTAP program defers sentencing and offers community-based residential drug treatment program, using a therapeutic community (TC) model, for 18–24 months. These two aspects of DTAP program eligibility—a felony drug sale with a prior felony conviction, and only accepting cases with strong evidence that are likely to result in a conviction—distinguish the DTAP program from most other prosecutorial diversion programs that accept only low-level or weaker cases (Hillsman, 1982).

Program completers have their sentence vacated, guilty plea withdrawn, and original charges dismissed; dropouts are brought back to court by a special warrant enforcement team for sentencing on the original charges. Between the DTAP program's inception in October 1990 and October 2005, 6,284 defendants were screened for the program. Of these, 2,184 (35%) were admitted (Hynes & Swern, 2006), and 892 have graduated. Of those not admitted, 22% refused the option and 43% were rejected after further screening. Over its 15-year existence, the DTAP program has annually screened an average of 419 offenders, admitted 146, and graduated 64; 317 were in the program as of October 2005.

Screening and Admission Process

At the initial criminal court arraignment, "paper-eligible" defendants (i.e., the appropriate felony charge and one-plus prior nonviolent felony convictions) are identified by DTAP program screeners. The bureau chief of the KCDA Alternative Programs Bureau assesses the evidentiary strength and facts of each case. The DTAP program warrant enforcement team verifies community contacts to ensure the ability to locate the defendant in the event of treatment failure; those with weak ties are rejected. Those with weak cases also are rejected, given that they are likely to have their charges reduced or dismissed and thus not face mandatory prison sentences. Other reasons for rejection include major drug trafficking involvement, significant histories of violence not on a person's criminal record, or a determination that a person is unsuitable for long-term residential TC treatment (e.g., those with serious psychological problems). For defendants already on probation or parole, their probation or parole officer is contacted and must approve their participation in the DTAP program. The TASC program screeners also interview the defendant and assess her or his suitability for treatment. Finally, the judge presiding over the case must approve the defendant's placement in the DTAP program. Although the program has a high level of coercion once a defendant is admitted, initial participation is not mandatory: defendants may refuse to enter the DTAP program and elect to be prosecuted in the standard manner. Reasons for refusal include claiming innocence, not perceiving that they have a drug problem, or not wanting to attend long-term residential treatment.

The Treatment Programs

The DTAP program uses several TC treatment providers. Except for those with special needs, new participants are assigned to programs on a rotating basis, and based on bed availability. The providers adhere to a traditional TC philosophy, emphasizing social learning, behavioral, and cognitive-behavioral approaches in a highly structured environment working toward a healthy prosocial lifestyle characterized by abstinence (De Leon, 1985; Lang & Belenko, 2000). The DTAP program participants receive similar treatment as other residents. Residents move through successive phases in a peer community, assuming increasing responsibility for program governance: an orientation phase (3 weeks) facilitates assimilation into TC. The goal is for residents to learn the policies and procedures of the program and to gain initial insight into the core issues of their drug abuse. The primary treatment phase (4–18 months, usually at an upstate facility) focuses on resolving personal and relationship problems through individual, group, and family counseling. In addition, residents participate in vocational training and job skills development, gain work experience, and are given housing and employment assistance to ease their return to the community. During the reentry phase (3 months), participants return to a program facility in New York City, acquire jobs and save money, and move toward the final aftercare phase. After securing a job and appropriate living arrangements, gradual reentry into the community begins. The treatment focus shifts to maintaining sobriety, preventing relapse, and adjusting to independent living.

The Impact of the DTAP Program
on Participants: Key Findings

A comprehensive NIDA-funded external evaluation of the DTAP program was conducted from 1995 to 2003 by Belenko and his colleagues (see Belenko et al., 2004; Lang & Belenko, 2000; Sung & Belenko, 2006), in collaboration with the KCDA office. The evaluation included several substudies: an impact evaluation of the DTAP program's effects on recidivism, relapse, health, and social functioning; an economic analysis of the net costs and economic benefits; and research on the impact of legal pressure on program retention and recidivism, compared to other types of criminal justice-supervised treatment. In this section key findings from this research are summarized.

The quasi-experimental design included an experimental sample of 150 offenders admitted into the DTAP program and a comparison sample of 130 offenders sentenced to state prison, matched on arrest charges, prior felony convictions, age, race, gender, drug use, and desire for drug treatment. An extensive battery of intake interview instruments includes items on drug use, prior treatment history, criminal activity, employment and earnings, physical and psychological health, HIV risk behaviors, and social stability. Follow-up interviews with the same assessments were conducted 6 months after DTAP program completion (for graduates) or prison release (for DTAP program dropouts and comparisons). Recidivism data (new arrests, convictions, and incarceration sentences) were collected from official records for up to 5 years after DTAP program completion/release from prison. Details on sampling, data collection procedures, and data sources are presented elsewhere (Belenko et al., 2004; Lang & Belenko, 2000; Young & Belenko, 2002; Zarkin, Dunlap, Belenko, & Dynia, 2005).

Program Retention

Research indicates that the effectiveness of drug treatment is related to the treatment length (see, e.g., De Leon, 1991; Hubbard et al., 1989; Simpson et al., 1997). In long-term residential programs, a minimum stay of 3–4 months appears to be critical for positive outcomes, with longer stays improving behavior (De Leon, 1991; Simpson et al., 1997). However, attrition rates are high in residential programs, with a majority terminating within 3 months (Simpson et al., 1997). One assumption about criminal justice-mandated treatment is that the certainty, celerity, and/or severity of the consequences of treatment failure improve retention (Young & Belenko, 2002).

From its inception through October 2005, the DTAP program has had an overall 12–month retention rate of 71% and a 24–month retention rate of 55%. Comparing the deferred prosecution model to the deferred sentencing model, there was a significant improvement in retention after 1998, as program planners had anticipated—1-year and 2-year retention rates for the 1990–1997 cohort were 64% and 50%, respectively, compared to 75% and 59% for the 1998–2005 cohort. The largest difference in the dropout rate was observed during the first 6 months of treatment, indicating that the improved retention rate for the period 1998–2005 for DTAP program participants was achieved by lowering the early dropout rate, probably through the more lenient readmission policy. The DTAP program's retention rates are substantially higher than those reported nationally for general residential treatment clients (e.g., Hubbard et al., 1989; Simpson et al., 1997) and comparable to the highest rates reported for coerced criminal justice clients (Belenko, 2001; Hiller, Knight, Broome, & Simpson, 1998).

Prosecution and Sentencing of Program Failures

Of the 946 participants who failed treatment through October 2005, 93% were returned to court for prosecution and possible sentencing in a median of 14 days (Hynes & Swern, 2006). Among DTAP program failures, 80% were convicted of a felony and sentenced to prison, and 7% were convicted with another sentence (Hynes & Swern, 2006). Data on defendants who refused to enter the DTAP program or were rejected as ineligible by the screeners confirm that a prison-bound population was targeted—65% of the defendants who refused DTAP program participation and 78% of those rejected by program screeners were indicted on felony charges or entered felony pleas mandating prison sentences (Hynes & Swern, 2006).

Impact on Recidivism

Recidivism is arguably the most important measure of effectiveness for a treatment diversion program for chronic felony offenders. Lower recidivism increases public safety (Clear & Braga, 1995; Dynia & Sung, 2000) and reduces incarceration (Fluellen & Trone, 2000), generates cost-savings (Belenko, Patapis, & French, 2005; Gerstein, Johnson, Harwood, Fountain, Suter, & Malloy, 1994), and provides political credibility (Belenko, 2001). The DTAP program participation resulted in significant reductions in multiple recidivism measures, compared with similar offenders sentenced to prison, or offenders receiving treatment under standard criminal justice models (Belenko et al., 2004; Dynia & Sung, 2000; Young, Fluellen, & Belenko, 2004).

The analyses indicate that DTAP program participation reduces recidivism, and that although differences narrow over time, these reductions are still statistically significant across all recidivism measures after 4 years of follow-up (Belenko et al., 2004). Over the full follow-up period, DTAP program participants had a significantly lower rearrest prevalence (57% vs. 75% for the comparison sample), as well as a significantly lower prevalence of reconviction, new jail sentence, or new prison sentence. Both the mean number of arrests and the annualized arrest rate adjusted for time at risk in the community were significantly lower for DTAP program participants.

Among those with at least 3 years of follow-up, 34% of DTAP program participants and 62% of comparisons were reconvicted; reconviction was significantly lower for every crime except nondrug felonies. New time sentenced to jail or prison also was significantly lower—DTAP program participants averaged 2.6 months of new prison time (including those with no prison time) compared to 6.8 months for comparisons. Over the entire follow-up, 7% of DTAP program participants versus 18% of comparisons received a new prison sentence and 30% versus 51% a new jail sentence.

Survival analyses using Cox regression found that DTAP program participation significantly delayed the number of months to first rearrest (p < .001), controlling for criminal history and other factors (Belenko et al., 2004). Controlling for other factors, multivariate logistic regression analyses indicated that DTAP program participation decreased the odds of a rearrest after release from prison or treatment completion by 42% (Belenko et al., 2004). A multiple regression analysis of the adjusted annual rearrest rate found that in addition to significant effects from several measures of drug use, prior drug treatment, and prior criminal record, DTAP program participation was marginally significant in terms of predicting lower rearrest rates relative to the comparison group (t = −1.91, p = .06).

These results suggest that compared to incarceration, the DTAP program is effective in reducing crime among chronic, high-risk drug felons. The recidivism reduction from DTAP program participation is more meaningful because the study samples were matched on age and criminal history, two strong predictors of recidivism (Laub & Sampson, 2001).

Relapse to Drug Use

Among DTAP program research subjects available for 6-month follow-up interviews, we found that DTAP program participation resulted in reductions in drug use. Because we were able to interview a higher percentage of completers than dropouts,[5] the analyses weighted the data to reflect the original percentage of dropouts in the prospective sample (40% vs. 17% of those with 6–month follow-up interviews). Despite this weighting, caution is needed in interpreting those data because of the small number of dropouts and comparisons available for follow-up in the community.

At follow-up, significantly smaller percentages of DTAP program participants reported use of cocaine, crack, marijuana, or any illegal drug in the past 30 days than comparisons, with 5% of DTAP program subjects reporting cocaine use, 2% crack use, 5% marijuana, and 20% any drug. In contrast, 17% of comparisons reported cocaine use, 22% crack, 20% marijuana, and 52% any drug. After controlling for other factors (including baseline drug use) in logistic regression analyses, DTAP program participants significantly reduced their use of crack, marijuana, and any drug at follow-up. However, there were no significant effects on heroin or marijuana use the previous 30 days. Controlling for other factors in multivariate analyses, DTAP program participants also spent significantly less money on drugs in the 30 days prior to the follow-up interview. There were no significant differences in committing crimes to get money for drugs, or number of days with drug problems. The DTAP program dropouts had significantly worse outcomes than DTAP program completers, however (more days with drug problems, higher rates of positive opiate urine, likelier to sell drugs to get drug money).

These findings indicate that DTAP program participation reduces relapse 6 months after treatment compared to incarceration, although the effects were not consistent across all drug use measures. More generally, drug use and other measures of drug-related problems decreased substantially from pre-DTAP program levels.

Employment and Income

The DTAP program participation resulted in significant improvements in employment. At the 6-month follow-up period, 71% (weighted data) of all DTAP program participants were employed ($p < .05$, controlling for baseline employment status), compared to 52% of the comparisons. They also had a significantly higher mean number of weeks worked in the past 6 months (16.7 weighted) than comparisons (13.9, $p < .05$), but wage income was not significantly higher. Relative to comparisons, DTAP program participants had fewer days with employment problems in the 30 days prior to the follow-up interview.

The DTAP program participation also resulted in statistically significant decreases in money earned from drug dealing. Over the prior 90 days, earnings from dealing decreased from an average of $7,866 at baseline to $623 (weighted) at the 6-month follow-up period among all DTAP program subjects, compared to a decrease from $13,370 to $1,512 for comparisons.

These employment findings are consistent with our analyses of data from other DTAP program samples that indicate high and stable employment rates among graduates. This may reflect the attention that DTAP program planners and administrators have placed on employment since the beginning of the program. Program graduates are required to have a job or to be in school at graduation, and the DTAP program job counselor and the Business Advisory Council are available to assist graduates.

Economic Impact

Zarkin et al. (2005) conducted analyses of the costs and benefits of the DTAP program. The analysis was conducted from the perspective of the CJS and focused on CJS costs associated with recidivism, comparing the prospective sample of DTAP program participants to the matched sample of prison comparisons who entered treatment or prison in the period 1995–1996 and tracking recidivism for 6 years.

A program such as the DTAP incurs a number of additional costs, including the costs of eligibility screening and community ties checks, pretrial detention prior to admission, treatment, the warrant enforcement team, and program monitoring and administration. Zarkin et al. (2005) estimated the per-person costs for each of these components, as well as the per-person costs for each CJS activity (e.g., court processing, pretrial detention, jail or prison time, and parole); all DTAP program and CJS costs were estimated by year and cumulatively after 6 years. To allow comparability, all costs were calculated in 2001 dollars, and the discounted present value was estimated as of Year 1, using the standard 3% discount rate (Gold, Siegal, Russell, & Weinstein, 1996). Year 1 is the year of initial sample arrest.

Net DTAP program economic benefits were calculated as the difference in per-person CJS costs between the DTAP program and prison comparison groups. After the costs of the DTAP program and the CJS benefits were estimated, we compared the benefits and costs of the DTAP program annually and cumulatively over 6 years (Zarkin et al., 2005). The estimated average total DTAP program cost was $40,718 per participant, and the estimated total CJS cost was $124,955 for the comparison group. The DTAP program participants had significantly lower estimated CJS costs ($36,441; p < 0.01). Thus over a 6-year follow-up period, the cumulative benefits accrued per DTAP program participant were $88,554. Combined to DTAP program costs of $40,718, these savings yield a benefit-cost ratio of 2.17 ($88,554/$40,718). Stated another way, the DTAP program saved $47,836 in CJS costs per participant over 6 years, or $7.13 million over 6 years for the cohort of 149 DTAP program participants included in our analyses.

Role of Perceived Legal Pressure

The idea of conducting research on the coercive properties of mandatory treatment programs emerged in the early years of the DTAP program. Researchers at the Vera Institute of Justice, consulting with DTAP program planners, conducted a literature search on coercion and mandatory treatment to inform DTAP program design and development. For the most part, that search revealed little extant information about the impacts of specific coercive program practices, despite an emerging literature supporting the use and expansion of mandatory treatment programs (e.g., De Leon, 1988; Young, 1996). The DTAP program's high retention rates, evidenced from its early years (Hynes, 1994), suggested the need for research to determine what accounted for this retention.

Young and Belenko (2002) compared levels of perceived legal pressure in three types of mandated treatment: DTAP, TASC, and a probation/parole comparison group. They reviewed program policies and other documents, interviewed program and treatment personnel, and conducted exploratory quantitative analyses of the perception of legal pressure (PLP) measure developed by Young (2002). The PLP was administered to samples of clients in the programs (DTAP N = 130; TASC N = 124; comparison group N = 76). Analyses explored the relationship between the programs' coercive strategies and retention in treatment through 1 year post-admission.

Participants with moderate and high PLP scores were retained at similar rates at 1 year post-admission; those with low scores terminated earlier at higher rates. Retention rates for low-PLP clients were 15%–20% below the other two groups during the 6–12 months post-admission period. The DTAP program clients were retained at higher rates beginning early in treatment. The TASC program and comparison groups showed similar rates through about 150 days post-admission, when the retention rates of the comparison group began to decrease. The difference between the DTAP program and the comparison group was significant in 6-month multivariate models, and marginally significant in 1-year analyses.

Lessons Learned

The KCDA office established the DTAP program to divert and treat prison-bound drug sellers with the goals of reducing drug use, lowering recidivism, and reducing incarceration costs. To achieve these goals, the DTAP program utilizes legal coercion, long-term residential treatment, close monitoring, and case management as key program components. In contrast to most previous prosecutorial diversion programs, the DTAP program targets chronic drug felons facing mandatory prison sentences. Findings from extensive research on the program have been quite encouraging and indicate achievement of the program's major goals. Its ability to target prison-bound felons for diversion has enabled it to avoid the net-widening typical of traditional diversion programs that target low-risk or first-time offenders. A number of important lessons for developing prosecutorial responses to drug-involved offenders can be learned from the KCDA office's experiences with the DTAP program.

Benefits of Diverting High-Risk, Prison-Bound Drug Sellers

Targeting a population previously avoided by prosecutorial diversion programs—drug sellers and other high-risk, prison-bound felons—was a political risk for DA Hynes. However, the DTAP program's experiences and research and theory on the risk principle have consistently demonstrated that diverting high-risk offenders into treatment provides substantial benefits in terms of avoided incarceration and increased public safety (through reduced drug use) and benefits the offender who avoids the stigma and danger of incarceration (where access to treatment is limited), as well as the difficulties of reintegrating into society following release (Petersilia, 2001).

The automatic exclusion of drug sellers from treatment diversion programs and drug courts may be shortsighted. Most drug sellers in the state and local criminal court systems are low-level street dealers who also have drug abuse problems (Kleiman & Smith, 1990; Zimring & Hawkins, 1992). Accordingly, if programs such as DTAP can successfully treat drug abuse problems among sellers, then sellers would be less likely to continue dealing drugs. In addition, diverting repeat felons means that they can avoid mandatory lengthy incarceration from the persistent felony offender or the "three-strikes" laws that exist in most states. Given the high cost of long-term or residential treatment needed by many offenders, diversion or alternative sentencing programs targeting only low-risk or first-time offenders might not be cost-beneficial.

Obtaining and Sustaining Collaborative and Political Support

Although the DTAP program was spearheaded by the prosecutor, a key to the program's successful launch was the early involvement of all related agencies. By inviting the assistance of other entities, the KCDA office strove to reduce suspicion that the DTAP program would not be a true diversion program. Because the concerns of all agencies were thoroughly aired and addressed, all parties had a stake in the DTAP program's success. Additionally, this teamwork minimized later misunderstandings about procedures and goals. Following implementation, frequent contact between KCDA office staff, the TASC program, treatment providers, and defense attorneys about particular treatment candidates and participants has ensured swift problem resolution before becoming systemic and jeopardizing the program. In short, open lines of communication and a constant flow of information and feedback have ensured that the DTAP program's collaborative efforts would be sustained.

The DTAP program's initial success helped attract funding, and the program's ability to sustain and expand its operations also had an important influence in attracting more widespread political support. Thus prosecutorial oversight makes the DTAP program more palatable to law enforcement groups and others who may recognize that community-based drug treatment can reduce recidivism and save incarceration costs but might worry about public safety risk. Such fears are allayed by the DTAP program's careful prosecutorial case screening and by its Warrant Enforcement Team. At the same time, as a prosecution-run program, DTAP has demonstrated to the community that a district attorney's office can operate a collaborative treatment diversion program—a prosecutor's office need not be just about incarcerating offenders but also can be about reducing and preventing future crimes by addressing substance abuse and addiction.

Finally, the role of DA Hynes in sustaining collaborations and in gaining political support has been very important. As head of a large urban prosecutor's office, he has continuously and publicly expressed his complete support of the DTAP program, writing articles and speaking publicly about the program, including testifying before Congress, rather than relying on subordinates, and thus he has inspired others' confidence in the program. The defense bar, judiciary, and treatment community know that the DTAP program is a top-priority program for this prosecutor, and that he is committed to making it work.

Building in Program Flexibility

Another unique program aspect has been a willingness to examine program activities, to use research findings, and to modify the DTAP program to resolve problems or improve operations. This flexibility is evidenced by the major structural changes made in 1998 in response to data on retention and dropout, and other periodic changes in target populations and treatment providers. In addition, the DTAP program has built in clinical flexibility: each participant completes the program when deemed clinically appropriate and when the DA considers that the defendant no longer poses a risk to public safety.

Role of Research Partnerships

A unique aspect of the DTAP program's planning and implementation has been the involvement of internal and external research. From the inception of the DTAP program, planners and administrators have demonstrated an interest in gathering data, monitoring and evaluating program operations, and using research findings to inform operations. This openness to research and evaluation, especially by outside evaluators, has had a number of benefits. First, researchers helped develop data systems and a framework for monitoring program operations and producing management reports and statistics that track DTAP program retention, targeting, and case-flow data. Second, the research activities have helped identify areas in need of operational change. Third, research partnerships have helped produce empirical evidence to generate program funding and external political and policy support. The regular dissemination of program data and findings through annual reports, conference presentations, and academic articles has provided evidence of the DTAP program's success and increased policy-maker confidence, as well as continued interest and visibility.

Deferred Prosecution versus Deferred Sentencing Models

The DTAP program began as a *deferred prosecution* program but shifted to a *deferred sentencing* program in January 1998. This increased certainty of punishment enhanced political support by further signaling that offender accountability was taken seriously, and that treatment diversion was not "soft on drugs and crime." The increased certainty of incarceration for program dropouts was intended to enhance perceptions of legal coercion, which preliminary research indicated increased retention (Young, 1996). As a program modification reform that held program dropouts even more accountable and increased legal pressure to stay in treatment, the shift from deferred prosecution to deferred sentencing proved to be a scientifically sound and politically important restructuring.

Role of Perceived Legal Coercion in Treatment Retention

Compared to conventional approaches, the DTAP program has more structured protocols for informing clients about the contingencies of participation and the legal consequences of failing treatment. It also differs in its use of behavioral contracts and in the number of criminal justice agents—prosecutors, judges, defense attorneys, and warrant investigators—who monitor clients. Our findings also support the DTAP program's policy of having formal agreements with treatment programs and requiring treatment staff to reinforce messages about contingencies and consequences. Also, the structured and consistent approach to enforcement and monitoring has been reflected in relatively high perceived legal pressure by its participants and has likely contributed to higher retention rates.

Importance of Long-Term Treatment

Relatively few drug-involved offenders receive treatment while incarcerated (Belenko & Peugh, 2005), and available treatment opportunities often are too limited and short term, especially given offenders' high rates of other social and health problems (Belenko & Peugh, 2005; Hammett et al., 2001). Although data are lacking on the effectiveness of short-term or "outpatient" correctional treatment, residential treatment during incarceration, followed by continuing care in the community, yields a reduction in recidivism and relapse to drug use (see, e.g., Inciardi et al., 2004; Prendergast et al., 2004). However, long-term residential treatment beds are generally scarce for offenders, and such treatment is not typically an option for offenders in diversion or alternative sentencing programs. The DTAP program has demonstrated that many high-risk offenders can be successfully engaged in long-term intensive treatment, with positive results.

Reducing Criminal Justice System Costs

Our economic analyses have identified key CJS costs and benefits associated with treatment diversion and provide an economic justification for programs such as DTAP that target high-risk offenders (Griffith et al., 1999) and use relatively expensive long-term residential treatment. Because of the high upfront costs of long-term residential treatment, most of the economic benefits of the DTAP program do not begin to accrue until the second year.

Accordingly, our data suggest the need for a longer-term perspective in esti-mating the economic benefits of treatment diversion. Because of the poten-tial long-term reductions in rearrest and reincarceration from programs such as DTAP, analyses that are limited to short-term outcomes are likely to underestimate net economic benefits.

Emphasis on Social Integration

The DTAP program has capitalized research on the effects of stable employ-ment on reductions in drug relapse and recidivism (Sung, 2001; Uggen, 2000). Effective drug treatment thus should also seek to bridge a return to society as productive citizens through emphasis on education and employment training and placement (Walker & Leukefeld, 2002). In addition to in-treatment edu-cational and vocational training that enhances graduates' marketable skills, the DTAP program seeks to strengthen its graduates' ties to the legitimate labor market through specialized employment counseling, its Business Advisory Council, and the networking and information sharing facilitated by the DTAP Alumni Association. As an important supplement to long-term resi-dential drug treatment, these services may help remediate their human and social capital deficits and greatly improve their chances to maintain sobriety, stable employment, and a crime-free lifestyle.

Notes

1. "Drug-involved offenders" include those charged with drug crimes as well as those charged with nondrug crimes who have an underlying drug abuse problem.

2. These programs are now usually called Treatment Accountability (or Alter-natives) for Safer Communities.

3. A nonprofit organization focusing on federal regulations of confidentiality, the privacy of substance abusers, and criminal justice program planning.

4. In "buy-and-bust" arrests, undercover police officers pose as drug users to buy drugs; other officers then capture the sellers. Conviction rates for these cases are very high because of their evidentiary strength—undercover agents testify as witnesses and recover prerecorded marked buy money. Other nonviolent felony cases are now DTAP-eligible.

5. Due to the length of time they spent in prison and the lack of sufficient fol-low-up time (six consecutive months) in the community during the period of the research project.

References

Andrews, D., & Bonta, J. (1998). *The psychology of criminal conduct* (2nd ed.). Cincin-nati, OH: Anderson.

Anglin, M., Longshore, D., & Turner, S. (1999). Treatment alternatives to street crime: An evaluation of five programs. *Criminal Justice and Behavior, 26*, 168–195.

Baker, S. H., & Sadd, S. (1981). *Diversion of felony arrests: An experiment in pretrial intervention: An evaluation of the Court Employment Project.* New York: Vera Institute of Justice.

Belenko, S. (1993). *Crack and the evolution of anti-drug policy.* Westport, CT: Greenwood Press.

Belenko, S. (2000). *Drugs and drug policy in America: A documentary history.* Westport, CT: Greenwood Press.

Belenko, S. (2001). *Research on drug courts: A critical review. 2001 update.* New York: The National Center on Addiction and Substance Abuse at Columbia University.

Belenko, S. (2002). Drug courts. In C. Leukefeld, F. Tims, & D. Farabee (Eds.), *Treatment of drug offenders: Policies and issues* (pp. 301–318). New York: Springer.

Belenko, S., & Dumanovsky, T. (1993). *Special drug courts: Program brief.* Washington, DC: U.S. Department of Justice, Bureau of Justice Assistance.

Belenko, S., Foltz, C., Lang, M., & Sung, H-E. (2004). The impact on recidivism of residential treatment for high risk drug felons: A longitudinal analysis. *Journal of Offender Rehabilitation, 40*, 105–132.

Belenko, S., Patapis, N., & French, M. T. (2005). *Economic benefits of drug treatment: A critical review of the evidence for policy makers.* Philadelphia: Treatment Research Institute.

Belenko, S., & Peugh, J. (2005). Estimating drug treatment needs among state prison inmates. *Drug and Alcohol Dependence, 77*, 269–281.

Blumstein, A., & Beck, A. J. (1999). Population growth in U.S. prisons, 1980–1996. In M. Tonry & J. Petersilia (Eds.), *Prisons*, vol. 26 of *Crime and justice: A review of research* (pp. 17–62). Chicago: University of Chicago Press.

Boldt, R. C. (1998). Rehabilitative punishment and the drug treatment court movement. *Washington University Law Quarterly, 76*, 1205–1306.

Bureau of Justice Assistance. (1997). *Improving the nation's criminal justice system: Findings and results from state and local program evaluations.* Washington, DC: Office of Justice Programs.

Clear, T. R., & Braga, A. A. (1995). Community corrections. In J. Q. Wilson & J. Petersilia (Eds.), *Crime* (pp. 421–444). San Francisco: ICS Press.

Clines, F. X. (1993, January 20). Dealing with drug dealers: Rehabilitation, not jail. *New York Times*, p. B1.

Cooper, C. S., & Trotter, J. (1994). Recent developments in drug case management: Reengineering the judicial process. *Justice System Journal, 17*, 83–98.

De Leon, G. (1985). The therapeutic community: Status and evolution. *International Journal of the Addictions, 20*, 823–844.

De Leon, G. (1988). Legal pressure in therapeutic communities. *Journal of Drug Issues, 4*, 625–640.

De Leon, G. (1991). Retention in drug-free therapeutic communities. In R. Pickens, C. Leukefeld, & C. Schuster (Eds.), *Improving drug abuse treatment* (no. 106, pp. 160–177). Rockville, MD: NIDA.

Drug Court Clearinghouse. (2005). *Drug court activity report, 2005.* Washington, DC: American University Justice Programs Office.

Dynia, P., & Sung, H. (2000). The safety and effectiveness of diverting felony drug offenders to residential treatment as measured by recidivism. *Criminal Justice Policy Review, 11*, 299–311.

Farabee, D., Hser, Y.-I., Anglin, M. D., & Huang, D. (2004). Recidivism among an early cohort of California's Proposition 36 offenders. *Criminology & Public Policy, 3*, 563–584.

Feeley, M. (1983). *Court reform on trial: Why simple solutions fail?* New York: Basic Books.

Festinger, D. S., Marlowe, D. B., Lee, P. A., Kirby, K. C., Bovasso, G., & McLellan, A. T. (2002). Status hearings in drug court: When more is less and less is more. *Drug and Alcohol Dependence, 68*, 151–157.

Fluellen, R., & Trone, J. (2000). *Do drug courts save jail and prison beds?* New York: Vera Institute of Justice.

Gerstein, D. R., Johnson, R. A., Harwood, H., Fountain, D., Suter, N., & Malloy, K. (1994). *Evaluating recovery services: The California Drug and Alcohol Treatment Assessment (CALDATA).* Sacramento, CA: State of California Department of Drug and Alcohol Programs.

Goerdt, J., & Martin, J. (1989). The impact of drug cases on case processing in urban trial courts. *State Court Journal, 13*, 4–12.

Gold, M. R., Siegal, J. E., Russell, L. B., & Weinstein, M. C. (1996). *Cost-effectiveness in health and medicine.* New York: Oxford University Press.

Goldkamp, J. S., & Weiland, D. (1993). *Assessing the impact of Dade County's felony drug court: Final report to the National Institute of Justice.* Philadelphia: Criminal Justice Research Institute.

Griffith, J. D., Hiller, M. L., Knight, K., & Simpson, D. D. (1999). A cost-effectiveness analysis of in-prison therapeutic community treatment and risk classification. *The Prison Journal, 79*, 352–368.

Hammett, T. M., Roberts, C., & Kennedy, S. (2001). Health-related issues in prisoner reentry. *Crime and Delinquency, 47*, 390–409.

Harrison, P. M., & Beck, A. J. (2005). *Prisoners in 2004.* Pub. No. NCJ 210677. Washington, DC: U.S. Department of Justice, Bureau of Justice Statistics.

Hiller, M., Knight, K., Broome, K., & Simpson, D. D. (1998). Legal pressure and treatment retention in a national sample of long-term residential programs. *Criminal Justice and Behavior, 25*, 463–481.

Hillsman, S. T. (1982). Pretrial diversion of youthful adults: A decade of reform and research. *Justice System Journal, 7*, 361–387.

Hora, P. F., Schma, W. G., & Rosenthal, J. (1999). Therapeutic jurisprudence and the drug treatment court movement: Revolutionizing the criminal justice system's response to drug abuse and crime in America. *Notre Dame Law Review, 74*, 439–537.

Hubbard, R. L., Marsden, M. E., Rachal, J. V., Harwood, H. J., Cavenaugh, E. R., & Ginzburg, H. M. (Eds.). (1989). *Drug abuse treatment: A national study of effectiveness*. Chapel Hill: University of North Carolina Press.

Hynes, C. J. (1994). *Drug Treatment Alternative-to-Prison: Fourth annual report*. Brooklyn, NY: Kings County District Attorney's Office.

Hynes, C. J., & Swern, A. (2006). *Drug Treatment Alternative-to-Prison program: 15th annual report*. Brooklyn, NY: Office of the Kings County District Attorney.

Inciardi, J. A., Martin, S. S., & Butzin, C. A. (2004). Five-year outcomes of therapeutic community treatment of drug-involved offenders after release from prison. *Crime & Delinquency, 50*, 88–107.

Jacoby, J. E., & Gramckow, H. P. (1994). Prosecuting drug offenders. In D. MacKenzie & C. Uchida (Eds.), *Drugs and crime: Evaluating public policy initiatives* (pp. 151–171). Thousand Oaks, CA: Sage Publications.

Kleiman, M. A. R., & Smith, K. (1990). State and local drug enforcement: In search of a strategy. In M. Tonry & N. Morris (Eds.) *Drugs and crime* (pp. 151–171). Chicago: University of Chicago Press.

Lang, M., & Belenko, S. (2000). Predicting retention in a residential Drug Treatment Alternative-to-Prison program. *Journal of Substance Abuse Treatment, 19*, 145–160.

Langan, P. A., & Levin, D. J. (2002). *Recidivism of prisoners released in 1994*. Washington, DC: Bureau of Justice Statistics, U.S. Department of Justice.

Laub, J. H., & Sampson, R. J. (2001). Understanding desistance from crime. In M. Tonry (Ed.), *Crime and justice: A review of research, Vol. 28* (pp. 1–69). Chicago: University of Chicago Press.

Marlowe, D. B. (2003). Integrating substance abuse treatment and criminal justice supervision. *NIDA Science & Practice Perspectives, 2*, 4–14.

Martinson, R. (1974). What works? Questions and answers about prison reform. *Public Interest, 35*, 22–54.

Mumola, C. J. (1999). *Substance abuse and treatment of state and federal prisoners, 1997*. Pub. No. NCJ 172871. Washington, DC: U.S. Department of Justice, Office of Justice Programs, Bureau of Justice Statistics.

National Institute on Drug Abuse (NIDA). (1988). *Compulsory treatment of drug abuse: Research and clinical practice*. Rockville, MD: NIDA.

New York State Commission on Drugs and the Courts. (2000). *Confronting the cycle of addiction and recidivism: A report to Chief Judge Judith Kaye*. New York: New York State Commission on Drugs and the Courts.

Nolan, J. L. (2003). *Reinventing justice: The American drug court movement*. Princeton, NJ: Princeton University Press.

Petersilia, J. (2001). Prisoner reentry: Public safety and reintegration challenges. *The Prison Journal, 81*, 360–376.

Powers, S., & Dynia, P. A. (1992a, November). Diverting prison-bound felony drug offenders from prison: A prosecutor's strategy. Paper presented at the annual meeting of the American Society of Criminology.

Powers, S., & Dynia, P. A. (1992b, November). Drug Treatment Alternative-to-Prison: Process evaluation and preliminary research report. Paper presented at the annual meeting of the American Society of Criminology.

Prendergast, M. L, Hall, E. A., Wexler, H. K., Melnick, G., & Cao, Y. (2004). Amity prison-based therapeutic community: 5–year outcomes. *Prison Journal, 84*, 36–60.

Simpson, D., Joe, G., Broome, K., Hiller, M., Knight, K., & Rowan-Szal, G. A. (1997). Program diversity and treatment retention rates in the Drug Abuse Treatment Outcome Study (DATOS). *Psychology of Addictive Behaviors, 11*, 279–293.

Sung, H-E. (2000). Employment and recidivism. *Alternatives-to-Incarceration, 6*, 14–15.

Sung, H-E. (2001). Rehabilitating felony drug offenders through job development: A look into a prosecutor-led diversion program. *Prison Journal, 81*, 271–286.

Sung, H.-E., & Belenko, S. (2006). From diversion experiment to policy movement: A case study of prosecutorial innovation. *Journal of Contemporary Criminal Justice, 22*, 220–240.

Thanner, M., & Taxman, F. (2003). Responsivity: The value of providing intensive services to high-risk offenders. *Journal of Substance Abuse Treatment, 24*, 137–147.

Uggen, C. (2000). Work as a turning point in the life course of criminals: A duration model of age, employment, and recidivism. *American Sociological Review, 65*, 529–546.

U.S. Government Accountability Office (U.S. GAO). (2005). *Adult drug courts: Evidence indicates recidivism reductions and mixed results for other outcomes*. Washington, DC: Author.

Walker, R., & Leukefeld, C. (2002). Employment rehabilitation. In C. G. Leukefeld, F. Tims, & D. Farabee (Eds.), *Treatment of drug offenders: Policies and issues* (pp. 69–79). New York: Springer.

Young, D. (1996). *Retaining offenders in mandatory drug treatment programs: The role of perceived legal pressure*. New York: Vera Institute of Justice.

Young, D. (2002). Impacts of perceived legal pressure on retention in drug treatment. *Criminal Justice and Behavior, 29*, 27–55.

Young, D., & Belenko, S. (2002). Program retention and perceived coercion in three models of mandatory drug treatment. *Journal of Drug Issues, 32*, 297–328.

Young, D., Cocoros, D., & Ireland, T. (1995). *Diverting drug offenders to treatment: Year three of DTAP (Drug Treatment Alternative-to-Prison) expansion.* New York: Vera Institute of Justice.

Young, D., Fluellen, R., & Belenko, S. (2004). Criminal recidivism in three models of mandatory drug treatment. *Journal of Substance Abuse Treatment, 27*, 313–323.

Zarkin, G. A., Dunlap, L. J., Belenko, S., & Dynia, P. A. (2005). A benefit-cost analysis of the Kings County District Attorney's Office Drug Treatment Alternative to Prison (DTAP) Program. *Justice Research and Policy, 7*, 1–25.

Zhang, Z. (2004). *Drug and alcohol use and related matters among arrestees, 2003.* Washington, DC: U.S. Department of Justice, National Institute of Justice.

Zimring, F. E., & Hawkins, G. (1992). The search for rational drug control. *Economist, 323*, 96.

Chapter Seven

Project Safe Neighborhoods and the Changing Role of the U.S. Attorney's Office

SCOTT H. DECKER and JACK McDEVITT

Introduction

This chapter examines the effect of implementing Project Safe Neighborhoods (PSN) strategies on U.S. Attorneys' offices nationally as well as PSN as a case study of organizational change. This is a particularly appropriate topic to examine in light of the highly structured, hierarchical, and formalized nature of U.S. Attorneys' offices and the general lack of attention to the organizational dynamics of these offices.[1] Because PSN calls for using strategic problem solving approaches, it represents a stark contrast to the typical legal approach where cases that are presented often drive the direction of many U.S. Attorneys' offices. Indeed, legal reasoning and strategic problem solving are distinct and often contradictory methods of addressing challenges.

Project Safe Neighborhoods presents researchers with a rare opportunity to study prosecutorial change, nested in theories of organizational change. In particular, the clash between legal reasoning and problem-solving cultures is important in this context. Prosecution, particularly federal prosecution, is built on "legal thinking"—one case at a time, the use of analogies, and precedents. Such thinking emphasizes the uniqueness of cases. Strategic problem solving, on the other hand, is based on the analysis of patterns across a large number of cases. It rejects a focus on a single case, in particular, on outliers or exceptional cases. Instead it seeks to aggregate cases, and it looks for patterns or trends. A consistent training theme for PSN has been that it (PSN) is not about cases, it is about strategies. This suggests that, in the end, PSN produced some level of organizational change, particularly for U.S. Attorneys' offices.

A Description of Project Safe Neighborhoods

According to the Web site that supports PSN,

> Project Safe Neighborhoods is a nationwide commitment to reduce gun violence by networking existing local programs that target gun crime and providing these programs with additional tools necessary to be successful. The goal is to take a hard line against gun criminals through every available means in an effort to make our streets and communities safer. Project Safe Neighborhoods seeks to achieve heightened coordination among federal, state, and local law enforcement, with an emphasis on tactical intelligence gathering, more aggressive prosecutions, and enhanced accountability through performance measures. The offensive will be led by the U.S. Attorney in each of the 94 federal judicial districts across America. (PSN, 2006)

Five core principles encompass PSN: (1) partnerships, (2) strategic planning, (3) training, (4) outreach, and (5) accountability (Executive Office for U.S. Attorneys, 2002). The PSN strategy has at its core leadership by the U.S. Attorney in each of the 94 federal judicial districts. U.S. Attorneys were charged by the president and the attorney general with creating and coordinating a response to gun crime in their districts. The response is meant to involve local, state, and federal authorities that involve prosecutors, law enforcement, probation and parole, juvenile courts, appropriate community and governmental agencies, and a research partner. It was to be the job of the research partner to develop an understanding of the gun crime problem in the jurisdiction based on data that reflected the patterns and trends of gun crime. A strategic plan was to be developed based on that empirical understanding that would address gun crime in each district that reflected three national priorities—increased prosecution, increased enforcement of federal gun laws (Title 18, USC), and increased enforcement of laws regulating possession of firearms, particularly "prohibited persons" (USC 922.g.1). Also recognized by PSN, however, is that the nature of gun crime is highly variable both across districts as well as within districts. Training is the third core principle of PSN. The description of the strategy (EOUSA, 2002, p. 3) notes eight separate training activities related to the strategy, three of which specifically are directed at prosecutors, and three others that have relevance for prosecution.

Outreach, the fourth core principle, was to include community outreach and public awareness. In this regard, each district was to employ a media outreach partner to work in conjunction with the National Crime Prevention Council (NCPC) to create a local campaign of advertising in support of task force activities. The final principle in the strategy was accountability. The PSN strategy emphasized that for strategic efforts to reduce gun crime to be successful, they must be constantly evaluated. Prosecutions were defined as outputs, not outcomes, and the focus was to be on outcomes. The training emphasized that PSN was not about *cases prosecuted*, it was about lowering the level of gun crime in a community. In this regard, prosecutions were a means to an end, not the end in itself. This represented one key point of organizational change for U.S. Attorneys' offices under PSN. Despite the emphasis on outcomes, however, the most recent PSN Fact Sheet (2006) emphasized the increase in the number of federal firearms prosecutions, a 62% increase since fiscal year (FY) 2000, along with other initiatives and crime reduction.

The Bush administration has committed more than $1.5 billion to PSN since 2001. The initial grant program through the Bureau of Justice Assistance funded local gun prosecutors at the district's or state's attorney level of jurisdiction. In addition, most districts received funding to hire additional assistant U.S. Attorneys to prosecute gun crime or support to hire an assistant U.S. Attorney to prosecute juvenile gun offenders and coordinate Project Sentry activities in addressing juvenile gun crime. Since that time, additional funding has been made available for research partners, media partners, task force activities, prevention and intervention programs, and Bureau of Alcohol, Tobacco, and Firearms (ATF) gun trace and investigation efforts.

According to PSN guidelines, the U.S. Attorney is responsible for convening the task force in each district and is held accountable for the success of the strategy. In each district, an assistant U.S. Attorney was named a PSN coordinator. In 93 of the 94 districts, that coordinator also prosecuted gun cases; the 94th district lost its full-time coordinator when she was named a state judge in 2004. In addition to the PSN coordinator, a Project Sentry (a parallel juvenile crime prevention program) coordinator was named to oversee prosecutions of juvenile gun crimes covered by federal law.

From a social science perspective, little research exists that described the functioning of federal prosecutors' offices. What does exist involves local prosecutors' offices. For example, in their discussion of felony courts, Eisenstein and Jacob (1977) described the courtroom work group. Such work groups had several common elements, most notably an environment in which routine activities are based more on personal relationships than formal structures and rules. The work group is comprised of multiple actors, including prosecutors, defense attorneys (especially public defenders, who are more "constants" than private counsel), judges, and other courtroom functionaries. Working together on a regular basis, a normative set of expectations is developed for disposing of what Sudnow (1965) has called "normal crimes." Such expectations help members of the work group reduce uncertainty, process large numbers of cases ("bulk"), develop routinized methods of identifying what the common features of routine cases might be, and minimize conflict. In this way, the work group promotes efficiency. Such efficiencies can be seen most clearly in the large number of cases that are plea bargained, and the routine manner in which such plea bargaining exists.

Work group research has been confined almost exclusively to state-level felony courts either at the adult (Clynch & Neubauer, 1981; Eisenstein & Jacob, 1977; Fleming, Nardulli, & Eisenstein, 1988) or juvenile level (Clarke & Koch, 1980; Feld, 1993; Knepper & Barton, 1997; Burruss & Kempf-Leonard, 2002). Few attempts have been made to understand the organizational dynamics of the federal court; most studies have examined the impact of sentencing guidelines (Nagel & Schulhofer, 1992; Wilmot & Spohn, 2004) or examinations of political influences in federal prosecution (Whitney, 1975). Eisenstein's (1978) work remains the major study of federal prosecutors as a work group. PSN represents a fundamental challenge to federal prosecution, as it reflects the clash of cultures, legal thinking (one case at a time, analogies) versus strategic problem solving (looking for patterns).

Strategic Interventions

Four specific interventions were developed through the training, technical assistance and leadership of PSN coordinators: homicide case review, offender notification meetings, MVP lists, and gun case review. These interventions emerged from PSN precursor programs such as the Boston Ceasefire Program (McDevitt, Braga, Nurge, & Buerger, 2003), the National Institute of Justice Strategic Approaches to Community Safety Initiative (SACSI) (Dalton, 2002), and the Richmond Ceasefire Strategy (APRI, 2002).

Source of the Strategy

The case review strategy emerged in a number of districts. Many of the districts observed that offenders did not view criminal penalties for gun possession as having much deterrent value. In state courts, many gun possession cases, even when offenders had significant felony records, resulted in trivial penalties, providing little deterrent value. In many districts, the U.S. attorney's office was somewhat isolated from local law enforcement and state prosecution. Often relationships did not exist between federal and state prosecutors and between federal prosecutors and local law enforcement. Also, in most U.S. Attorneys' offices, the prosecutors had few relationships with the local community, which also inhibited a strategic approach to dealing with gun crime.

In addition, there was a lack of familiarity on the part of local law enforcement with what the U.S. Attorney's office could do and what penalties were provided by federal statute. These problems led to the conclusion in many districts that in order for criminal penalties to pose a realistic threat to offenders, the system needed to be fixed.

Goals

The goals of case review reflect the principles of the overall PSN strategy. Specifically, the goal is to find the best venue for prosecution, and that can be done only by sharing information in a team approach. Effective prosecution is applying sentences to offenders in ways that send a deterrent message to those individuals, as well as to other offenders—and potential offenders—in the community. It is important for the choice venue to also correspond to the ongoing strategic gun violence efforts in each jurisdiction. The case review process seeks to demonstrate that coordination of resources can make the system more effective.

Twenty-seven districts report having a formal gun case review process in 2005, nearly all of the PSN task forces report some type of gun case screening mechanism, and most report working with local prosecutors in this case screening process. Achieving the goal of effective prosecution is contingent upon a variety of factors. A key challenge faced by case review is to find the most appropriate venue for prosecution. In many states, federal gun laws provide for more severe penalties than do state laws. With the strategic goal of finding the most appropriate venue for prosecution, the case review process seeks to identify relevant elements of a gun case or a gun offender's criminal record that have an impact on this decision. Then the process seeks to gather as much information as possible and make strategic decisions about not only where the longest sentence can be obtained but also where conviction is most likely and where the impact of punishment is likely to be the greatest. The goal is not simply to increase the number of federal gun cases but to increase the deterrent effect of gun laws. The consideration of the impact of a punishment on other offenders is a key factor in such reviews. This calls for increased cooperation on several fronts. First, the different sectors of law enforcement, including local, state, and federal enforcement agencies, must cooperate on a regular basis. Second, levels of prosecution must be better coordinated—state, federal, and municipal prosecution must work together. Finally, there must be cooperation across the sectors of the criminal justice system, so that law enforcement, prosecution, and aftercare supervision (probation and parole) work together to review data, make decisions about cases, and follow through on decisions. While this type of coordination has begun in many communities over the past several years, often the U.S. Attorney was not involved. PSN is the broadest national effort to include the U.S. Attorney as a leader in these coordinated efforts.

If successful, case review should have an impact on gun crime that is measurable. First, increased federal prosecutions can be an integral part of communicating the PSN strategy to offenders. This can be true both for the specific offenders who receive federal sentences for gun offenses as well as for their cohorts who also are engaged in gun crime and the community where awareness of the PSN strategy is communicated well to the public. Second, cases at the state level can be strengthened, thereby resulting in increased incarceration time, more convictions, or both. Because of the critical role of information sharing and strategic decision making in PSN, gun case reviews can be an effective means of developing a stronger case against an offender, thus ensuring more appropriate penalties for gun offenders. This is particularly true in those communities where simple gun possession has been de facto decriminalized. Many local jurisdictions report that there are few, if any, penalties for simple illegal gun possession because of the large volume of such cases and their "routine" nature. The case review process can help solve this problem by providing more information about the criminal histories of the offenders as well as working with local law enforcement to improve the quality and quantity of information about the cases.

In addition to its impact on gun crime, an effective case review process should produce changes in the way the system works, or what have come to be known as "system fixes." A number of PSN jurisdictions report that one of the challenges they faced was the number of gaps that presently exist in the criminal justice system. It became immediately apparent to many districts that there were gaps between agencies of the criminal justice system. Whether those gaps were between federal and local law enforcement, federal- and state-level prosecution, or across functions, the gaps resulted in cases not being dealt with as successfully as possible. In addition, the penalties for gun crimes in many districts had little or no deterrent effect. Accordingly, many jurisdictions set out to fix those challenges in the system, typically through better communication among themselves and better information the cases being prosecuted. In addition, producing a credible deterrent message was viewed as an important part of fixing the system. In the Eastern District of Missouri, the PSN coordinator has taken it as his charge to make offenders more fearful of the criminal penalties for carrying a gun than they are of being caught on the street by local gang rivals without their gun. Prior to PSN, too many cases in this district were either not presented to the U.S. Attorney's office or were not prepared in sufficient detail for federal prosecution.

The Western District of Tennessee reported that a significant problem it faced was that a combination of weak state gun laws and a large volume of gun cases led to the belief that it was "no big deal" to be caught with a gun.

Unfortunately that view also had begun to permeate many aspects of the criminal justice system. This led the U.S. Attorney's office to implement a case-tracking system that reviewed all gun cases that met the federal gun statute. This appears to be a critical element for success; by reviewing every gun case, the task force better understands the nature of gun crime in the jurisdiction, improves the overall quality of case materials, reinforces to local law enforcement the importance of gun cases, and makes better strategic decisions. In addition, the research partner, as required in each PSN jurisdiction, can contribute to the discussion of the nature of gun crime in a jurisdiction, making the discussion broader and the decisions more strategic. Thus there are latent functions—cooperation, strategic problem solving, better knowledge of gun crime—that may outweigh the value of prosecution itself.

Roles in the Gun Case Review Process

Leadership from the U.S. Attorney's office is a key to effective case review. Prior to PSN, in many districts the U.S. Attorney did not play a leadership role in local crime control, as she or he was focused on "federal" cases. However, PSN and the gun case review process have thrust both U.S. Attorneys and assistant U.S. Attorneys into a more prominent role in addressing local gun crime. The U.S. Attorney in the Western District of Tennessee attended police roll call trainings to demonstrate the importance of good cooperation. Similarly, in both the Middle and Southern Districts of Alabama, the U.S. Attorney traveled the district, visiting local police departments and asking them to bring appropriate guns cases to the U.S. Attorney's office. An added benefit of this process has been the demystification of the U.S. Attorney's office. For many in the local and state criminal justice systems, the U.S. Attorney's office has long been a source of isolation and has not been actively involved in what were perceived to be "local" crime problems. In fact, in many jurisdictions, the only experience local law enforcement has had with the U.S. Attorney was public corruption cases. Breaking down those barriers by making the U.S. Attorney's office and its staff more accessible and increasing knowledge about the federal process are important, indirect benefits of the case review process.

U.S. Attorney's Office. The gun review team in the Western District of Tennessee can be viewed as a model. In addition to the assistant U.S. Attorney PSN coordinator, the task force includes two district attorneys, a U.S. marshal, two ATF agents, seven representatives of the Memphis Police Department, one Shelby County Sheriff, and the research partner. In the Eastern District of Missouri, there has been strong collaboration between the U.S. Attorney's office (USAO), the St. Louis City Circuit Attorney's Office (CAO), the

St. Louis Bureau of Alcohol, Tobacco, and Firearms (ATF), and the St. Louis Metropolitan Police Department (STLMPD). This cooperation grew out of a number of local and federal initiatives to reduce gun violence in the city of St. Louis, including Ceasefire, Weed and Seed, the Juvenile Accountability Incentive Block Grant, and the Strategic Approaches to Community Safety Initiative (SACSI). In St. Louis, the gun review process was modeled after work piloted by the Western District of Tennessee. This highlights one of the most valuable features of PSN, the ability to learn of successful models in other districts and adapt them for implementation in new venues. It also illustrates the nature of communication across the district.

State prosecution. The state prosecutor has a key role to play in reducing gun violence, since the bulk of cases will continue to be prosecuted by this office. In St. Louis, the chief warrants officer sits on the Case Review Committee, which leads to more effective charging decisions. For example in California, Illinois, and Massachusetts, state gun law often provides for a more serious penalty than federal statutes, so the role of the state prosecutor is enhanced in these jurisdictions. The substantial involvement of state-level prosecutors clearly is essential to the effectiveness of gun review task forces.

Local law enforcement. Local law enforcement makes the majority of arrests and provides key information for the case review process. It can safely be said that without local law enforcement, the case review process cannot work. Yet historically, cooperation between U.S. Attorneys and local law enforcement has, for a variety of reasons, left much to be desired, in part because the increase in federal prosecution has come largely from arrests of "prohibited persons" (922.g.1). In many jurisdictions, local police officers are assigned to the PSN task force on a permanent basis, in some they rotate in and out, and in others they rotate into the task force as they have cases to be presented. Many jurisdictions also have employed sheriffs' deputies in their task forces, reflecting the mobile nature of gun offenders as they move in and out of jurisdictions.

One unique component to the case review team in St. Louis is the police internship with the USAO. The purpose of the internship is to allow local law enforcement to gain a better understanding of the federal justice system and how federal prosecutors put together cases at this level. In St. Louis a local police officer is assigned to this internship. For each case review meeting, the police intern compiles a summary of each case offender's history, with particular attention to whether the case meets the requirements of federal jurisdiction.

Federal law enforcement. The Bureau of Alcohol, Tobacco, Firearms, and Explosives (BATFE) also is an important player in the case review process.

Such agents can enhance the efficiency of the review process, as ATF agents have extensive information about federal firearms laws and make a number of their own cases. In the District of Nevada, an ATF agent gives a briefing about each gun case, and the assistant U.S. Attorney and assistant district attorneys then ask questions about elements of the case that may make for a more successful prosecution in one of their venues. The U.S. Marshal's service is playing an increasingly important role in PSN, particularly through its ability to apprehend fugitives, and its role in several gun task forces has grown over time. In the Western District of Tennessee, local law enforcement officers have been cross-deputized as U.S. Marshals, enhancing cooperation across agencies. In other jurisdictions, the Drug Enforcement Agency also has played a key role in gun review groups.

Probation and parole. Various other PSN partners have been included in the case review process. Because of their knowledge of offender histories and current supervision status, some jurisdictions may choose to include state probation and parole in the case review process, in part because by definition parolees and probationers have a prior felony conviction and are, by definition, "prohibited persons." Such individuals often have a handle on individuals about to be released from prison, as well as associates and some aspects of prior records that are unique contributions to the process. Here again, because of the role of federal probation and federal parole, many U.S. Attorneys did not have existing relationships with local parole and probation agents until the initiation of PSN.

Description of Intervention

Criteria for Choosing Federal Cases

The way in which cases are chosen first for review and then for assignment to the appropriate prosecution is a crucial step in the gun case review process. As noted earlier, the most successful processes review every gun case in the jurisdiction. The process of reviewing cases for the best venue for prosecution is one of the areas where a strategic problem-solving approach is most important.

Because of their extensive use of this process, and its history, we present detailed descriptions of two districts with considerable experience with the gun case review process. In the Eastern District of Missouri the review committee meets biweekly in order to determine the most appropriate jurisdiction for prosecution, and if the case can be opened by the USAO. Three questions are asked: (1) Does the case violate federal law, (2) Is the federal prison length more severe than the state sentence? and (3) Is there a strategic reason that this case should be prosecuted federally? Cases come from local law enforcement, ATF, and the CAO. The ATF reviews all firearm arrests from the local police department for potential federal prosecution and then compiles criminal histories, examines the firearms, conducts traces and test-firings, obtains information regarding felony convictions, performs fingerprinting, and then forwards the case to the USAO, recommending federal prosecution when possible. Once a case is taken by the USAO, a specific ATF agent is assigned to follow the case through federal prosecution.

The CAO compiles all gun cases for which local police have applied for warrants. Because of both the volume of firearm cases in St. Louis and the focus on felons in possession of a firearm, the CAO prosecutes all robberies, assaults, and so on where a gun was recovered. The cases that the CAO can relinquish to the USAO, along with the cases prepared by the ATF, are discussed in the case review meeting. On average, 8 to 12 cases are reviewed in each meeting, and 2 to 4 may be taken federally.

Before each review meeting the police intern for the U.S. Attorney's office compiles the police reports for each case that will be discussed at the meeting and locates additional information that would be helpful prior to the actual meeting. After the decision has been made to prosecute federally, the assistant U.S. Attorney gathers information and communicates with other necessary agencies. If a case is declined by the USAO, then a letter is sent to the police officer assigned to the case, saying that the case was reviewed, is now being deferred to the CAO, and the reasons for the referral. If a case is accepted by the USAO, then a letter also is sent to the police reporting the acceptance and the name of the assistant U.S. Attorney who assigned the case. During a 9-month period in 2003, this team screened 130 cases, with 53 resulting in a federal indictment.

In the Western District of Tennessee, a dual tracking system for cases has been instituted. Cases are tracked through both the DA's office as well as the USAO. When the case review process was initiated, it confronted several obstacles faced by many districts, including a low priority placed on many gun cases and the widespread belief among offenders that the penalties for gun crimes were only minor inconveniences. There was an extensive training process, and a policy manual was developed to guide the process. The Western District of Tennessee found that inviting a large number of people was an effective way to build teamwork. The committee meets weekly to review every case that involved a gun, obliterated serial number, or ammunition, and it focuses particular attention on prohibited persons. No gun case can be disposed of by the DA's office without a review by the committee. The goal is to find federal "triggers," elements of a case that would make it eligible for federal prosecution. A "Handgun Offense Review Sheet" has been developed to identify all of the potentially relevant aspects of the case so that cases can be tracked effectively and the necessary information is available to prosecutors. Specifically, this form includes a summary of the offense, charts the offender's criminal history, identifies federal triggers present, and includes the "arrest ticket," evidence reports, and the "Rights Waiver Form." Arresting officers now have a copy of a "Rights Waiver Form" that includes the appropriate federal triggers that would make a case eligible for federal prosecution. The goal is to have every arrest involving a firearm accompanied by the inclusion of this form. The increased availability of information produces better cases, regardless of where they are ultimately prosecuted, and leads to more appropriate charging.

Federal prosecution often is used as a hammer to leverage state pleas. Offenders are frequently faced with the threat of federal prosecution or offered the chance to plead guilty in state court to a charge that does not include probation, a 30-day hearing, and no chance for early release from prison. In this way, cases that are prosecuted by the DA still carry the threat of federal prosecution and include enhanced sentencing for gun use. The Western District of Tennessee has used this process for 3 years, attesting to its staying power and importance to the participants.

There is considerable anecdotal information that the message about fixing the gaps in the system is beginning to have an impact on offenders. In the Western District of Tennessee, jailhouse telephone calls have specifically mentioned PSN and enhanced gun prosecution in warnings by arrestees to co-offenders on the street. The presence of an ATF officer was met with comments about the "922–G" man in the house. When arrestees begin to know the federal statutes by number, the message is clearly being sent. In the Eastern District of Missouri, offenders now tell the research partner during periodic interviews in the jail that they do not want to be "walked across the street," from state court to federal court, because of increased federal prosecution and penalties for gun cases. In the Middle District of Alabama, arrestees are reported to have told arresting officers, "Don't ICE me," ICE being the acronym for the PSN program.

Publicizing the efforts of such task forces is a key to their sustainability. The assistant U.S. Attorney in the Eastern District of Missouri distributes a monthly newsletter to the local police department, reporting cases that have been opened for federal prosecution, including the officer assigned to that case, updates on open cases, and sentence lengths, when given. The U.S. Attorney's office circulates an online newsletter as well as a local newspaper, informing both government agencies and the public about firearm cases being prosecuted at the state and federal levels in the city of St. Louis. Additionally, the assistant has spoken to police recruit classes to train new police officers about federal jurisdiction and the PSN initiative in general and the case review process specifically. In this jurisdiction, a weekly newsletter detailing prosecutions is provided to local media. One source in particular, *The Evening Whirl*, a local newspaper read primarily in the

African American community, details gun prosecutions under headlines such as "Gun Toters, Dopers Feel the Wrath of Ceasefire," "The 'G'², Lady 'Justice' Want the Message Out: Jail for Guns," "Ceasefire, 'G-Man' Gruender Sending 'Em Away in Packs," "Ceasefire Takes Down More Hoodlums," and "Ceasefire Lands Even More Bad Boys in State and Federal Pens." Again, this is new for many U.S. Attorney offices that have worked under a veil of secrecy for years—having to "get the message out" about their work on gun prosecutions places them in unfamiliar territory.

Program Successes

This increased openness and broadened partnerships between federal and local criminal justice agencies have led to successes in a number of areas. Interviews with members of gun review teams and a review of PSN documentation revealed three primary areas where nationally case review teams feel they have achieved the greatest success. These include information sharing, the increase in federal firearms cases being prosecuted, and public safety. Many agency representatives agree that the cooperation among the team from the beginning of the case review process has increased remarkably. Prior to the case review, the local police, state prosecutor, and federal prosecutor often could be working on the same case without the knowledge that another agency was looking at the case. The procedures allowed through the case review have greatly reduced these duplicating efforts. This increases the effectiveness as well as the efficiency of the system, both through the lack of duplication and the increased information that each partner brings to the case. It is important to note that the information is both of the formal case history, as well as experience with the individual, because even in large cities with high crime rates, many chronic offenders are well known to officials in the criminal justice system.

The next success most often cited for the case review process is the number of cases now being federally prosecuted. Cases with federal elements can be identified more clearly, and the state prosecutor understands the federal elements as the USAO understands the state elements of a gun case. There is now a concrete mechanism for identifying federal cases that, if prosecuted at the state level, would result in probation or a minimal prison sentence. In many states, low-level firearm cases get more time and have a higher probability of incarceration when prosecuted federally.

Finally, there is emerging evidence that public safety has been enhanced as a result of the PSN case review process. By aggressively prosecuting suspects in the arena that can provide the harshest sentence, more criminals are being taken off the streets. In many cities there is little deterrent at the state level, as defendants rarely receive a jail sentence for gun offenses.

Program Challenges

The case study of St. Louis can be illustrative of a number of the challenges being faced by PSN task forces across the country. Through separate interviews with representatives from all of the agencies involved, overall, a few problems were expressed about the case review process in St. Louis. The police intern relayed that while local police are becoming more familiar with federal firearm prosecution, it would be beneficial to be able to provide more information for all police officers about what the federal guidelines are. Currently each police officer receives a card, about the size of a business card, with limited information about what constitutes federal jurisdiction. The officer suggested putting out this information in the monthly newsletter or via periodic departmental e-mails to relay this information to all St. Louis police officers.

The assistant U.S. Attorney reported few problems. The one concern that was expressed was predictive in nature, suggesting a problem that may arise, but has not become problematic at this point in time. The U.S. Attorney's office is wary of local district attorneys trying to rush their cases through state prosecution before the defendant can be indicted in federal court. To date, this has only happened in two cases. This observation appears to be based on the impression that the cases that go federal are seen as the "best cases," with strong public support.

The primary source of difficulty is the amount of time and effort required for the case review process, including not only the process itself and the information gathering required but also the added tasks of newsletters and updating all of the agencies involved. In addition, there is a need for better data collection in order to track cases through the system to better gauge the level of success of all of these initiatives. These minor complaints are greatly offset by the many positive aspects that have resulted from the initiation of the case review process in St. Louis.

The local prosecutor, or chief warrant officer (CAO), in St. Louis has only one concern—the amount of time it takes the USAO to file a complaint or an indictment so the CAO can dismiss the case. Before the case goes federal, a substantial amount of time has already been spent by the CAO reviewing and developing cases. The chief warrant officer did note that the USAO is aware of this concern and has been trying to figure out a solution. If the USAO could proceed with its own charges at an earlier stage in the process, then wasted time and resources would not be expended at the state level. Despite this concern, the communication flow that has resulted from the case review has diminished, but not ceased, these overlapping efforts.

Nationally, as with any innovation, several potential hurdles must be overcome in initiating a successful case review process. Several districts have reported that representatives of the federal bench have been resistant to taking some of the new gun cases generated by the PSN process. In some instances, judges have not regarded these gun cases as "serious enough" to merit federal attention. This hurdle can potentially be overcome by educating the judiciary, as well as by careful case presentation. This is the specific strategy that the Western District of Missouri has employed by educating federal judges on the volume of gun crime in their district. Issues of territoriality between agencies and levels of government also can arise. In some federal districts, there has been a history of distrust or conflict between the U.S. Attorney's office and local law enforcement. In other cases, federal prosecution and state prosecution have competed for cases, or the federal prosecutor has been perceived to "cream" the best cases and leave the bulk of gun cases to the state prosecutor. Again, the means to overcome these challenges to successful implementation is to have a clear set of goals and procedures in place before beginning a case review process. Another hurdle can occur several months into this process, when things seem to be going well. Changes in personnel often mean that successful programs are abandoned or changed in ways that do not reflect the most efficient means for running the program. Developing ways to institutionalize the practices is a key to overcoming this potential challenge. Training, procedure manuals, and buy in from key leaders are ways to address this potential hurdle.

Keys to Successful Implementation

There are a number of keys to successfully implementing an effective case review process. The key issue is building trust between members of the task force. As indicated earlier, in many districts significant suspicion exists about the U.S. Attorney's office, and only time and communication can reduce or eliminate this initial bias. This can best be accomplished by regular meetings over specific cases where each agency shares information that reflects the key features of the cases. Having a shared set of expectations about what will be accomplished by the case review process is an important part of this process.

Another important part of a successful case review process involves integrating local law enforcement into the process in a real and substantive role. Local law enforcement is the backbone of any gun strategy, and their expertise and record keeping must be integrated into the review of cases. That said, ATF also has a critical role to play in the review of gun cases. If ATF can provide timely trace data for guns recovered in crime, then the deterrent effect, both for the suspect as well as for those involved in obtaining the gun, will be greatly enhanced.

A number of districts have found that providing feedback to participants has been especially important in achieving success. In particular, in a number of U.S. Attorneys' offices, staff have provided letters of commendation for the work done by local police in preparing cases that were prosecuted in a federal venue. Such letters have been very well received by individual officers, who previously would only know about a case if they were called to testify. Such letters are highly valued by officers whose efforts are validated by this process.

The gun case review process can work most effectively in concert with other interventions, particularly incident reviews, most violent offender lists, and offender notification meetings. Each of these approaches is based on a common set of PSN principles, including strategic prosecution, the use of data to guide decisions, a task force approach, and spreading the deterrence message to high-risk offenders.

Conclusion

It is important to place the gun case review process in a broader context. First, the expansion of the role of the U.S. Attorney's office was made easier by the existence of several earlier efforts, notably Weed and Seed, a federal program that emphasizes the role of the U.S. Attorney's office in federally prosecuting cases to help clean up neighborhoods. The distinct problem-solving approach and use of teamwork between the U.S. Attorney and other enforcement and community partners mirror the form of PSN, though not the focus on gun crime. Weed and Seed represented a distinct shift for the U.S. Attorney's office involving them more heavily in local crime problems. In addition to Weed and Seed, and following on the heels of the successful Boston Ceasefire Gun Strategy, 10 communities (with leadership from their U.S. Attorney) implemented the Strategic Approaches to Community Safety Initiative. This strategic, problem-solving approach to gun violence contained many of the principles included in PSN. The experience with these programs made it easier for U.S. Attorneys to engage in strategic, problem-solving approaches necessitated by PSN.

In many ways it is not surprising that there has been an increase in cases prosecuted, as prosecutors at all levels understand the impetus and mechanisms to generate cases. The fact that some form of case review process has been the most common intervention reflects what federal prosecutors know and do best—prosecute cases. On the other hand, markers of institutional change indicate that many U.S. Attorneys' offices have undergone fundamental shifts in how they define crime, the approaches they choose, and the way they approach their partners. The first of these indicators is the move beyond federal agencies to generate a definition of crime and cases for prosecution. Local law enforcement has always generated a large number of cases for federal prosecution; in the case of PSN, however, its role has been highlighted in that "lesser" cases that would not have received federal attention are now being prosecuted. State and local probation and parole also have been involved in the PSN initiative, another shift away from a strictly federal focus. Involvement with these agencies has led to the second shift in how gun crime has been defined by U.S. Attorneys' offices. PSN has led to a fundamental involvement in what was heretofore considered "local" crime. Indeed, a city's homicide rate has hardly been the standard by which a U.S. Attorney has been judged, and it is likely the case that most U.S. Attorneys knew little about their cities' homicide rates. PSN has changed that, prompting attention to the nature of decline (or increase) in a neighboring jurisdiction's homicide rate. A third fundamental change has been the involvement of nonenforcement partners, such as community groups, neighborhood residents, and the faith-based community. These individuals sit at the table when strategic decisions are being made about approaches to use, targets for enforcement, and the development of innovative strategies. The final change of note is the use of strategic approaches rather than simply prosecuting cases. The case review process forces teams of prosecutors and law enforcement personnel to ask questions about where the largest deterrent effect may lie, rather than whether the case is winnable. Whether the changes in U.S. Attorneys' offices outlive PSN is an empirical question, but the changes in the offices have been real.

Notes

1. For a rare exception, see Eisenstein (1978).

2. "G" is former U.S. Attorney Ray Gruender, and "Lady Justice" is Circuit Attorney Jennifer Joyce.

References

American Prosecutors Research Institute (APRI). (2002). *The Richmond exile project.* Alexandria, VA: APRI.

Burruss, G. W., & Kempf-Leonard, K. (2002). The questionable advantage of defense counsel in juvenile court. *Justice Quarterly, 19*, 37–68.

Clarke, S. H., & Koch, G. C. (1980). Juvenile court: Therapy or crime control, and do lawyers make a difference? *Law and Society Review, 14*, 263–308.

Clynch, E. J., & Neubauer, D. (1981). Trial courts as organizations: A critique and synthesis. *Law and Policy Quarterly, 3*, 69–94.

Dalton, E. (2002). *Lessons in Preventing Homicide: Project Safe Neighborhoods.* East Lansing, MI: Michigan State University.

Eisenstein, J. (1978). *Counsel for the United States.* Baltimore, MD: Johns Hopkins University Press.

Eisenstein, J., & Jacob, H. (1977). *Felony justice: An organizational analysis of criminal courts.* Boston: Little Brown.

Executive Office for U.S. Attorneys (EOUSA). (2002, January). *Project Safe Neighborhoods: A network to make America's communities safer*. U.S. Attorneys' Bulletin, 1–5.

Feld, B. (1993). *Justice for children: The right to counsel and the juvenile court*. Boston: Northeastern University Press.

Fleming, R., Nardulli, P. & Eisenstein, J. (1988). *The craft of justice: Politics and work in criminal court communities*. Philadelphia: University of Pennsylvania Press.

Knepper, P., & Barton, S. M. (1997, June). The effect of courtroom dynamics on child maltreatment proceedings. *Social Service Review, 71*, 289–307.

McDevitt, J., Braga, A., Nurge, D., & Buerger, M. (2003). Boston's youth violence prevention program: A comprehensive community-wide approach. In S. Decker (Ed.), *Policing youth gangs and youth violence* (pp. 53–76). Belmont, CA: Wadsworth.

Memphis Police Department. (2004, July 13). *Project Safe Neighborhoods: Standard operating procedures*. Unpublished manuscript.

Nagel, I. H., & Schulhofer, S. (1992). A tale of three cities: An empirical study of charging and bargaining practices under the federal sentencing guidelines. *University of Southern California Law Review, 66*, 501–546.

Pillsbury, S., Reed, L., Henderson, E., & Janikowski, R. (2002, February–2004, May). *The PSN Case Process* (Working Paper No. 6). Unpublished manuscript.

PSN. (2006). *Project Safe Neighborhoods*. Retrieved May 16, 2006, from http://www.psn.gov/about/faqs.html.

PSN Fact Sheet. (2006). *Project Safe Neighborhoods: America's network against gun violence*. Retrieved May 2, 2006, from http://www.usdou.gov/opa/pr/2006/May/06_ag_263.html.

St. Cyr, J., & Decker, S. H. (2003). *St. Louis gun case review study*. Unpublished manuscript.

Sudnow, D. (1965). Normal crimes. *Social Problems, 12*, 255–276.

Whitney, S. (1975). *United States Attorney: An inside view of justice in America under the Nixon administration*. New York: Morrow and Company.

Wilmot K. A., & Spohn, C. (2004). Prosecutorial discretion and real-offense sentencing: An analysis of relevant conduct under the federal sentencing guidelines. *Criminal Justice Policy Review, 15*, 324–343.

Chapter Eight

Anticipatory Prosecution in Terrorism-Related Cases

ROBERT CHESNEY

Introduction

What practical impact has 9/11 had on the charging decisions of federal prosecutors in terrorism-related cases? Consider the following scenario: The FBI learns from a confidential informant that John Doe, an American citizen, has expressed considerable hostility toward the U.S. government, an interest in Islamic fundamentalism and the idea of an obligation to take up arms in defense of oppressed Muslims, and a desire to obtain military-style training from a camp in Pakistan. The FBI then determines that Doe currently is in Pakistan attending such a camp and is scheduled to return to the United States the next week. Is intervention to incapacitate Doe desirable at this stage? If so, would federal prosecutors have statutory grounds to act?

Regarding the desirability of early intervention, the "John Doe" scenario involves considerable tension between the benefits to be gained from a strategy oriented toward the prevention of harm and the costs that might be incurred as a result of an increased rate of false positives. Perhaps in response to that tension (and perhaps also out of a pragmatic desire to exploit the situation for intelligence purposes) the traditional response in this scenario would not involve immediate prosecution. Rather, the more likely outcome would be to allow Doe to remain at liberty while surveilling him in order to gather information regarding his potential plans (and to identify other persons who may also be of interest to the FBI). Eventually, should sufficient evidence arise to indicate that he actually is planning to carry out an attack, Doe might then be incapacitated by the criminal justice system on traditional inchoate crime charges of attempt or conspiracy (McCormack, 2005). In that circumstance, some uncertainty would remain as to how Doe would have acted if not for the intervention, but the risk of a false positive would be offset to some degree by the requirement of proving Doe's specific intent to commit (or assist others in committing) the attack in question.

Under the terrorism-prevention paradigm adopted by the U.S. government in the aftermath of the 9/11 attacks, events might unfold differently. Senior government officials with a voice in national security decision making might prove unwilling to follow the surveillance-oriented approach, preferring instead to incapacitate Doe at the earliest possible moment in order to minimize the risk of an attack.[1] That decision might result in the use of military detention (as illustrated, at least for a time, by Jose Padilla). But it remains possible—indeed, likely—that the task instead would be given to the Justice Department. And so the question arises: If asked, could the Justice Department successfully prosecute at a preliminary stage in anticipation of the harm that Doe might cause?

The United States does not have an explicit preventive detention statute for terrorism, although other countries confronted with similar problems have experimented with such an approach, and there has been a considerable amount of academic debate concerning that subject (Breyer, 2006; Rosenzweig & Carafano, 2004). Congress did enact a wide array of new statutory authorities in the wake of 9/11 (they are, for the most part, collected in the USA PATRIOT Act), but the vast majority of these provisions advance the goal of prevention by enhancing the investigative and intelligence-gathering powers of the federal government, not by creating substantive criminal statutes of a preventive nature (Yeh & Doyle, 2006; Doyle, 2002). And yet federal prosecutors *have* taken action in the John Doe scenario since 9/11. Through the creative enforcement of existing statutes, prosecutors have established a substantial capacity for anticipatory prosecution in terrorism-related cases.

The Post-9/11 Terrorism Prevention Paradigm

Post-9/11 prosecutions and related law-enforcement measures are best understood as expressions of a multitiered strategy designed to achieve prevention on both a targeted and an untargeted basis.

Conventional Targeted Prevention

The first of these tiers—and the least controversial with respect to the goal of prevention—involves the scenario in which a particular individual is associated with a particular act of violence, whether completed or inchoate (i.e., the subject of an attempt or a conspiracy). In such cases, the suspect is personally and directly linked to the potential act of violence, and the primary goal of the prosecution is to incapacitate the suspect through conviction on charges that arise directly out of that linkage (Chesney, 2005).

Conventional targeted prosecutions have long been the bread and butter of federal criminal law enforcement relating to terrorism. Significant examples from the pre-9/11 era include the prosecutions of a number of individuals for an array of plots, including the 1993 World Trade Center bombing, the planned "Day of Terror" bombing campaign in New York City, and other planned attacks (*United States v. Yousef*, 2003; *United States v. Rahman*, 1999; *United States v. Salameh*, 1998), and also of Timothy McVeigh in connection to the bombing of the Murrah Federal Building in Oklahoma City in 1995 (*United States v. McVeigh*, 1998).

Not surprisingly, this approach has continued to play a significant role in the Justice Department's counterterrorism efforts since 9/11. A review of the charges in terrorism-related prosecutions instituted during the 3-year period between September 2001 and September 2004 shows that at least 27 individuals were prosecuted during this period for completed acts of violence or attempts or conspiracies to commit particular acts of violence (Chesney, 2005). Some of these defendants are well known, such as Zacarias Moussaoui and Richard Reid (*United States v. Moussaoui*, 2004; *United States v. Reid*, 2002). Others are somewhat obscure, as demonstrated by the indictment and conviction of Gale Nettles in connection to a plot to attack a federal building in Chicago (*United States v. Nettles*, 2005).

Not all post-9/11 terrorism prosecutions fit the description of conventional targeting, however. On the contrary, the vast majority of terrorism-related cases since 9/11 differ in one of two ways from the conventional targeted approach. Some are not targeted at all, at least not in the sense described earlier, in which prosecutors believe that the defendant is personally involved in terrorism or potential terrorism. Others are targeted in just that way, but for lack of evidence the crime charged does not pertain directly to that underlying suspicion. I explain both categories in more detail next.

Untargeted Prevention

Analysts have long understood that terrorism cannot be prevented solely through targeted measures, because inevitably there will be situations in which the government does not learn of the threat posed by a particular individual or group in time to take action (McCormack, 2005). Accordingly, the government combines its conventional targeted efforts with various forms of untargeted prevention (Heymann, 1998).

The traditional methods of untargeted prevention involve intelligence-gathering activities and a variety of passive-defense, target-hardening measures, such as the installation of surveillance and access-restriction equipment at potential targets for terrorist attacks (Heymann, 2003). There also is a prosecutorial role in untargeted prevention, however, and this role has become an integral part of the overall post-9/11 strategy (Chesney, 2005).

First, the Justice Department can allocate its investigative and prosecutorial resources to generate a system-wide increase in the enforcement of laws relating to activities thought to be significant to the preparatory and logistical stages of a terrorist attack. Making it harder for anyone to carry out various illegal but relatively innocuous precursor activities such as immigration fraud, identity fraud, and money laundering contributes to prevention in several ways. First, potential terrorists may incidentally be jailed and thus incapacitated at least temporarily. Second, the increased difficulty of carrying out certain illegal precursor tasks without detection or arrest may delay or even render unworkable a particular plot. Third, systemically increased enforcement of precursor crimes may generate information that in turn can be used to pursue targeted approaches (Chesney, 2005). Recent research indicates that a similar approach has been undertaken by state and local law enforcement authorities (Nugent, 2005).

A second aspect of the diffused prevention method involves enforcement of 18 U.S.C. § 2339B, the federal statute prohibiting the provision of "material support or resources" to groups that have been formally designated by the secretary of state to be "foreign terrorist organizations." The primary purpose of § 2339B is to reduce the flow of resources to foreign terrorist organizations. This limits (if only marginally) their capacity to cause harm, even without knowledge of what particular harms might thereby be averted. Because this strategy seeks to achieve a degree of prevention without knowledge of which individuals might actually carry out a terrorist attack, enforcement of § 2339B in most instances counts as a method of untargeted prevention; in the typical material support case, the defendant is not viewed as a potentially dangerous person in his or her own right but rather as someone whose conduct facilitates the danger posed by others (Chesney, 2005).

Prosecutions under § 2339B were rare during the period between the statute's enactment in 1996 and the 9/11 attacks. The statute appears to have been charged on just four occasions during those 5 years, twice in cases involving the provision of funds and equipment to Hezbollah and twice in cases involving the provision of support to the Iranian dissident group Mujahedin-e Khalq. In the 3 years following 9/11, in contrast, at least 32 individuals have been charged under § 2339B for providing support to various designated foreign terrorist organizations (Chesney, 2005). Examples include the prosecution of Sami al-Arian and a number of other individuals charged with raising funds for Palestinian Islamic Jihad (PIJ) and with facilitating the fraudulent entry into the United States of PIJ members (*United States v. al-Arian*, 2004) and the prosecution of Muhammed Hamid Khalil Salah for attempting to provide funds and weapons to Hamas (*United States v. Marzook*, 2005).

Unconventional Targeted Prevention

The third tier of the Justice Department's prevention strategy returns to a focus on particular individuals suspected of involvement in terrorism. In this context, the government suspects that the individual may be a terrorist but lacks evidence to pursue a conventional targeted prosecution. As noted earlier, the traditional response to this scenario is to engage in surveillance and other information-gathering activities until sufficient evidence can be developed. The post-9/11 strategic imperative of prevention has, however, led federal prosecutors to develop several alternative approaches that permit direct incapacitation of such potentially dangerous persons.

One such alternative involves the use of "preventive charges," an approach also known as "pretextual prosecution," or the "Al Capone strategy" (Richman & Stuntz, 2005). Under this heading, prosecutors pursue any criminal charge that may happen to be available to incapacitate a suspected terrorist, however unrelated to terrorism the charge may be.[2]

The efficacy of the preventive charging approach is inherently difficult to assess. In most instances there will be nothing in the indictment to reveal that the underlying investigation was motivated by terrorism concerns. Even if such a linkage comes to light informally, moreover, litigation of the pretextual charge by definition will not put that alleged linkage to the test. It thus is difficult both to identify the cases that count as instances of terrorism-related preventive charging and to determine whether any given prosecution of this type does in fact contribute to terrorism prevention (Chesney, 2005). This approach—as well as the strategy of systematically increasing the enforcement of precursor crimes, described earlier—accordingly presents significant difficulties of measurement, and thus of accountability as well (Richman & Stuntz, 2005).

This is not to say, however, that these approaches do not actually make useful contributions. In any given case, such a prosecution may or may not tend to prevent future harms; in most instances, one cannot say one way or the other with any certainty. Thus it would be inappropriate to simply assume that a prosecution under either approach necessarily contributes to the terrorism-prevention mission, but it also would be a mistake to assume the contrary. With all of that said, the preventive charging strategy—including, in particular, the use of relatively minor charges involving matters such as Social Security fraud—clearly constitutes an important thread in the Justice Department's post-9/11 strategy (Webb, 2002).

A second and more controversial option available to prosecutors who wish to incapacitate a potentially dangerous person in these circumstances involves the federal material witness detention statute, 18 U.S.C. § 3144, authorizes the government to seek a warrant for the arrest and detention of a person where that individual's testimony is "material in a criminal proceeding" and there are grounds to believe that "it may become impracticable to secure the presence of the person by subpoena" (18 U.S.C. § 3144). In that circumstance, the statute allows the arrest and detention of the witness for as long as is reasonably necessary to secure his or her testimony.

Although the statute is designed for purposes of preserving witness testimony, there is little doubt that it has been used since 9/11 in order to at least temporarily incapacitate suspected terrorists. "Aggressive detention of . . . material witnesses is vital to preventing, disrupting, or delaying new attacks," said then attorney general John Ashcroft in October 2001 (Ashcroft, 2001). Specific information about such "pretextual" uses of the material witness detention statute is difficult to come by, but one report estimates that approximately 70 suspects have been detained on material witness grounds in connection to the post-9/11 investigation (Human Rights Watch, 2005). In any event, although the practice has received judicial approval (*United States v. Awadallah*, 2003), it nonetheless remains the subject of sharp criticism (Human Rights Watch, 2005), with the Justice Department's Office of Professional Responsibility undertaking a review of the issue in 2006 (Office of the Inspector General, 2006).

Anticipatory Prosecution?

Return for a moment to the John Doe scenario with which the chapter began, and consider the extent to which the foregoing methods would be available to federal prosecutors in the event that the decision is made to intervene immediately rather than to continue surveillance. A conventional targeted prosecution might be difficult to maintain in these circumstances, as prosecutors would have difficulty establishing Doe's specific intent to carry out a particular attack. On the facts given, moreover, Doe has not coincidentally violated any statutes unrelated to terrorism and thus does not appear to be vulnerable to the "Al Capone" preventive charging strategy. Nor is he likely to be caught up by happenstance in a systemic increase in prosecutions of crimes, such as identity fraud. True, he might be detained for a time as a material witness, but the brevity of the resulting detention means that this approach would provide relatively little benefit unless prosecutors could use the time gained in order to indict.

In short, none of the options described earlier seems promising as a ground for intervention in the John Doe scenario. And yet prosecutors faced with this scenario since 9/11 on several occasions have managed to bring what might be described as anticipatory prosecutions in order to incapacitate potentially dangerous persons. The next section describes how they have done so.

Anticipatory Prosecution and the Creative Use of Existing Statutes

The John Doe scenario is not fictional, or at least not entirely so. In fact, versions of it have arisen on a number of occasions since the 9/11 attacks and are likely to continue to arise periodically for the foreseeable future. On two occasions—one involving Jose Padilla and another involving a citizen of Qatar, Ali Saleh Kahlah Al-Marri—the government has responded by eschewing prosecution (at least for a time) in favor of simply placing these individuals in military detention (*Padilla v. Hanft*, 2005; *Al-Marri v. Hanft*, 2005).[3] On several other occasions, however, similarly situated individuals have been prosecuted. In light of the previous discussion regarding the limits of the Justice Department's capacities for preventive intervention, how has this been achieved?

In the years since 9/11, federal prosecutors have established two grounds for anticipatory prosecution in this context, each depending on criminal statutes that already were on the books as of 9/11. The first option applies to the situation in which the defendant can be linked to a group that has been formally designated by the secretary of state a "foreign terrorist organization." This option, which arguably amounts to a variation on the Al Capone preventive charging strategy, involves prosecution under 18 U.S.C. § 2339B, the "material support or resources" statute described earlier. The second option comes into play in the increasingly important circumstance where the defendant cannot be linked to a designated organization. This option, which is more in the nature of a conventional targeted prosecution, typically involves a combination of 18 U.S.C. § 2339A (a close cousin to § 2339B, but one that does not require a link to a designated group) with either 18 U.S.C. § 956 (criminalizing conspiracies to kill, kidnap, or maim outside of the United States) or 18 U.S.C. § 2332b (criminalizing transnational attacks where the harm occurs in the United States). I discuss each of these options in more detail in the pages that follow.

Anticipatory Prosecution with a Specific Organizational Link

The discussion of untargeted prevention strategies in the preceding section emphasized the important role played by 18 U.S.C. § 2339B, the law prohibiting the provision of "material support or resources" to groups formally designated by the secretary of state to be foreign terrorist organizations. The paradigmatic material support defendant in that context is someone who does not pose a personal threat of violence but whose conduct in providing support might facilitate the ability of others to cause harm. But § 2339B's utility turns out not to be limited to the paradigm case. Because of the breadth of the definition of "material support or resources," prosecutors also have been able to employ the statute as a vehicle for anticipatory prosecution of persons who are potentially dangerous in and of themselves (McCormack, 2005; Chesney, 2005; Breinholt, 2004).

The phrase "material support or resources" is defined to refer to a broad range of activities, including the following: currency, monetary instruments, and financial securities; lodging, facilities, and safehouses; training, expert advice or assistance, and financial services; false documentation or identification; communications equipment; weapons, lethal substances, and explosives; transportation; personnel; and any "other physical assets, except medicine or religious materials" (18 U.S.C. § 2339A(b)). For present purposes, the key term in the definition is the reference to "personnel." At least since 9/11 the government has taken the position that one can provide "personnel" to a designated foreign terrorist organization by submitting one's own self to that group's direction and control (Executive Office for United States Attorneys, 2006, pp. 9–91, 100); in effect, one violates § 2339B simply by becoming a member (on more than a merely nominal basis) of a designated foreign terrorist organization (Chesney, 2005). And, significantly, attendance at a training camp operated by such a group may contribute to a finding that the defendant did provide himself or herself as "personnel" to the group (*United States v. Lindh*, 2002). Both qualities—being a member of a terrorist organization, or having attended a designated group's training camp—are precisely the type of factors likely to give rise to the John Doe scenario in the first place. They are highly salient proxies for future dangerousness, and their inclusion within the scope of § 2339B's prohibition is what gives that statute its capacity to be used for anticipatory prosecutions.

The leading example of the use of § 2339B for anticipatory prosecution is the so-called "Lackawanna Six" case, which involved six Yemen-American men from Lackawanna, New York, who traveled to Afghanistan in the summer of 2001 in order to attend an al Qaeda-affiliated training camp. The men had returned to the United States later that summer and resumed their normal lives. Though the FBI surveilled them closely after learning of their activities in Afghanistan, there was little other evidence suggesting that the men constituted a sleeper cell. Eventually, however, a suspicious e-mail sent by one of the men—one that arguably read like a coded message about an upcoming attack—prompted senior government officials to insist that the men be incapacitated as soon as possible (Purdy & Bergman, 2003). Vice President Cheney and Secretary of Defense Rumsfeld suggested placing the men in military detention, ala Jose Padilla, but Attorney General Ashcroft made a convincing case for employing criminal prosecution instead (Isikoff & Klaid-

man, 2004). Relying on the "personnel" aspect of the material support definition, the men were prosecuted under § 2339B (*United States v. Goba*, 2002).
Deputy Attorney General Larry Thompson announced that the government
had captured "a Qaeda-trained terrorist cell on American soil" (Thompson,
2002). Eventually, the men reached plea agreements with the government and
are now incarcerated (Purdy & Bergman, 2003).

Is the Lackawanna Six prosecution an example of timely intervention
that prevented a terrorist attack, or instead were the men merely misguided
adventurers who never had any intention of carrying out an attack in the
United States? The ambiguities surrounding their case have prompted considerable media attention (Public Broadcasting Service, 2003; Purdy &
Bergman, 2003). The journalist Stuart Taylor Jr. has well summarized both
the uncertainty and the stakes potentially involved:

> Were they on their way to committing mass murder? Were they a bunch
> of harmless guys who had blundered unwittingly into a terrorist training
> camp while on a religious quest without ever intending to become ter-
> rorists? Nobody really knows. If we throw all such suspects into military
> brigs, we risk becoming more like a police state. If we let those who can-
> not be prosecuted roam free, some might pull off catastrophes dwarfing
> 9/11. (Taylor, 2004, p. 1320)

An attack potentially (but by no means certainly) averted, injustice potentially
(but by no means certainly) inflicted, this is the inherent dilemma of anticipatory prosecution.

It should be noted that federal courts have been confronted with a
range of arguments challenging § 2339B prosecutions both in the John Doe
scenario and the more straightforward, pure-support context described previously. Some litigants have argued, for example, that the material support
prohibition unconstitutionally interferes with freedom of expression and of
expressive association. This argument has been consistently rejected
(*Humanitarian Law Project v. Reno*, 2000). But arguments that certain terms
in the definition of material support or resources—including the term *personnel*—might be unconstitutionally vague have met with some success
(*Humanitarian Law Project v. Reno*, 2000).[4] In response, the Justice Department in 2004 obtained an amendment to the statutory definition clarifying
that the term *personnel* includes the provision of "1 or more individuals who
may be or include oneself" (Intelligence Reform and Terrorism Prevention
Act, 2004, § 6603). Whether this amendment will suffice to preclude further
adverse rulings on vagueness grounds remains to be determined. In any
event, no court has yet rejected the proposition that the term *personnel* can
apply to one's self. On the contrary, on the two occasions on which this issue

has been discussed in a published opinion, the courts endorsed the government's interpretation (*United States v. Lindh*, 2002; *United States v. Goba*,
2002). Thus far, then, the statutory interpretation that enables § 2339B to
serve as a vehicle for anticipatory prosecution (in addition to its primary
function of reducing the flow of resources to designated organizations) has
had considerable traction in the courts.[5]

In practical terms, this interpretation of § 2339B has the effect of out-
lawing active membership in designated foreign terrorist organizations and
thus brings U.S. criminal law into line (albeit indirectly) with the approach to
prevention favored by a number of European allies, including, in particular,
the United Kingdom (Walker, 2002). This step is a controversial one in light
of the potential chill on expressive and associational rights that such measures
entail (Gross, 2002). But even setting aside civil liberty concerns, there is a
fundamental flaw from the security perspective in any strategy of prevention
that depends upon linking the potentially dangerous person to a designated
foreign terrorist organization. Sometimes the threat of terrorism cannot easily or even possibly be linked to any specific group, let alone one that already
has been formally designated by the secretary of state; in such cases, § 2339B,
by definition, has no application. And as many scholars have observed, the
threat of terrorism in the 21st century often will emanate not from organizations as such but instead from decentralized networks of individuals sharing
common ideological inspirations but little else in the way of formal organization (Sageman, 2004).[6] How (if at all) may prosecutors intervene?

Anticipatory Prosecution in the Absence of a Specific Organizational Link

This question already has arisen on several occasions, and prosecutors once
more have drawn upon existing statutory authorities to establish a capacity for
anticipatory prosecution. In particular, they have pursued a modified form of
the "conventional targeted prosecution" model described earlier, one in which
the defendant is prosecuted not under § 2339B but instead under an earlier
iteration of the material support statute, 18 U.S.C. § 2339A (Breinholt, 2004).

Liability under § 2339A requires proof of two elements: an act, and a
particular mental state. The act element requires that a defendant engage in
conduct that falls within the scope of the definition of "material support or
resources," which as noted earlier is understood by the government to include
one's provision of one's self as "personnel." In contrast to § 2339B, however,
there is no requirement under § 2339A that this support be rendered to a designated foreign terrorist organization; any recipient of the support qualifies.

The mental state element under § 2339A is more complicated. Whereas
§ 2339B requires no proof that the defendant intended to facilitate any
unlawful acts or knew such acts would follow (§ 2339B in this sense functions

as a strict liability offense), § 2339A does require culpable intent or knowledge on the part of the defendant. In particular, § 2339A requires proof that the defendant knew or intended that the "material support or resources" were "to be used" in connection to a violation of any of several dozen predicate crimes listed in the statute (18 U.S.C. § 2339A(a)). These predicate offenses range widely, but for present purposes the two most significant are 18 U.S.C. § 956 (criminalizing conspiracies to kill, kidnap, or maim persons outside of the United States where certain jurisdictional prerequisites are satisfied) and 18 U.S.C. § 2332b (criminalizing transnational attacks where the harm occurs inside of the United States).

Whichever predicate is involved, the critical point is that § 2339A by its own terms does not require proof that the predicate offense actually occurred. On the contrary, by the statute's own terms, it is enough if the support was intended "to be used in *preparation* [italics added] for" such an offense (18 U.S.C. § 2339A(a)). Perhaps for this reason, the Justice Department's Criminal Resource Manual (part of the United States Attorneys' Manual) instructs federal prosecutors that § 2339A

> requires only that the supplier of the material support have knowledge of its intended use. Section 2339A, unlike the aiding and abetting statute (18 U.S.C. § 2), does not require that the supplier also have whatever specific intent the perpetrator of the actual terrorist act must have to commit one of the specified offenses. (Executive Office for United States Attorneys, 2006, p. 15)

As the cases examined next demonstrate, the net effect of this language—particularly when combined with an understanding of "material support or resources" that includes the provision of one's self as "personnel"—is to permit prosecution under § 2339A at a very early stage of the John Doe scenario, extending the scope of criminal liability beyond the reach of a traditional conspiracy or attempt charge.

Consider the indictment of Syed Haris Ahmed and Ehsanual Islam Sadequee, two U.S. citizens living in Georgia. According to the indictment, Ahmed and Sadequee engaged in "rudimentary paramilitary training to prepare for participation in violent jihad," and went to Toronto to meet with likeminded individuals "to discuss how to participate in, facilitate, and otherwise further violent jihad activities in the United States and other foreign nations" (*United States v. Ahmed*, 2006, p. 3). Combined with allegations that the defendants "cased" landmarks in the Washington, DC area in order to "establish their credentials with other supporters of violent jihad," these claims formed the basis for charging the men with several material support violations under 18 U.S.C. section 2339A (predicated on potential violations of Title 18, United States Code, Sections 956 [conspiracy to kill, kidnap, maim, or injure persons or damage property in a foreign country] and 2332b [acts of terrorism transcending national boundaries]) (*United States v. Ahmed*, 2006, pp. 1–13).

Assuming these facts are true, the first question that arises is whether the Justice Department could pursue a conventional targeted prosecution strategy against Ahmed and Sadequee by charging them directly under § 956 or § 2332b (or both). Arguably, it could not. The potential difficulty lies in the lack of specificity regarding the unlawful act that the defendants may have been planning. Conspirators need not agree as to the particular details of an anticipated offense, but they must at least agree as to the type of offense to be committed (Chesney, 2007). It may be, of course, that the government later will obtain such evidence and thus become more clearly able to prosecute him directly under § 956 or § 2332b, and it also is possible that the government already has such evidence but for reasons unrelated to the merits has decided at least for the moment not to charge conspiracy directly. But assuming, for the sake of argument, that the government is not currently in a position to prove the nature of the offense that these individuals may have contemplated, a question then arises as to how he can instead be charged with violating § 2339A based on predicate violations of §§ 956 and 2332b. It is probable that the defendants' alleged contribution of material support consists of their actions in making themselves available to the others involved in the Toronto meeting (i.e., that they provided themselves to the group as "personnel"). But no matter how clearly his conduct might fall within the definition of "material support or resources," is it possible for their actions to trigger § 2339A liability if the government is unable to prove the existence of an underlying violation of § 956 or § 2332b?

The answer appears to be yes. As noted earlier, § 2339A does not require proof of a completed violation of the underlying predicate offense (in this case, §§ 956 and 2332b). Instead, it is enough if their support was intended to *prepare* for the commission of such a violation (18 U.S.C. § 2339A(a)). Thus it would suffice if they intended to facilitate the formation of a § 956 conspiracy (i.e., preparation), even if that conspiracy had not yet actually formed and regardless of whether they could be shown to have the *mens rea* required to prove their involvement in the conspiracy itself (Executive Office for United States Attorneys, 2006, p. 15). In this way, § 2339A has the capacity to expand the anticipatory reach of federal criminal law beyond the traditional inchoate crimes of conspiracy and attempt.

Further evidence of the use of § 2339A as a mechanism for anticipatory prosecution comes from the recently concluded prosecution of Hamid Hayat, an American citizen from Lodi, California.[7] Hayat had been arrested by the FBI in the spring of 2005 shortly after his return to the United States from a

2-year trip to Pakistan. The indictment did not contend that Hayat was involved in any specific terrorist plot, nor did it link him to any designated foreign terrorist organization. Instead, it rested on allegations that Hayat was a militant who had traveled to Pakistan in 2003 to learn paramilitary skills at a "jihadist training camp" of unspecified affiliation, and had returned to the United States with the general purpose of carrying out an unspecified type of attack at some point in the future (*United States v. Hayat*, 2005, p. 5).

As in *Ahmed*, prosecutors in *Hayat* built their case around § 2339A, predicated on a violation—or, rather, preparation for a violation—of § 2332b. The particular target of the predicate § 2332b plot was entirely unspecified, precluding a direct charge that Hayat had conspired (let alone attempted) to carry out a § 2332b violation. In light of the "preparation" option under § 2339A, however, prosecutors could prosecute nonetheless. As explained in the government's proposed jury instructions in *Hayat*,

> the government ... need *not* [italics in original] establish that defendant actually committed a violation of § 2332b. The government must establish that defendant knew or intended that the material support *be used in preparation for or in carrying out* [italics in original] an act [in violation of § 2332b]. (*United States v. Hayat*, 2006, p. 49)

Ultimately, Hayat was convicted and now faces a potential sentence of up to 39 years in federal prison (Tempest & Bailey, 2006).[8]

Conclusion

In this chapter I addressed the impact of 9/11 on federal prosecutors by examining the statutory tools that have been used since 9/11 to achieve prevention in terrorism-related cases. By and large, this is not a story of newly enacted statutes. Federal prosecutors have instead found that existing statutory authorities—particularly the two material support statutes, 18 U.S.C. §§ 2339A and 2339B—are sufficient to bring what might be described as anticipatory prosecutions at relatively early stages in terrorism-related cases.

These changing prosecutorial strategies draw attention to a significant, possibly intractable, policy dilemma associated with the prioritization of prevention. On the one hand, it is laudable to take steps to reduce the odds that a suspected terrorist will succeed in causing harm before the government can intervene to incapacitate that individual. On the other hand, the earlier that prosecutors intervene—and, in particular, the evidence there is concerning a defendant's particular intentions—the greater the odds are that the prosecution will involve a false positive (in the sense that the defendant would not in fact have gone on to attempt to cause harm). Complicating matters, unduly early intervention through prosecution also runs the risk of undermining security in the long term by (1) contributing to feelings of injustice (warranted or not) in communities of particular significance (including, in particular, the Muslim and Arab American communities in the United States) from the perspective of intelligence-gathering and law enforcement cooperation and (2) foregoing opportunities to conduct additional intelligence-gathering through surveillance of the suspect (Chesney, 2007). Ultimately, bearing in mind the tremendous anticipatory sweep of statutes such as § 2339A and § 2339B, fair consideration of these inherent tensions suggests that the Justice Department would do well to avoid the reflexive resort to prosecution at the earliest possible opportunity, focusing instead on calibrating the point of intervention on a case-by-case basis with reference to the full range of both liberty and security concerns.

Notes

1. As Judge Posner recently has written, "Often the best strategy is not to arrest or charge at the earliest stage of terrorist plotting but instead to monitor the individuals in an effort to learn the scope, intentions, membership, and affiliations of the terrorist or proto-terrorist cell" (Posner, 2006, p. 96). The policy merits of an early intervention strategy are, however, beyond the scope of this chapter.

2. Noncriminal enforcement of the immigration laws also forms part of the preventive charging strategy (Chesney, 2005).

3. Three individuals have been held as military detainees in the United States since 9/11. The U.S. government does, of course, hold many thousands of other detainees in military (or other) custody outside of the United States in connection to the war on terrorism and the war in Iraq (Chesney, 2006).

4. With respect to "personnel," the argument is that the statute is insufficiently clear regarding whether a person's First Amendment-protected activities might trigger the application of the statute (*Humanitarian Law Project v. Reno*, 2000).

5. From 2005 onward, prosecutors have had a new tool that could be brought to bear on some variations of the John Doe scenario. A new criminal statute—18 U.S.C. § 2339D—expressly criminalizes the act of obtaining military-type training from a designated foreign terrorist organization. Section 2339D is very much designed for purposes of anticipatory prosecution, but it suffers from two crucial limitations: it has no application where the entity providing the training has not already been designated by the secretary of state as a foreign terrorist organization, and in any event it applies only to conduct occurring postenactment (Chesney, 2005).

6. The problem is particularly acute with respect to the ideological movement generally associated with bin Ladin—often referred to in the literature as Salafism, militant Wahhabiism, or simply the jihad movement—but it is by no means limited to Islamist fundamentalism. Indeed, the "leaderless resistance" model advanced among homegrown, far-right-wing extremists in the United States poses a similar problem (Stern, 2003).

7. The indictment against Jose Padilla that resulted in his transfer from military to civilian custody in November 2005 also arguably makes use of § 2339A and § 956 in this way; interestingly, however, § 956 also is charged separately in that case (*United States v. Hassoun*, 2005).

8. The government simultaneously prosecuted Hamid Hayat's father, Umer Hayat, for making false statements to the FBI in connection to his son's alleged activities. That prosecution resulted in a mistrial on all counts in April 2006; prosecutors intend to retry the case (Marshall, 2006).

References

Al-Marri v. Hanft. 378 F. Supp.2d 673 (D.S.C. 2005).

Ashcroft, J. (2001). Press conference, October 31 2001. Retrieved January 21, 2008, from http://www.usdoj.gov/archive/ag/speeches/2001/agcrisisremarks10_31.htm.

Breinholt, J. (2004). *Counterterrorism enforcement: A lawyer's guide*. Washington, DC: U.S. Department of Justice, Executive Office for United States Attorneys.

Breyer, S. G. (2006). Symposium on terrorism, globalization, and the rule of law: An introduction. *Cardozo Law Review, 27*, 1981–1985.

Chesney, R. M. (2005). The sleeper scenario: Terrorism-support laws and the demands of prevention. *Harvard Journal on Legislation, 42*, 1–89.

Chesney, R. M. (2006). Leaving Guantanamo: The law of international detainee transfers. *Richmond Law Review, 40*, 657–752.

Chesney, R. M. (2007). Beyond conspiracy? Anticipatory prosecution and the challenge of unaffiliated terrorism. *Southern California Law Review, 80*, 425–502.

Doyle, C. (2002). *The USA PATRIOT Act: A legal analysis*. Washington, DC: Congressional Research Service. Retrieved January 20, 2008, from http://www.fas.org/irp/crs/RL31377.pdf.

Executive Office for United States Attorneys. (2006). *United States Attorneys' manual*. Retrieved January 20, 2008, from http://www.usdoj.gov/usao/eousa/foia_reading_room/usam/index.html.

Gross, E. (2002). The influence of terrorist attacks on human rights in the United States: The aftermath of September 11, 2001. *North Carolina Journal of International Law and Commercial Regulation, 28*, 1–101.

Heymann, P. B. (1998). *Terrorism and America: A commonsense strategy for a democratic society*. Cambridge, MA: MIT Press.

Heymann, P. B. (2003). *Terrorism, freedom, and security: Winning without war*. Cambridge, MA: MIT Press.

Human Rights Watch and the American Civil Liberties Union. (2005). *Witness to abuse: Human rights abuses under the material witness law since September 11*. Retrieved from http://www.hrw.org/reports/2005/us0605/index.htm.

Humanitarian Law Project v. Reno. 205 F.3d 1130 (9th Cir. 2000).

Intelligence Reform and Terrorism Prevention Act. (2004). Pub. L. No. 108-458, 118 Stat. 3638.

Isikoff, M., & Klaidman, D. (2004, April 26). The road to the brig: After 9/11, justice and defense fought over how to deal with suspected terrorists. How a new system was hatched. Newsweek, 26.

Marshall, C. (2006, May 6). Government will retry terror case. *New York Times*, p. A11.

McCormack, W. (2005). Inchoate terrorism: Liberalism clashes with fundamentalism. *Georgetown Journal of International Law, 37*, 1–60.

Nugent, M. E., Johnson, J. L., Bartholomew, B., & Bromirski, D. (2005). *Local prosecutors' response to terrorism*. Alexandria, VA: American Prosecutors Research Institute.

Office of the Inspector General. (2006). *Report to Congress on the Implementation of Section 1001 of the USA PATRIOT Act*. Washington, DC: U.S. Department of Justice.

Padilla v. Hanft. 423 F.3d 386 (4th Cir. 2005).

Posner, R. A. (2006). *Uncertain Shield: The U.S. Intelligence System in the Throes of Reform*. New York: Rowman & Littlefield Publishers, Inc.

Public Broadcasting Service. (2003). *Frontline: Chasing the sleeper cell*. Retrieved January 20, 2008, from http://www.pbs.org/wgbh/pages/frontline/shows/sleeper.

Purdy, M., & Bergman, L. (2003, October 12). Where the trail led: Between evidence and suspicion: Unclear danger: Inside the Lackawanna terror case. *New York Times*, p. A1.

Richman, D. C., & Stuntz, W. J. (2005). Al Capone's revenge: An essay on the political economy of pretextual prosecution. *Columbia Law Review, 105*, 583–639.

Rosenzweig, P., & Carafano, J. J. (2004). *Preventive detention and actionable intelligence*. Retrieved January 20, 2008, from http://www.heritage.org/Research/ HomelandDefense/lm13.cfm.

Sageman, M. (2004). *Understanding terror networks*. Philadelphia: University of Pennsylvania Press.

Serrano, R. A. (2003, June 4). Two guilty in terrorism trial: Jury in Detroit convicts the Arab immigrants of aiding terror in the first major case tied to 9/11; Two others are cleared of conspiracy charges. *Los Angeles Times*, p. 1.

Stern, J. (2003). *Terror in the name of God: Why religious militants kill*. New York: HarperCollins.

Taylor, Jr., S. (2004, May 5). The fragility of our freedoms in a time of terror. *National Journal, 36*, 1319–1320.

Tempest, R., & Bailey, E. (2006, April 26). Conviction for son, mistrial for father in Lodi terror case. *Los Angeles Times*, p. A1.

Thompson, L. (2002). Press conference. Retrieved from http://www.usdoj.gov/dag/speech/2002/091402dagremarks.htm.

United States v. Ahmed. No. 06 Cr. 147 (N.D. Ga. 2006) (indictment).

United States v. al-Arian. 329 F. Supp.2d 1294 (M.D. Fla. 2004).

United States v. Awadallah. 349 F.3d 42 (2d Cir. 2003).

United States v. Goba. 220 F. Supp.2d 182 (W.D.N.Y. 2002).

United States v. Hassoun. No. 04 Cr. 60001 (S.D. Fla. 2005).

United States v. Hayat. No. 05 Cr. 240 (E.D. Cal. 2005) (first superseding indictment).

United States v. Hayat. (2006, February 10). Government's proposed jury instructions; annotated set.

United States v. Lindh. 212 F. Supp.2d 541 (E.D. Va. 2002).

United States v. Marzook. 383 F. Supp.2d 1056 (N.D. Ill. 2005).

United States v. McVeigh. 153 F.3d 1166 (10th Cir. 1998).

United States v. Moussaoui. 382 F.3d 453 (4th Cir. 2004).

United States v. Nettles. 400 F. Supp.2d 1084 (N.D. Ill. 2005).

United States. v. Rahman. 189 F.3d 88 (2d Cir. 1999).

United States v. Reid. 206 F. Supp.2d 132 (D. Mass. 2002).

United States v. Salameh. 152 F.3d 88 (2d Cir. 1998).

United States v. Yousef. 327 F.3d 56 (2d Cir. 2003).

Walker, C. (2002). *Blackstone's guide to the anti-terrorism legislation*. Oxford: Oxford University Press.

Webb, J. K. (2002). Use of the Social Security fraud statute in the battle against terrorism. *United States Attorneys' Bulletin, 50*, 1–12.

Yeh, B., & Doyle, C. (2006). *USA PATRIOT Improvement and Reauthorization Act of 2005: A legal analysis*. Congressional Research Service. Retrieved January 20, 2008, from http://www.fas.org/sgp/crs/intel/RL33332.pdf.

PART IV

Community Prosecution
and Problem Solving

Chapter Nine

Evolving Strategies in 20th-Century American Prosecution

CATHERINE M. COLES

How the prosecution dealing with contemporary issues.

Introduction

Public prosecutors and the offices they lead constitute an important part of society's efforts to control crime, enhance security, and assure justice for victims and offenders. Uniquely positioned because of their authority, strategic position between police and courts, and linkages to those in the executive and legislative branches, American prosecutors exercise considerable power and discretion. Nevertheless, the 20th century ended with two actively competing visions of prosecution—one dominant for the last 50 to 75 years, a second emerging to challenge the first.[1] The outcome is not merely academic: when fundamental changes take place in the role and function of the organization headed by the chief law enforcement officer in the community, as are many district attorneys, the implications are significant for other justice agencies, for justice processes, and for crime control efforts as a whole in local communities.

During much of the last century, district attorneys achieved their goals primarily through efficient and effective felony case processing, governed by twin principles of adhering to a standard of order through treating like cases alike while attempting to handle individual cases fairly. They concentrated primarily on "serious" violent felonies and sought, for the most part, maximum penalties supported by the evidence available. Today, considerable change is visible in the scope and functions of prosecution, especially in large urban offices. Key elements include a new concern with crime prevention and low-level crimes, adopting a problem-solving approach to matters of public safety, collaborating closely with other justice and governmental agencies, and building a working partnership with citizens in the community (Coles, 2002b; Coles & Kelling, 1999). Controversy looms over whether the new practices are merely temporary; whether they will remain additions to the core felony case processing capacity or be fully institutionalized; and whether they fall legitimately within the purview of prosecutorial discretion or pose a threat to constitutional safeguards traditionally thought to limit prosecutors' activities. Little unanimity has emerged regarding how to assess the significance of prosecutors' attempts to address crime and safety problems in these new ways.

Such developments echo experiences in policing, making it reasonable to ask whether prosecution might be on a course analogous to the transformation from an earlier "professional" policing model to the more recent community-policing era, driven by problem solving and a community orientation. In a seminal paper two decades ago, George Kelling and Mark Moore used the concept of an organizational or a corporate strategy to interpret American policing history in terms of three eras—political, reform, and community policing—each dominated by a particular strategy, a "professional ethos that defines standards of competence, professionalism, and excellence in policing. . . . Sometimes this . . . ethos has been explicitly articulated . . . [by] leaders of their profession. . . . Other times, the ethos is implicit—accepted by all as the tacit assumptions that define the business" (Kelling & Moore, 1988, p. 2). Boundaries between eras might not be sharply defined, nor did every organization adopt the dominant strategy—yet the ethos shaped standards and practices powerfully. In writing, Kelling and Moore were concerned with a rocky transition in policing from the reform era (1920s–1930s through the 1970s) to the community problem-solving era (arriving 1970s–1980s) and the dangers they saw in the failure to recognize the significance of this paradigm change. Their idea of a shift in strategy, in particular, characterizing the new strategy as community policing, provoked heated debate even though community and problem-oriented policing now dominates the field.

Although the outcome for prosecution may be less certain today, pressures for change are considerable. Unlike police in the 1980s, prosecutors are surrounded by community and problem-oriented innovations throughout the justice system—in community courts, community-based probation, and corrections, even among public defenders (Clarke, 2001). Positive outcomes of new trends in prosecution (often in combination with policing) are evident—lowered crime rates in targeted neighborhoods, increased satisfaction and decreased fear among citizens, enhanced working relationships between prosecutors and other justice agencies, more effective coordination and delivery of justice and local government services to address crime and safety, and growing acceptance by citizens of their own responsibility for creating safe communities. Since elected prosecutors can be blamed at the ballot box for failure of leadership or the appearance of impeding positive change, at the very least in mid-size and large cities they will need to position themselves to respond to the achievements and impetus for change around them.

This chapter interprets current developments in prosecution through the prism of an organizational strategy, a framework that offers prosecutors a new way of thinking about their goals, functions, and organizations in the face of changing, and often competing, demands. The analysis first identifies the ethos that defined American prosecution through much of the 20th century—the felony case processing strategy; it then considers historical forces that posed a challenge to this strategy from the late 1980s to the mid-1990s and drove some prosecutors into rethinking their function; explores the emergence of a community prosecution strategy, so-named because of prosecutors' partnerships with and growing accountability to citizens in neighborhoods; constructs a model of the new strategy; and, finally, assesses briefly the strengths of and challenges posed by community prosecution.

Thinking in Terms of Organizational Strategies of Prosecution

Interpreting current changes in prosecution as the emergence of a new organizational strategy recognizes them as a transformation through which the dominant paradigm of one era replaces that of another (Kuhn, 1970). Other researchers have contributed to understanding changes in *particular aspects* of prosecutors' activities: closer alignment of prosecutors with the community (Forst, 1993, p. 297); prosecutorial leadership style, interaction with the local environment, adoption of crime prevention (Jacoby, 1995);[2] and new problem-solving activities in response to evolving crime configurations (Boland, 1996, 1998, 1999). Yet the framework set forth by an organizational strategy is more comprehensive in scope than these analyses.

Components of an Organizational Strategy of Prosecution

As used here an organizational strategy includes seven elements (Miles & Snow, 1977; Andrews, 1980):

1. mission or definition of the function of prosecution
2. sources of authority, legal and moral, plus public support, resources, and funds necessary to carry out the mission
3. sources of demand for prosecutors' products or services, as well as marketing and management of demand

4. organizational structure and administrative processes in the prosecutor's office, including personnel issues
5. tactics, core capacities, operations, and activities by which the organization achieves its goals
6. external environment within which the prosecutor's office operates, including political context, task environment, and interaction with other justice agencies, private and public institutions, and groups in the community
7. measurable outcomes related to organizational mission: What does it seek to accomplish through tactics and supporting organizational and administrative features?

Comprised of distinct yet interrelated components, the framework of an organizational strategy offers a conceptual means for clarifying and assessing the significance of specific changes in prosecution, such as the introduction of problem solving or assigning prosecutors to work with citizens in neighborhoods, and what they require in order to succeed. Kelling and Moore point out the danger of misconstruing a practice that represents a fundamentally new strategy as merely another tactic, warning that it could doom the strategy to failure. Such was the fate of team policing during the 1960s and 1970s, when police worked closely with citizens, yet which vanished because "it was a strategy that innovators mistakenly approached as a tactic . . . a competing strategy with different assumptions about every element of police business . . . one did not fit into the other" (Kelling & Moore, 1988, p. 13). A similar struggle is evident today in many prosecutors' offices where community prosecution units or activities are created as "add-ons" to traditional functions, compete for scarce resources in an organization whose culture values felony prosecutions most highly, and operate more or less successfully—then languish or disappear. Incompatible with the overall felony case processing strategy adopted by that office, they probably will achieve only limited success. In other contexts, such innovations may be part of a conscious attempt by the prosecutor to reorient office functions in line with a new definition of prosecution—a new strategy—with a better chance of flourishing.

The appearance of a new organizational strategy signals a fundamental alteration in the function of the prosecutor in the justice system and the "business" of prosecution. To describe this change, two models of prosecution are set forth here—models that do not necessarily represent the strategy of a particular office but identify dominant strategies for prosecution as an institution. Each represents a set of ideals, a professional ethos rather than a mere description of current practices, although it derives in part from observing practices. Not all organizations need to adopt or fully implement a strategy for it to serve as a normative model, to guide and inspire.

Organizations and Strategies in 20th-Century American Prosecution

Since the mid-20th century, the position of American prosecutors in the justice system, crime control, and local political communities has become extraordinarily powerful. Prosecutors' discretion over charging "the single most important decision made in an individual case" (Remington, 1993, p. 98; American Bar Association (hereafter ABA), 1970, p. 93, 1980) is crucial. Limits placed on the discretion of police (with court decisions restraining police activity, the removal of police prosecutors, and screening moving under prosecutorial control) and the judiciary (with mandatory and determinate sentencing) added to discretion exercised by prosecutors. Prosecutors have moved into a position of prominence in juvenile courts, and increasing numbers of states have given them power over waiver of juvenile offenders into adult criminal courts (Coles & Kelling, 2002). Most are elected officials with political bases, and in many cities they have emerged as acknowledged leaders in criminal justice.

Yet accretion of greater power to prosecutors relative to other justice system actors did not happen overnight. More important, prosecutors' offices moved relatively slowly into a central coordinating and policy-making position, leading McDonald to describe prosecution as "the last of the main agencies of the justice system to develop into a major organizational force" (1985, p. 10). The history of American prosecution offers some clues to explain why. Prosecutors' roles since the 17th century portray a melding of European traditions and influences within myriad New World economic, cultural, and political contexts (U.S. National Commission on Law Observance and Enforcement (hereafter U.S. National Commission), 1931, pp. 6ff.; Kress, 1976; Jacoby, 1997a, b). Though a system of public prosecution developed, variation persisted in prosecutorial structures, functions, and jurisdiction: for example, prosecutors in New Jersey, Delaware, Connecticut, and Rhode Island are appointed, not elected; prosecutors' jurisdiction over misdemeanors is inconsistent as well. Another source of variation lies in differing demographic and urban, rural, or suburban contexts that influence policies governing office operations, and organizational structures and processes (Jacoby, 1980, chaps. 1, 2, 11; Eisenstein, Flemming, & Nardulli, 1988, pp. 262–273; Flemming, 1990).

The predominance of small offices in which prosecutors continued to serve part time well into the second half of the 20th century especially impacted organizational development. In 1990, only 53% of chief prosecutors were full time (Dawson, Smith, & DeFrances, 1992); by 2001, this number had increased to 77% (DeFrances, 2002), yet close to a quarter of offices still had part-time chief prosecutors, and the median staff size was nine (see DeFrances, 2001, 2003; DeFrances & Steadman, 1998; DeFrances, Smith, &

van der Does, 1996). The implications were significant: whereas in smaller jurisdictions prosecutors might rely on informal relationships with citizens and actors in other agencies and local government to cross agency boundaries and address problems, large urban offices are more bureaucratic, have larger numbers of staff and higher caseloads, and face greater challenges in institutionalizing consistent policies governing the use of discretion. They are likely to have more resources, their concerns may be influenced by higher crime rates, especially in large cities (Jacoby, 1980, chap. 2), and addressing problems jointly with other agencies may require formal collaboration. Many of these features are evident in histories of individual offices—such as former Suffolk County District Attorney Newman Flanagan's account of the years (1961–1992) he spent in various positions in his Boston office (Coles & Kelling, with Moore, 1998, App. B). Such experiences offer insight into prosecution's slow development as an institutional force and processes by which prosecutors' sense of professional and organizational self-consciousness developed later and perhaps less fully than that of police.

Regardless, for much of the 20th century, a single organizational strategy dominated in prosecution, traceable from pronouncements in the early crime surveys (Pound & Frankfurter, 1922; Illinois Association for Criminal Justice, 1929; Missouri Association for Criminal Justice, 1926) and Wickersham Commission's report on prosecution (U.S. National Commission, 1931) and formally validated in recommendations from the President's Commission on Law Enforcement and Administration of Justice (President's Commission, 1967a, b, c) in 1967. The strategy identified the mission of a prosecutor as a felony case processor, and for the last half century it provided the framework for development as prosecutors' offices increased in size. Standards crafted by professional organizations addressed the expanding scope of prosecutors' power and authority. Mainstream research explored, promoted, and refined practices central to the strategy. For prosecutors, the strategy defined the business and set out the appropriate tools for use.

The Felony Case Processor Strategy

The felony case processor strategy was rooted in Progressive Era attempts to professionalize criminal justice practices and remove them from corrupt political influence. Conclusions and recommendations in reports and crime surveys of the 1920s and 1930s set a foundation. For example, the Wickersham *Report on Prosecution* identified four functions of the prosecutor, all associated with case processing: criminal investigation; "determining who shall be prosecuted and who brought to trial"; preparation of cases for trial; and trying cases and arguing appeals. It also emphasized dangers inherent in the prosecutor's political role: "[I]t is vital to a combination of corrupt politics and orga-

nized crime to control the prosecutor's office, or . . . render its activities nuga-
tory. . . . [T]he prosecutor's office, with its enormous power of preventing
prosecutions from getting to trial, its lack of organization, its freedom from
central control, and its ill-defined responsibility, is a great political prize" (U.S.
National Commission, 1931, pp. 11–12; Moley, 1974).

Virtually all of the reports documented prosecutorial discretion and decision making in case disposal through charging, plea bargaining, and nol-pross-
ing (McDonald, 1979, pp. 32–35). The focus was on the processing of cases
reflecting, primarily, felonies in which police arrests had been made, subsequent
case attrition, and the supposed failure of the formal justice system to deal with
increased caseloads. The ideal was full prosecution under the law: case attrition
between arrest and conviction was attributed to "inadequately trained prosecutors, or political interference, or simple lack of prosecutorial will" (Walker, 1993,
p. 86). Plea bargaining represented failure—refusal to prosecute, try cases, or
arrive at punishment for an offender (Walker, 1992, p. 53). There was no appreciation for the context in which prosecutorial discretion was exercised or its
potential value in terms of other outcomes; the goal was to minimize, eliminate,
or tightly control its use. Successful prosecution of cases emerged as the measure of organizational performance, and recommended remedies focused primarily upon improving efficiency in office organization, working methods, and
administrative practices (U.S. National Commission, 1931, p. 180).

The next major study of prosecution, the American Bar Foundation
(ABF) Survey, conducted in the 1950s and 1960s, documented the "law in
action" (actual activities of prosecutors), and it thereby raised questions about
the dominant model (Miller, 1969; Remington, 1993). It has been described as
"discovering" discretion (Walker, 1993, p. 6); in fact, survey reports departed
from previous crime surveys by treating discretion differently. In the major
publication on prosecution, *Prosecution: The Decision to Charge a Suspect with a
Crime* (1969), Frank Miller explored aspects of prosecutorial discretion
involved in the decision not to charge (or charge fully) that were related not
directly to evidentiary concerns but to considerations such as achieving objectives more satisfactorily through formal alternatives, administrative procedures,
or civil sanctions; weighing potential harm to the victim or undue harm to the
suspect; and costs to the system (see LaFave, 1970; Remington & Logan,
1991). Yet these findings failed to take center stage. Instead, the felony case
processor model was reinforced by the work of President Johnson's Commission (1967a, b, c) and subsequent model codes and standards for prosecution.

The President's Commission report restated many ABF Survey findings
on the uses of discretion by prosecutors, while essentially accepting the role of
prosecutor as a case processor—similar to police under the reform organizational strategy (Kelling & Moore, 1988, pp. 4–9).[3] Discussion of prosecution
was placed within the commission's consideration of the courts: the prosecutor

was a court official, whose "crucial position in the law enforcement system" rested in his discretion to charge and to affect dispositions (1967a, p. 147). The *Task Force Report* identified three prosecution functions: "to determine whether an alleged offender should be charged to obtain convictions through guilty plea negotiations ... presenting government's case in court ... [and] often an investigator and instigator of the criminal process" (1967c, p. 72). Virtually all recommendations aimed at improving professionalism and performance in case processing. Not surprisingly, the ABA, the National Association of Attorneys General (NAAG), and the National District Attorneys Association (NDAA) followed this lead: they recommended hiring full-time staff and prepared manuals and guides to promote the standardization of screening and case management and to control line prosecutors' exercise of discretion, and they increased efficiency in office operations (see NDAA, 1976, 1973; NAAG, 1974; ABA, 1970, 1980, 1993).

Elements of the Strategy

In practice, the felony case processor strategy has been unevenly distributed across the country—found primarily in major urban centers and larger offices staffed by full-time associates. Today, many offices continue to operate within the framework set out by the model, or at least to recognize it as the professional standard. The basic elements follow:

1. *Mission.* The goal of the prosecutor and the prosecutor's office is to ensure the efficient and effective prosecution or disposition of cases presented for prosecution. Effective prosecution of criminal cases means ensuring that cases are prosecuted justly, with some resolution of the tension between individualization (each case should be decided fairly in light of its peculiarities, emphasizing maximum use of prosecutorial discretion) and standardization and equity concerns (in general, like cases should be treated alike). Prosecutors strive to get the most out of evidence presented to them and generally concentrate on "serious" cases, defined primarily in terms of "Part I" crimes. The operational goal becomes maximizing the felony conviction rate.

2. *Source of authority.* The support and legitimacy of the office are rooted in society's desire to hold offenders accountable for their offenses. The prosecutor is authorized to enforce the law, acting within its boundaries. Most often an elected official with a public mandate, as an attorney she or he also is expected to enforce the law in a professionally competent manner. Most offices are organized and seek to operate as professional felony case processing organizations, with a professional "mystique" attached to lawyers and their work.

3. *Demand.* The prosecutor's office markets itself primarily as a professional organization equipped to hold offenders accountable by obtaining guilty pleas or trial convictions, or in some cases diverting cases for treatment. The workload (demand for service) comes primarily from police in the form of cases. In this respect, prosecutors are relatively passive, reacting to cases coming to them rather than pursuing cases proactively. Nevertheless, they largely control what cases they accept and have discretion over how to handle them (Forst, 1993). At times they may obtain cases in other ways, such as through investigations initiated and pursued by special prosecution units in organized crime and public integrity.

4. *Organization.* In terms of structure, prosecutors' offices generally have been centralized geographically and operationally and organized functionally with special teams or units (for general felony prosecutions, misdemeanors, homicides, juveniles, domestic violence, or sex crimes). They tend to be relatively "flat" organizations (at least compared to police departments), typically with the district attorney, first assistant or deputy, executive staff (usually division or section heads), heads of units or trial teams, and line prosecutors. Offices are staffed primarily by attorneys, with few non-lawyers in key management or administrative positions, except where investigative units or divisions exist. During the 1970s and 1980s, however, victim witness advocates did begin working in larger urban offices. Newly appointed assistant prosecutors generally handle "simple" cases, as in juvenile or misdemeanor units, progressing with competence to complex cases involving violent felonies and homicide. Ideally, decision making by junior assistants is controlled through procedures and oversight mechanisms that ensure adherence to office policies governing screening, charging, plea bargaining, and sentencing recommendations. In practice the exercise of discretion varies considerably among offices (Eisenstein et al., 1988, pp. 151–153; Flemming, Nardulli, & Eisenstein, 1992, pp. 58–65; Eisenstein & Jacob, 1977, pp. 85–86, 116–117, 151–154). Traditionally the line of accountability by assistants has been inward to the organization, although more accountability grew later to victims and their families (Dawson et al., 1992; Forst, 1993, p. 297). Salaries of assistant prosecutors are low compared to the private sector; consequently, offices have fairly young staff and high turnover. Most assistants lack civil service protection and are not unionized: the district attorney enjoys considerable discretion over appointments and terminations. Each prosecutor's performance is generally measured by numbers of trials (violent crimes most highly valued), percentage of convictions (including pleas), and length of sentence for repeat and violent offenders (Eisenstein & Jacob, 1977, p. 47).

5. *Tactics.* The most important tactic used to reach the operational goal of maximizing the felony conviction rate is case preparation to support success

at trial and plea bargaining. Screening and charging are crucial elements: prosecutors may adopt different policies that govern decisions for the acceptance and disposal of cases, but such policies are applied primarily to weed out cases not considered strong enough to proceed to trial on legal sufficiency, evidentiary, or constitutional grounds, or in which the type of offense and record of the offender make diversion a viable alternative. Such policies may correspond to environmental features or resource availability (for example, when courts are overloaded and resources strained, a system efficiency policy may dictate the early disposal of weak cases) (Jacoby, 1980, chap. 7).[4] Yet they do not conflict with the goal of seeking to maximize convictions and obtain dispositions reflecting the maximum charge evidence can reasonably sustain.

6. *Environment.* Within the political and task environment, prosecutors' offices have strong, impermeable boundaries and operate with relative independence. Many key operations that prosecutors perform are largely hidden from the lay public. Furthermore, since the American prosecutor is part of the executive branch of government, her or his policies are not subject to judicial and legislative review (Forst, 1993, p. 294). Prosecutors are not part of the local government structure, and no real premium is placed on working closely with it. The prestige of the office vis-à-vis other agencies in the local community may be as high as the prosecutor's ability to capture public attention. This prestige differential also exists in relationships between assistant prosecutors and police, often causing considerable conflict. Population size, demographics, and the structure of other organizations affect and shape the structure and day-to-day operations of the prosecutor's office (Jacoby, 1980, p. 76). Prosecution trial teams may be linked to specific courts to handle cases assigned there. Court processes and interactions with judges, defense attorneys, and courtroom staff require constant adjustment and negotiation by line prosecutors as they carry out their functions, whether in line with policies dictated by the district attorney or through the exercise of individual discretion (Eisenstein et al., 1988; Eisenstein & Jacob, 1977). Nevertheless, the position and functions of the prosecutor in justice processes and the power of a chief prosecutor to set her or his own goals and political "style" are potent forces in shaping office policies (Flemming, 1990, pp. 47–48).

7. *Outcomes.* The primary organizational outcome measures sought as part of the felony case processor strategy have been the number of trials (particularly involving Part I crimes), convictions, and length of sentences. Both the media and public judge the prosecutor's office on its ability to prosecute cases successfully (Eisenstein & Jacob, 1977, p. 47).

The Impetus for Change in Prosecution

The origins of current changes in prosecution are in many senses intertwined with police experiences since the 1960s. These were not easy years in policing: during the 1960s and 1970s, police came under intense scrutiny from the courts, especially with regard to investigatory practices and search and seizure. Many riots were blamed on police actions. In the years following, as crime began to rise, larger numbers of police failed to produce anticipated crime reductions; at the same time research into core police competencies—preventive patrol, criminal investigation, and rapid response to calls for service—called into question the very ability of police to control or affect serious crime. Police experienced nothing less than a crisis of confidence in their professional integrity and competence. Yet these "failures" led to self-reflection, and by the mid-1980s police began crafting a new strategy. Their function would be preventing crime and problem solving—not just responding after the commission of a crime (Goldstein, 1979, 1990; Eck & Spelman, 1998). They rediscovered citizens' roles in crime prevention, providing support and authority for police, identifying problems, and helping to establish police priorities (Wilson & Kelling, 1982). Recognizing citizens as their partners in crime control, police returned to tactics and allocation methods that fostered close linkages to communities—foot and bicycle patrol and permanent beats—and redesigned beats and precincts to match neighborhood boundaries. To enable police to respond more effectively to local priorities, decision-making authority was devolved to lower levels of police organizations. All of these became part of "community policing" (Kelling & Moore, 1988; Moore, 1998).

Although police and prosecutors faced the same set of crime problems from the late 1960s on, they experienced them differently. When police began moving "out of the box," prosecutors did not immediately take a similar path. Prosecutors never faced a loss of public confidence in their mission and tactics. While policing was relatively public and accessible, the day-to-day work of prosecutors was less visible (Forst, 2000, p. 23), and no one challenged seriously prosecutors' core business of case processing. Nevertheless, from the mid-1980s to the early 1990s, prosecutors in many cities began to believe that they were no more immune to blame than police were for criminal justice agencies' failure to deal with exploding violence and disorder on city streets. In spite of innovations that produced increasingly sophisticated and efficient prosecutions, crime remained high, urban quality of life was eroding, and jails and prisons were filled to overcapacity. Changes in policing offered a powerful example of the benefits of problem-solving and community-oriented operations and tactics.

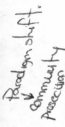

Paradigm shift·
Community Prosecution

Motivating Factors and Prosecutors' Responses

Prosecutors who adopted a community-oriented prosecution strategy at this time were motivated by the following three key factors to think about what they might do differently:

problem solving

1) *Addressing drug crime and quality of life through problem solving.* Many prosecutors point to the dramatic increase in drug-related crime as an impetus for changing their views of what a prosecutor's mission should be. In Kansas City, Missouri, Jackson County Prosecutor Albert Reiderer (in office from 1980 to 1992) recalls a surge in such crime (especially crack cocaine) when one of every two arrests involved a drug user and 80% of all crimes involved illegal drugs (Coles & Kelling, with Moore, 1998, App. D). In Boston, youth gang violence reached unprecedented highs: in 1990, 152 people were killed, 73 age 24 and under, and 18 age 17 or under; rival gangs shot up funerals of each others' members (Buntin, 1998). Initially, prosecutors responded by "getting tough" on perpetrators, but the strategy failed to check crime: a review of arrest dispositions in Los Angeles, Manhattan, San Diego, and Washington, D.C., with exploding drug cases, found when "felony drug arrests increased by 136 percent from 1982 to 1987, the number of imprisonments increased 317 percent" (Boland & Healey, 1993, p. 1).

By the late 1980s some practitioners were concluding that prosecuting cases was not enough. Prosecutors had already made headway against racketeering and organized crime by adopting broader tactics, including civil remedies such as forfeiture and injunctions (Goldstock, 1992; Blakey, Goldstock, & Rogovin, 1978). Responding to the surge in drug arrests and caseloads, other prosecutors sought a similar, more comprehensive approach: Norm Maleng in Seattle, Washington, Michael Schrunk in Portland, Oregon, Robert Macy in Oklahoma County, Oklahoma, and Janet Reno in Miami, Florida, all formulated problem-reduction strategies involving proactive, multifaceted attacks on drug abuse that included drug education, deterrence, and treatment, plus expedited prosecution. The formal use of problem solving by prosecutors to address crime problems began, then, with these efforts. Once adopted, problem solving could be applied to increase the efficiency and effectiveness of case processing, as well as to reduce the incidence of felony crime and quality-of-life offenses. It produced changes in prosecutors' activities, plus greater collaboration between prosecutors and other justice agencies—especially the police.

2. *Learning from citizens.* Accounts by prosecutors of how and why they began moving away from the felony case processor strategy emphasize the role played by citizens. In particular, victims, victims' rights organizations, and

members of minority groups heavily impacted by increases in crime and a worsening quality of life—yet alienated from justice institutions and political leadership—increasingly demanded more than arrests, prosecution, and incarceration. In Kansas City, Prosecutor Albert Reiderer saw the federal response pushing prosecution and policing into "drug-fighting" mode, losing sight of community concerns. He committed to work with African American community leaders, who sought to draw attention back to neighborhoods and who argued that drugs represented not just a crime problem but a public health issue requiring education and prevention. Using nuisance abatement and forfeiture laws to close drug houses and reduce sales, his prosecutors worked with citizens and the police to pressure landlords to remove drug dealers (Mills, 1996; Coles & Kelling, with Moore, 1998, App. D). In Austin, Texas, District Attorney Ronald Earle's tenure was strongly affected by vocal victims and victims' rights associations. During the 1980s, when incidents of child abuse rose and the child abuse unit he had created in his office produced lawyers "burned out" from heavy caseloads and emotionally draining cases, Earle founded the Institute for Community Family Treatment (which his office administered at first) to treat incest in families. Later he created the Children's Advocacy Center (which eventually passed to community control) and the Child Protection Team to handle intake and investigate cases of child abuse and neglect (Coles & Kelling, with Moore, 1998, App. A).

As the police had learned earlier, many citizens' concerns heard by prosecutors involved quality-of-life issues—prostitution, aggressive panhandling, loud music, youths hanging out in parks and intimidating elderly citizens, drug dealing and use on street corners and in public places, and graffiti (Wilson & Kelling, 1982). This message also came from the business community: Portland, Oregon, District Attorney Mike Schrunk responded to business owners concerned about the effects of crime for viable economic activity in an inner-city downtown area by assigning a special prosecutor to the district—and a neighborhood prosecutor program was born (Boland, 1998).

Changes in other justice agencies. Community policing provided a model for and in some cases put pressure on prosecutors: community policing "wins," the growing use of problem solving by police, the popularity of community policing with the public, and the increase in the number of police available—all were visible at the national level if not in every locality. Prosecutor Scott Newman described this pressure in Indianapolis, Indiana, during the 1990s: "If I didn't change the way I did business . . . the community would draw closer to the police department . . . and . . . blame [failures] . . . on me as the most visible proponent of the criminal justice system" (WG 1, April 19, 1996).[5] By the early 1990s, it was not only the police who engaged in community-oriented initiatives but also the courts, such as Manhattan's Midtown Community

Court (Sviridoff, Rottman, Ostrum, & Curtis, 2000) and problem-solving courts nationwide (Berman & Feinblatt, 2005), probation programs, such as Operation Nightlight in Boston (Clear & Corbett, 1998), and community sanctioning and corrections movements, such as those in Vermont (Bazemore, 1998). The elements that would comprise "community justice" began to emerge in many justice agencies: operations focused at the neighborhood level; problem-solving processes involving citizens; organizational trends toward decentralization of authority and accountability; and commitment to citizen priorities replacing extreme reliance on professionalism by criminal justice agencies (Clear & Karp, 1998).

Prosecution in Transition

Prosecution was not left out: from the late 1980s on, innovative prosecutors began creating programs and processes in which deputies worked more closely with citizens and made changes in the processing of cases to address citizens' priorities. Their experience in collaborative problem solving grew, as did insights gained through contact with citizens. Nevertheless, no critical mass had been reached across the country, and a synergy was lacking to propel leading professional organizations and the field as a whole into a new strategy. The dominant strategy of prosecution was in transition and flux—a fact not yet recognized by prosecutors themselves.

　　This unsettled state was evident in meetings of the Executive Session for State and Local Prosecutors, convened at the Program in Criminal Justice Policy and Management of the Kennedy School of Government, Harvard University, from 1986 to 1990. Discussions focused on the current state of prosecution, with differing conceptions put forth for the role of the prosecutor—pure jurist, sanction setter, problem solver, strategic investor, and institution builder. The first two were linked to the felony case processor model; the remainder departed from it. Two in particular recognized the complexity of prosecutorial functioning: *problem solvers* moved beyond criminal law to use all available authority and resources in the enforcement and regulatory communities to control crime. Complicated problem-solving activities involved mounting and leading an organized attack on problems by mobilizing agencies, seeking funding, creating specific programs, and using traditional enforcement mechanisms. *Institution builders* fostered the vitality of basic neighborhood institutions—families, schools, and civic and religious institutions—against criminal disruption and disorder, so that they could become self-sufficient and capable of regulating their own affairs. Underlying this approach was the assumption, based upon social science research, that severe stress and disorder could produce disengagement and withdrawal by citizens, the weakening of social ties, the collapse of supporting institutions, and an influx of increasing disorder and crime (Skogan, 1990; Kelling & Coles, 1996). Institution builders processed cases, considering in part the value of the institution threatened or damaged by the act and the potential benefit of prosecutorial action, but they also adopted the tactics of problem solvers (Tumin, 1990, pp. 7–15).

Among participants from around the country in the Executive Session, some concluded in retrospect that the discussions motivated them to reconsider their mission and adopt new tactics. Prosecutor Albert Reiderer, drawing on a background in tax law, conceived the idea of supporting a broad-based approach to drug crimes and related problems with a sales tax. He helped shape legislation and pass a 1/4 cent addition to a general-purpose, county-wide tax that raised approximately $14 million—for establishing prosecution, policing, juvenile and circuit courts, corrections, crime prevention, and rehabilitation programs. Community members assumed active roles: health and social service providers offered treatment options, citizens joined in neighborhood-oriented problem-solving, and crime prevention initiatives, and others served on the COMBAT Commission (Coles & Kelling, with Moore, 1998, App. D). But if individual prosecutors in the Executive Session talked about possibilities that might yet develop and to innovate in their own jurisdictions, the time was not ripe for a mass movement. The Executive Session produced no conclusive statement to suggest that a coherent new strategy might be emerging in prosecution, and no discernible impact on wider discourse about prosecutors' roles in criminal justice, or with respect to crime control.

The Community Prosecution Strategy *not less.*

Only a few years later, problem solving and a community-oriented approach had not only matured in policing but taken hold in growing numbers of prosecutors' offices. During the 1990s dramatic increases took place in prosecutors' offices nationwide in staff size, budgets for prosecutorial functions, and population served (DeFrances, 2002), and a new strategy of prosecution was gaining ground. At first prosecutors themselves sought to develop greater capacities for addressing crime problems having a grave impact on public safety—crack cocaine and, by this time, methamphetamine, organized crime, and gang-related violence. Increased collaboration with police and other justice agencies in a joint problem-oriented approach enhanced their efforts. As the developing community justice movement increased the pressure on justice agencies to question their mode of operation, prosecutors responded by offering the community a more direct role in affecting prosecution priorities and processes.

The convergence of these trends was obvious in the activities of a growing number of prosecutors around the country. Marion County (Indianapolis,

Indiana) prosecutor Jeff Modisett created a community prosecution program in 1993–1994 that placed deputy prosecutors in police district stations where they worked with police and citizens (Coles & Kelling, with Moore, 1998, App. C). Andrew Sonner, state's attorney in Montgomery County (Maryland), in 1991 reorganized his office into five teams assigned to handle cases from specific police districts and geographical areas and to work on problem solving with police and community organizations to reduce crime (Jacoby, 1995). District attorney Charles Hynes (Kings County, New York) also created felony community prosecution teams to work in five zones with police and to get to know the local community and its crime problems (Hynes, 1993). Such projects were observed and replicated by prosecutors all over the country. By 1989, district attorney Ronald Earle had written and secured passage of state legislation creating county community justice councils to oversee public safety planning. During the 1990s, he set up councils and task forces in which citizens and professionals jointly planned for the development and administration of local justice processes in Travis County (Texas) (Coles & Kelling, with Moore, 1998, App. A).

While changing practices were critical in the emergence of a new prosecution strategy, equally significant was the national dialogue that began reshaping the frame of reference. New leaders advanced goals substantively different from those accepted a generation ago. Yet changes in practice and thinking clearly were not universal, and at times new programs did not succeed and were withdrawn. All of these elements emerged clearly in a further series of meetings held at the Program in Criminal Justice, Policy, and Management at the Kennedy School of Government, as part of two studies of prosecution conducted there from 1995 to 2000. The first, "Prosecution in the Community: A Study of Emergent Strategies," looked in depth at four innovative prosecutors' offices, along with their local police departments, from 1995 to 1997: district attorneys Ralph Martin (Suffolk County, Boston, Massachusetts) and Ronald Earle (Travis County, Austin, Texas) and county prosecutors Claire McCaskill (Jackson County, Kansas City, Missouri) and Scott Newman (Marion County, Indianapolis, Indiana). Two working group meetings convened at the Kennedy School to test study findings and to obtain input from a wider range of prosecutors, researchers, scholars, and government officials from around the country (Coles & Kelling, with Moore, 1998). The second study, "Boston's Safe Neighborhood Initiatives (SNIs): Defining 'Community Partnership' and Measuring Performance in Community Based Prosecution," focused on four prosecutor-initiated collaborations in the Boston area (Coles, Carney, & Johnson, 2000). Three meetings took place (1998–2000), attended by prosecutors, police, judges, representatives of other justice agencies, and participating citizens, to address issues arising in the collaborations.

One participant in the first series of meetings, former prosecutor and then law professor Ronald Goldstock, summed up how prosecutors' thinking was being transformed: most were traditional "case processors," with a smaller group adopting broader crime prevention efforts, and finally a subset "who recognize that . . . crime can't always be reduced by investigation, prosecution, conviction and sanction . . . it's got to be through the use of other means . . . civil relief, suits, injunctions, eviction, the use of eminent domain, forfeiture and disruption . . . reports, hearings, instructional, institutional training . . . there are an enormous number of things that prosecutors can do" (WG 1, April 19, 1996). The four prosecutor-subjects of the studies and others who attended the meetings provided clear examples of Goldstock's last group. From their office operations, reflections, approaches, and thoughtful statements, the elements of a new strategy of prosecution emerged. Since that time ongoing research has documented prosecutors nationwide appearing to move in the same direction, both conceptually and in practice.

Elements of the Community Prosecution Strategy

Elements of the emerging community prosecution strategy include the following:

Mission. The overriding priority is to make communities safer for citizens. Community prosecution leaders retain effective felony case processing as a core capacity, yet "doing justice" brings new goals: reducing and preventing crime, addressing disorder and misdemeanor offenses as well as felony crime, and strengthening bonds with citizens, governmental and law enforcement agencies, and civic groups to establish and secure a community capacity for enhancing security and promoting justice (see Nugent, 2004a). Even where the district attorney's office lacks jurisdiction over misdemeanors and ordinance violations, or cedes that power to county or city prosecutors, these remain an important focus of problem-solving efforts.

Source of authority. Prosecutors are still authorized to enforce the law in a professionally competent manner, maintaining their status as elected officials and attorneys. Whereas their elected status in the felony case processor model was based on a plurality in a jurisdiction, community prosecutors derive additional authority through relationships with specific neighborhoods and communities. This increased authority emerges from the legitimacy they gain by responding to discrete problems in particular locations affecting particular individuals and groups—prosecutors draw support directly from leaders and ordinary citizens in these local areas. Correspondingly, citizens have a direct line to the prosecutor's office. Assistants as well as the district attorney gain added authority through these neighborhood relationships. As they respond to citizen priorities and share their thinking directly with citizens—about what they cannot do regarding problems and/or cases as well as what they can—their credibility is enhanced: they demonstrate expertise as lawyers and prosecutors as well as their problem-solving ability. Further authority and prestige accrue to the prosecutor through her or his ability to leverage discretionary resources for solving problems, whether federal funds or local tax initiatives.

Demand. In the community prosecution strategy demand continues to come from police in the form of cases presented for processing; however, it also comes directly from citizens. Where police engage in community policing and prosecutors have direct contact with citizens, this demand increasingly takes the form of requests from both police and citizens for prosecutors to handle not just felonies but also quality-of-life crimes affecting local neighborhoods, and for prosecutors' assistance in solving specific problems. The prosecutor markets the office's capacity for prosecuting cases, for leading (or joining) efforts to solve local public safety problems, and for serving as an effective partner in them. The traditional formal holds truth under community that still happens.

Organization. Broad changes in structure and administrative and personnel aspects of prosecutors' offices take place with the new strategy. Working with citizens who see problems locally pressures prosecutors to decentralize their operations. As a result, prosecutors may assign deputies to work with the police in precinct stations or neighborhood offices, focusing upon specific geographical areas; create bureaus or teams to carry out vertical prosecution and to handle all cases (even screening) from an area; and set up community prosecution sections and units. In some offices, specific roles, projects, and programs identified as part of a discrete community prosecution effort are established as additions to preexisting special units; alternatively, roles for assistants may be redefined across the office to include new tasks and responsibilities. Increasingly, more staff at all levels work in the community in a wide range of activities, from attending neighborhood association or crime watch meetings to joining high-level, regional, multiagency task forces concerning public safety issues, while also carrying out traditional supervisory and litigation-related duties (see Harp, Kuykendall, Cunningham, & Ware, 2004).

Transforming the culture of the prosecutor's office is fundamental to implementing the new strategy—continuing to value felony crime prosecution and prosecutors above all else can doom community prosecution. Aware of this challenge, prosecutors are devising new recruitment standards to require experience in and a commitment to community service and problem solving as well as litigation. Nonlawyer specialists in public health, the media, public relations, and social services—even former police officers—are sought and even elevated to executive positions. Measuring the performance of pros-

[handwritten margin note: if you are changing the mission you need to change the organization structure?]

ecutors in the range of new tasks remains a dilemma: as community prosecutors realize, most current measures are woefully inadequate, often failing to capture labor-intensive aspects of work with citizens, law enforcement partners, and in the community sufficiently to justify adequate funding.

✔ read

Tactics. The new strategy uses a greatly expanded "tool kit" compared to the felony case processing strategy. Tactics are grouped here into the following three categories:

(1) *Case processing* remains at the core, but it is one of several tactics and subject to greater influence from the public than was true previously. New priorities in prosecuting cases reflect determinations by citizens as to which offenses are most significant: quality-of-life offenses, while not overshadowing felonies, frequently rise in importance. Prosecutors also bring citizens more directly into court processes through community impact statements, court watch organizations, and regular reporting on the progress of cases to local neighborhoods.

(2) *Developing partnerships* of two types is fundamental to the strategy. Working in partnership with the community is part of the mission, a key tactic, and it affects organization and outcome goals. Establishing partnerships with other justice and government agencies and public and private organizations changes the nature of the prosecutor's relationships in the environment. Though prosecutors have always worked with citizens as victims and other criminal justice actors in case processing, today's broad-based, problem-solving efforts involve larger numbers of players coming to the table regularly, in a different setting (often in neighborhoods), and for different purposes (Kennedy, 1997). Different sets of issues face prosecutors in the two types of partnerships (Liddle & Gelsthorpe, 1994). Effective working relationships among justice and government agencies require decisions about which should be present; turf issues must be resolved; representatives who come together must have the authority to act and not simply be conduits of information back to the agency; and basic agreement must exist about the nature of problems and those means appropriate or desirable for addressing them. In partnership with citizens, prosecutors must decide who will represent the community and how they will be chosen, develop an agenda to the satisfaction of both citizens and justice agency representatives, including crime and safety priorities, and negotiate appropriate citizen roles: Will they be involved in identifying local problems as well as devising plans to address them? Will citizens eventually assume leadership of the problem-solving effort?

(3) *Problem solving to prevent and reduce crime* takes place within the office and as prosecutors join collaborative partnerships. Problems may be small, requiring short-term efforts, or broader in scope and in need of attention for months or years. Both problem identification and problem-solving

activities reflect citizen priorities, input, and cooperation and usually target particular neighborhoods. Problem-solving activities often are multifaceted and nearly infinite, involving such tactics as targeted and expedited criminal prosecutions, civil remedies, nuisance abatement, code enforcement, establishing new institutions (a day report center, or problem court), crafting legislation, developing working protocols among agencies, and fund-raising for new activities.

Environment. The prosecutor adopting community prosecution likely will develop new relationships with judges and courts, police, other justice agencies, governmental actors, business and citizen groups, and social service providers. Communication must flow to all of them about prosecutorial initiatives both inside and outside the courtroom, and insofar as possible partnerships must be established so that prosecution operations will be enhanced and not thwarted by lack of congruence in the strategy and performance of other agencies and citizen groups. With these partnerships, organizational boundaries demarcating the prosecutor's office from other agencies become increasingly permeable as representatives work together. The relationship between prosecutors and citizens also is fundamentally changed: prosecutorial decision making about how particular types of cases should be treated and the prosecutorial use of discretion become more accessible to citizens, while prosecutors' accountability to victims is broadened to the community.

Demands arising out of interagency relationships may place strains on prosecutors, as well as other organizations involved. For example, coalitions that bring treatment into the realm of criminal justice processes raise questions about the roles of partners and confidentiality issues—prosecutors working in case management or treatment settings may be exposed to information that could be used against an offender in a subsequent prosecution. Alternatively, where collaborative initiatives turn to city departments for help, prosecutors often are the ones expected to push city agencies to "do their job" with respect to code enforcement for health and safety violations, or liquor control and licensing. Where specific agencies are unresponsive, the temptation is to set them up as targets for the media, portraying them as part of the problem rather than the solution—charges also levied at the courts—and placing prosecutors in a potentially difficult position. These types of strains have not all been resolved.

Outcomes. In the new strategy, desired outcomes change and broaden, targeting improved quality of neighborhood life, crime prevention, management of problems, reduced levels of fear, and citizen confidence, satisfaction, and capacity to solve future problems. Former outcomes such as guilty verdicts in trials become the means to obtain improved neighborhood safety and crime

[handwritten: you have to measure the outcome. Is what you are doing is working? Are you achieving your mission.]

prevention rather than ends in themselves. Among the indicators that prosecutors have begun to use for measuring these broadened outcomes are lowered rates of crime and victimization, perceptions of increased personal safety by citizens in their neighborhoods, more frequent use of public spaces by citizens (as an indication of their perceptions of safety), greater involvement of citizens in crime prevention and reduction activities, and stronger relationships between citizens and police and other criminal justice agencies. Individual prosecutors grappling with the need for new measures are becoming increasingly creative in devising indicators to match their goals and tactics (Coles & Kelling, with Moore, 1998, p. 113). But the process is complicated—to mention just one issue, formulating indicators to measure project outcomes at the neighborhood level (the target for many activities) requires input from citizens with an intimate knowledge of local conditions. Yet the goals that citizens and other partners bring to the partnership with the prosecutor may diverge considerably. Citizens participating in a discussion of goals and outcome measures for Boston's SNIs in 1999 emphasized that they wanted prosecutors to develop a personal stake in their community, to "do business" in a different way by working to coordinate the delivery of services locally, and to address priorities relating to crime and safety that citizens brought to them (Coles, Carney, & Johnson, 2000). Designating outcomes and crafting indicators that are meaningful to citizens and other partners, as well as consistent with prosecutorial priorities, present a new challenge.

Summing Up: The Community Prosecution Strategy vs. Felony Case Processor

Comparing community prosecution and felony case processor strategies illustrates some similarity between them in terms of category content; however, the new strategy reflects a reformulation consistent with changes in principles and values underlying the broader mission (Table 9.1).

The mission offers a thematic basis for and shapes an entire strategy; yet no single element wholly defines that strategy. Conceived as an organizational strategy, community prosecution is not simply a collection of new tactics (such as addressing misdemeanors and quality-of-life issues, placing prosecutors in neighborhoods, or employing a problem-solving approach to crime problems). Any of these might be seen as expendable when resources grow scarce or an upsurge in crime occurs unless the prosecutor's mission, commitment to citizens and other justice partners, and measures for assessing achievements also have moved in the direction of community prosecution. The transition to a community prosecution strategy involves more than making a few changes in tactics or organization. The two prosecution strategies arise out of fundamentally different values, project different goals, hold different assumptions

198

TABLE 9.1
Comparing Prosecution Strategies:
Felony Case Processor versus Community Prosecution

	Felony Case Processor Strategy	Community Prosecution Strategy
Mission	Prosecute or dispose of cases presented by police; highest priority accorded violent crimes, repeat and/or violent offenders; operational goal to maximize felony conviction rate	Prevent, reduce, manage crime, and quality-of-life offenses; prosecute felonies and low-level crimes corresponding to citizen priorities; create partnership with community
Base of Authority	Law, professional status, plus broad electoral mandate	Law, professional status, electoral support from specific local areas and entire community
Demand	From police via cases presented to prosecutor's office; prosecutor markets office capacity for felony case processing; prosecutors as professionally able to hold offenders accountable by obtaining trial convictions/pleas and maximum penalties for violent repeat offenders	From police, political leadership, citizens in neighborhoods, and other partners; prosecutor markets collaborative problem-solving capacity of office, willingness to work with citizens and adopt their priorities, plus prosecute crimes committed
Organization	Offices generally centralized, organized functionally, "flat" hierarchy; most staff are lawyers; office culture values successful litigation, appellate skills; performance measures highlight case processing expertise, trial and plea negotiation outcomes; accountability inward to the organization	Decentralization, with focus on working in local neighborhoods and entire community; nonlawyer specialists hired; recruitment stresses problem-solving ability, community orientation, and litigation skills; new career track and performance measures for community prosecution
Tactics	Primary tactic is case preparation for efficient and effective felony case prosecution or plea negotiations	Criminal law and prosecution at the core, but civil remedies, code enforcement, other tactics added; problem solving a key tactic

(continued on next page)

TABLE 9.1 *(continued)*

	Felony Case Processor Strategy	*Community Prosecution Strategy*
Environment	Offices operate in relative isolation from other justice agencies	Close working relationship sought with other justice agencies, local government, private citizens, health and service providers, business and faith communities; accountability develops outward to partners in community
Outcomes	Measured in numbers of felony convictions, maximum sentences obtained, dispositions through plea negotiations	Quantitative measures reflect cases screened, pled, tried, dispositions; qualitative and quantitative indicators required to measure crime prevention and reduction, fear reduction, improved quality of life

concerning where accountability is owed, value and demand different attributes and capacities in staff, and define and seek to measure outcomes differently. Overall, the new strategy places a greater premium on the use of discretion by prosecutors in various aspects of their work (for example, with the community and in collaborative problem solving), even though it may be exercised within specific parameters. Organizational boundaries are less rigid as assistant prosecutors work with representatives of other justice agencies and community groups to whom they develop accountability. Finally, the organization and functioning of the prosecutor's office become more transparent with greater access by citizens and an increase in cross-boundary operations.

The Community Prosecution Strategy: Strengths and Challenges

The transition to a community prosecution strategy represents an innovative and a thoughtful professional response by prosecutors faced with a changing environment—one in which the capacity and tools of a felony case processing strategy could not meet late-20th-century challenges. Prosecutors have been called upon to offer new skills, assume new roles in the justice system and wider community, and exercise leadership in new contexts (Wolf & Worrall, 2004). As they take on these tasks, the strategy will no doubt develop further.

Recent reports by the American Prosecutors Research Institute (APRI) suggest that about half of prosecutors' offices engage in some practices associated with community prosecution (Nugent, 2004a). Whether these figures represent prosecutors actually implementing the community prosecution strategy, at least in part, or adopting it as the normative model for prosecution is not yet clear (see Nugent, 2004b); regardless, the new strategy appears to have gained considerable ground over the last decade. Prosecutors practicing community prosecution have accomplished much, yet they continue to face resistance and obstacles within and outside their own organizations and questions concerning the appropriateness of prosecution moving in this direction.

Opportunity and opposition in the prosecutor's office. Many prosecutors—both experienced and new to the job—thrive on the new tasks associated with community prosecution, taking satisfaction in positive outcomes in relationships with community and justice agency partners as well as in crime reduction and control. Nevertheless, prosecutors unfamiliar with community prosecution may see it as "social work" and view prevention activities as potentially interfering with ongoing investigations, threatening successful prosecutions, or diverting them from "serious" cases. For prosecutors facing a flood of incoming cases, reallocating resources and personnel from case processing to other types of work can be highly unpopular: crime prevention and problem solving may not yet be paying off in terms of reducing the number of cases they have to process. Community prosecutors' duties may lack the visibility and definitiveness of successfully prosecuted cases, and individual prosecutors may need more training and/or experience to do their new jobs effectively. Prosecutors in these roles may flounder if steps are not taken by the chief prosecutor. Often this involves waging a campaign within the office to highlight achievements of community prosecution, establish clearly that assistants are expected to engage fully in carrying out the new mission and tactics, and demonstrate that community prosecution offers a secure career path. If the message does not reach prosecutors at all levels, then old ways of operating will not only die hard but may not die at all.

Stress and success in the local environment. More than one police official has commented, "Community prosecution makes community policing work." Both prosecutors and police report policing benefits from closer prosecutorial collaboration; prosecutors say that prosecution benefits as well. With more accessible legal consultation, police improve their street activities and investigations; as prosecutors understand better what police face on the streets, their respect for police often rises; as prosecutors learn more about how particular offenders and criminal activity impact a local neighborhood, they generate more creative tactics to address problems (see APRI, 2004). Police and prosecutors also make extraordinarily effective teams in working with citizens. Prosecutors educate, explaining why police cannot legally undertake certain actions, why an offender was released on bail, or a decision was made not to prosecute; they may suggest how police and citizens can assist in a prosecution. Nevertheless, serious questions arise about where responsibilities of police and prosecutors begin and end, and the relationship between them. Are community prosecutors assuming police roles? How can prosecutors avoid co-optation by police? Does accountability to police ever override a prosecutor's accountability to her or his own office? Responsible prosecutors must address and work toward resolving these issues.

In addition to police, other potentially important partners for prosecutors include city attorneys and state attorneys general, who may be vitally interested in community prosecution (Coles, 2002a, 2002b). The work of many city attorneys constituted the essence of community prosecution long before district attorneys thought about it. Prosecutors' collaborations with city attorneys and attorneys general offices may lead to complementary policies for dealing with offenders and particular offenses, drafting legislation, collaborative problem solving on public safety issues, and sharing or cross-designating staff. Courts also are potentially important partners, but collaboration may pose a more formidable problem. Aligning prosecution trial teams with specific neighborhoods may conflict with trial court organization and procedures. Some judges see community involvement as threatening their objectivity and neutrality, but around the country, judges have joined prosecutors in problem-solving courts and other initiatives with great benefit, such as Newark's (New Jersey) Safer Cities Initiative.[6]

Connecting with citizens. The public must understand fully the change in the prosecutor's mission and tactics. Not only is community approval required to legitimize prosecutor actions, but citizens must embrace their new role as co-participants in producing public safety. Forming a community partnership can be difficult in high-crime areas and in impoverished minority communities where citizens have withdrawn from streets in fear, residents resent law enforcement officials, and neighborhood associations and crime watch groups do not function. In the Grove Hall SNI in Boston, it took more than a year of meetings before citizens, police, and prosecutors trusted each other enough to agree on priorities and procedures for collaborating and to get down to work (Coles et al., 2000). Once trust is established, however, citizens offer information that prosecutors never had before unless it came from police, allowing prosecutors to pursue cases that otherwise would be impossible and use the information in problem-solving efforts. Citizen satisfaction increases as residents see concrete results—more importantly, citizen initiative grows. Nevertheless, a host of issues need to be resolved concerning prosecutors' new roles in neighborhoods and relationships with citizens. Many relate to the need for guidance in the use of prosecutorial discretion about questions such as these: Who represents the community? How can the prosecutor avoid co-optation by one segment attempting to push its own agenda at the expense of others? Where are the legal, ethical, and professional boundaries for prosecutors working with citizens? What are citizens' responsibilities?

Pursuing public safety. Evidence documenting the impact of community prosecution in helping to reduce and prevent crime, improve quality of life, and increase local safety is accumulating slowly. Anecdotal data support a positive impact, but systematic evaluations are sorely needed (Thompson, 2002; Goldkamp, Irons-Guynn, & Weiland, 2002). Most evidence of success comes from cities where prosecutors and police have implemented a joint community-oriented strategy, using problem solving: even here parsing out results attributable to acts of prosecutors, or police, remains problematic (Braga, Kennedy, Waring, & Piehl, 2001). One outcome is clear—citizens who experience community prosecution want to see it continue. They lobby legislators and funders for financial backing, support sympathetic political candidates, and even continue to work with prosecutors and police when crime spikes in a community, such as Boston has experienced recently (Smalley, 2005). Nevertheless, legitimate questions exist about new tactics that prosecutors use as part of prevention and crime reduction efforts. Community prosecution and community policing are inherently more intrusive than traditional forms. Will more knowledgeable prosecutors misuse their discretion with dangerous consequences for offenders? Are appropriate safeguards in place and observed? These and related concerns raise serious policy issues.

Outstanding challenges in these and numerous other areas remind us that much remains to be settled regarding the development of community prosecution. Pressure in favor of adopting the new strategy emanates from leading prosecutors capitalizing on it, as well as from the community justice movement. This movement's power is understandable—proponents see it as the positive replacement for a failed system through which justice agencies can reestablish their authority in the community and reconnect with citizens (not merely victims or offenders), many of whom have been alienated for decades. Arising within the context of this movement, community prosecution's development has been intimately connected to similar changes in other justice agencies. For example, with the transition to community policing, order maintenance was increasingly recognized and sanctioned as part of police work, but to be carried out legally and taken seriously by other agencies, these activities required a switch in prosecutorial priorities. Community prosecutors changed their stance toward minor offenses. Similarly, problem-solving courts that focus on quality-of-life offenses and community-oriented probation and parole efforts all need prosecutors' commitment to function effectively.

Nevertheless, the felony case processing strategy exerts considerable pressure on prosecutors to continue along the same path they have for decades—in part because problem solving can be used to improve case processing, while research has refined and made it more efficient and equitable. Yet with the transition to the new strategy, prosecution as an institution is abandoning the notion that to do their job professionally and properly, prosecutors must be reactive case processors, removed from citizens and communities. In a sense, American prosecution has come full circle—under the private prosecution system early in the nation's history, citizens determined prosecution priorities; with the growth of police institutions and a public prosecution system, demand from citizens was increasingly screened and filtered through the criminal justice system, and citizens priorities were eventually abandoned. With community prosecution, professional groups and researchers can, as before, help establish guidelines and refine procedures for use with new tactics and processes (see APRI, 1995a, 1995b). Citizens' priorities move back into prosecution, accompanied by a stronger sense of prosecutorial accountability to the public.

Notes

Research here was supported in part by Grants No. 95-IJ-CX-0096 and No. 97-MU-MU-013, awarded by the National Institute of Justice, Office of Justice Programs, U.S. Department of Justice and the Pew Charitable Trust. Research was conducted by C. Coles as a research associate, Program in Criminal Justice Policy and Management, John F. Kennedy School of Government, Harvard University. Points of view are those of the author and do not necessarily represent the official position or policies of the U.S. Department of Justice, or of the Pew Charitable Trust. An earlier version of this chapter appeared by the author as *Community Prosecution, Problem Solving, and Public Accountability: The Evolving Strategy of the American Prosecutor* (Criminal Justice Working Paper No. 00-02-04). Cambridge, MA: Program in Criminal Justice Policy and Management, John F. Kennedy School of Government, Harvard University, 2000.

1. This chapter deals with prosecutors at the county level—district attorneys, county prosecutors, or state attorneys—whose titles are used interchangeably.

2. Jacoby uses "strategy" in a sense closer to the use of "tactics" here.

3. Although the President's Commission released its reports before publication of all of the major works emanating from the ABF Survey, survey results were made available to the commission.

4. Jacoby has written extensively on case handling, disposition, and devising tools for the standardization of procedures (see also 1977, 1976; Jacoby, Mellon, Turner, & Ratledge, 1982; Jacoby, Mellon, Turner, & Smith, 1982; Jacoby, Mellon, Turner, & Ratledge, 1982).

5. These comments are from a working group meeting held for the project "Prosecution in the Community." Remarks are cited as WG 1 or WG 2, plus the date. For confidentiality reasons, transcripts from the meetings are not available for distribution (see Coles & Kelling, with Moore, 1998).

6. The Safer Cities Initiative is organized by the Police Institute, School of Criminal Justice, Rutgers University, Newark, New Jersey.

References

American Bar Association (ABA). (1970). *Standards relating to the prosecution function and the defense function.* Chicago: American Bar Association.

American Bar Association (ABA). (1980). *Standards relating to the prosecution function: ABA standards for criminal justice* (Vol. 1). (2nd ed.). Boston: Little, Brown.

American Bar Association (ABA). (1993). *ABA standards for criminal justice. Prosecution function and defense function.* Washington, DC: American Bar Association.

American Prosecutors Research Institute (APRI). (1995a). *Community prosecution: A guide for prosecutors.* Alexandria, VA: American Prosecutors Research Institute.

American Prosecutors Research Institute (APRI). (1995b). *Community prosecution implementation manual.* Alexandria, VA: American Prosecutors Research Institute.

American Prosecutors Research Institute (APRI). (2004). *Unwelcome guests: A community prosecution approach to street-level drug dealing and prostitution.* Alexandria, VA: American Prosecutors Research Institute.

Andrews, K. R. (1980). *The concept of corporate strategy.* Homewood, IL: Richard D. Irwin.

Bazemore,G. (1998). *Evaluating community youth sanctioning models: Neighborhood dimensions and beyond.* Research Forum. Crime and Place: Plenary Paper, 1997 Conference on Criminal Justice Research and Evaluation. Washington, DC: National Institute of Justice.

Berman, G., & Feinblatt, J. (2005). *Good courts: The case for problem-solving justice.* New York: The New Press.

Blakey, G. R., Goldstock, R., & Rogovin, C. H. (1978). *Rackets bureaus: Investigation and prosecution of organized crime.* Washington, DC: U.S. Government Printing Office.

Boland, B. (1996, August). What is community prosecution? *National Institute of Justice Journal, 231,* 35–40.

Boland, B. (1998). Community prosecution: Portland's experience. In D. R. Karp (Ed.), *Community justice: An emerging field* (pp. 253–277). Lanham, MD: Rowman & Littlefield.

Boland, B. (1999). *Community prosecution in Washington, DC: The U.S. Attorney's fifth district pilot project* (Grant No. 97-IJ-CX-0058). Washington, DC: National Institute of Justice.

Boland, B., & Healey, K. M. (1993). *Prosecutorial response to heavy drug caseload: Comprehensive problem-reduction strategies.* Washington, DC: National Institute of Justice.

Braga, A. A., Kennedy, D. M, Waring, E., & Piehl, A. M. (2001). Problem-oriented policing, deterrence, and youth violence: An evaluation of Boston's Operation Ceasefire. *Journal of Research in Crime and Delinquency, 38,* 195–225.

Buntin, J. (1998). *A community responds: Boston confronts an upsurge of youth violence.* Cambridge, MA: Harvard University, John F. Kennedy School of Government Case Program.

Clarke, C. (2001). Problem-solving defenders in the community: Expanding the conceptual and institutional boundaries of providing counsel to the poor. *Georgetown Journal of Legal Ethics, 14,* 401–458.

Clear, T. R., & Corbett, R. P., Jr. (1998). *The community corrections of place.* Crime and Place: Plenary Papers, 1997 Conference on Criminal Justice Research and Evaluation. Washington, DC: National Institute of Justice.

Clear, T. R., & Karp, D. R. (1998). The community justice movement. In D. R. Karp (Ed.). *Community justice: An emerging field* (pp. 3–28). Lanham, MD: Rowman and Littlefield.

Coles, C. M. (2002a). *City attorneys and corporation counsel: The original community prosecutors and problem solvers.* Criminal Justice Working Paper No. 02-02-06. Cambridge, MA: Program in Criminal Justice Policy and Management, John F. Kennedy School of Government, Harvard University.

Coles, C. M. (2002b). *Community prosecution: District attorneys, county prosecutors, and attorneys general.* Criminal Justice Working Paper No. 02-02-07. Cambridge, MA: Program in Criminal Justice Policy and Management, John F. Kennedy School of Government, Harvard University.

Coles, C. M., Carney, B., & Johnson, B. (2000). Crime prevention through community prosecution and community policing: Boston's Grove Hall Safe Neighborhood Initiative. In C. Brito & C. & E. Gratto (Eds.), *Problem-oriented policing: Crime-specific problems, critical issues, and making POP work* (Vol. 3) (pp. 55–99). Washington, DC: Police Executive Research Forum.

Coles, C. M., & Kelling, G. (1999, Summer). Prevention through community prosecution. *The Public Interest, 136,* 69–84.

Coles, C. M., & Kelling, G. (2002). New trends in prosecutors' approaches to youthful offenders. In G. Katzmann (Ed.), *Securing our children's future, new approaches to juvenile justice and youth violence* (pp. 28–83). Washington, DC: The Brookings Institution.

Coles, C. M., & Kelling, G., with Moore, M. H. (1998). *Prosecution in the community: A study of emergent strategies. A cross site analysis* (Grant No. 95-IJ-CX-0096). Washington, DC: National Institute of Justice. Case Studies (Appendices): A (Austin); B (Boston); C Indianapolis); D (Kansas City, Missouri). Available at http://www.ksg.harvard.edu/criminaljustice/publications/cross-site.pdf.

Dawson, J. M., Smith, S. K., & DeFrances, C. J. (1992). *Prosecutors in state courts, 1990.* Washington, DC: Bureau of Justice Statistics.

DeFrances, C. J. (2001). *State court prosecutors in large districts, 2001.* Washington, DC: Bureau of Justice Statistics.

DeFrances, C. J. (2002). *Prosecutors in state courts, 2001.* Washington, DC: Bureau of Justice Statistics.

DeFrances, C. J. (2003). *State court prosecutors in small districts, 2001.* Washington, DC: Bureau of Justice Statistics.

DeFrances, C. J., Smith, S. K., & van der Does, L. (1996). *Prosecutors in state courts, 1994.* Washington, DC: Bureau of Justice Statistics.

DeFrances, C. J., & Steadman, G. W. (1998). *Prosecutors in state courts, 1996.* Washington, DC: Bureau of Justice Statistics.

Eck, J. E., & Spelman, W. (1998). Problem solving; Problem-oriented policing in Newport News. In G. Alpert & G. & A. Piquero (Eds.), *Community policing* (pp. 63–77). Prospect Heights, IL: Waveland Press.

Eisenstein, J., Flemming, R. B., & Nardulli, P. F. (1988). *The contours of justice: Communities and their courts.* Boston: Little, Brown.

Eisenstein, J., & Jacob, H. (1977). *Felony justice.* Boston: Little, Brown.

Finn, P. et al., & Abt Associates. (1999). *Jackson County, Missouri, COMmunity-Backed Anti-Drug Tax (COMBAT) evaluation* (NIJ Grant #91-IJ-CX-0091). National Institute of Justice & Ewing Marion Kauffman Foundation. Washington, DC: NIJ.

Flemming, R. B. (1990). The political styles and organizational strategies of American prosecutors: Examples from nine courthouse communities. *Law and Society Review, 12,* 25–50.

Flemming, R. B., Nardulli, P. F., & Eisenstein, J. (1992). *The craft of justice: Politics and work in criminal court communities.* Philadelphia: University of Pennsylvania Press.

Forst, B. (1993). The prosecutor and the public. In B. Forst (Ed.), *The socio-economics of crime and justice* (pp. 291–302). Armonk, NY: M. E. Sharpe.

Forst, B. (2000, Spring). Prosecution's coming of age. *Justice Research and Policy, 2(1),* 21–46.

Goldkamp, J. S., Irons-Guynn, C., & Weiland, D. (2002). *Community prosecution strategies: Measuring impact.* Bulletin. Washington, DC: Bureau of Justice Assistance.

Goldstein, H. (1979). Improving policing: A problem-oriented approach. *Crime and Delinquency, 25,* 236–258.

Goldstein, H. (1990). *Problem-oriented policing.* New York: McGraw-Hill.

Goldstock, R. (1992, Fall). The prosecutor as problem solver. *Criminal Justice, 7,* 3–9, 48–49.

Harp, C., Kuykendall, M., Cunningham, C., & Ware, T. (2004). *Juvenile delinquency and community prosecution: New strategies for old problems.* Alexandria, VA: American Prosecutors Research Institute.

Hynes, C. J. (1993). The urban criminal justice system can be fair. *Fordham Urban Law Journal, 20,* 419–430.

Illinois Association for Criminal Justice. (1929). *The Illinois crime survey.* Montclair, NJ: Patterson Smith.

Jacoby, J. E. (1976). *Pre-trial screening in perspective.* Washington, DC: Law Enforcement Assistance Administration, National Institute of Law Enforcement and Criminal Justice.

Jacoby, J. E. (1977). *The prosecutor's charging decision: A policy perspective.* Washington, DC: Law Enforcement Assistance Administration, National Institute of Law Enforcement and Criminal Justice.

Jacoby, J. E. (1980). *The American prosecutor: A search for identity.* Lexington, MA: Lexington Books, D. C. Heath.

Jacoby, J. E. (1995). Pushing the envelope—leadership in prosecution. *The Justice System Journal, 17(3),* 291–307.

Jacoby, J. E. (1997a, May–June). The American prosecutor in historical context. *The Prosecutor,* 33–38.

Jacoby, J. E. (1997b, July–August). The emergence of local prosecutors. *The Prosecutor,* 25–30.

Jacoby, J. E., Mellon, L. R., Ratledge, E. C., & Turner, S. H. (1981). *Prosecutorial decision making: A national study.* Washington, DC: National Institute of Justice.

Jacoby, J. E., Mellon, L. R., & Smith, W. F. (1982). *Policy and prosecution.* Washington, DC: National Institute of Justice.

Jacoby, J. E., Mellon, L. R., Turner, S. H., & Ratledge, E. C. (1982). *The standard case set. A tool for criminal justice decision makers.* Washington, DC: National Institute of Justice.

Kelling, G. L., & Coles, C. M. (1996). *Fixing broken windows: Restoring order in American cities.* New York: Martin Kessler Books/Free Press.

Kelling, G. L., & Moore, M. H. (1988, November). *The evolving strategy of policing* (Perspectives on Policing, 4). Cambridge, MA: National Institute of Justice & Program in Criminal Justice Policy and Management, John F. Kennedy School of Government, Harvard University.

Kennedy, D. M. (1997). Pulling levers: Chronic offenders, high-crime settings, and a theory of prevention. *Valparaiso Law Review, 31(2),* 449–483.

Kress, J. M. (1976, January). Progress and prosecution. *Annals of the American Academy of Political and Social Sciences, 423,* 99–116.

Kuhn, T. (1970). *The structure of scientific revolutions* (2nd ed.). Chicago: University of Chicago Press.

LaFave, W. R. (1970). The prosecutor's discretion in the United States. *American Journal of Comparative Law, 18*, 532–548.

Liddle, M., & Gelsthorpe, L. (1994). *Crime prevention and inter-agency cooperation* (Crime Prevention Unit Series Paper 53). London: Home Office Police Research Group.

McDonald, W. F. (1979). The prosecutor's domain. In W. F. McDonald (Ed.), *The prosecutor* (pp. 15–51). Beverly Hills, CA: Sage Publications.

McDonald, W. F. (1985). *Plea bargaining: Critical issues and common practice.* Washington, DC: National Institute of Justice.

Miles, R. E., & Snow, C. C. (1977). *Organizational strategy, structure, and process.* New York: McGraw-Hill.

Miller, F. W. (1969). *Prosecution: The decision to charge a suspect with a crime.* Boston: Little, Brown.

Mills, G. (1996). *Community Backed Anti-Drug Tax: COMBAT in Jackson County, Missouri.* Program Focus. Washington, DC: National Institute of Justice.

Missouri Association for Criminal Justice. (1926). *Missouri crime survey.* New York: Macmillan.

Moley, R. (1974). *Politics and criminal prosecution.* New York: Arno Press.

Moore, M. H. (1998). Problem solving and community policing. In B. Alpert & A. Piquero (Eds.), *Community policing* (pp. 327–375). Prospect Heights, IL: Waveland Press.

Nardulli, P. F., Eisenstein, J., & Flemming, R. B. (1988). *The tenor of justice. Criminal courts and the guilty plea process.* Urbana: University of Illinois Press.

National Association of Attorneys General (NAAG). (1974). *The prosecution function: Local prosecutors and the attorney general.* Raleigh, NC.

National District Attorneys Association (NDAA). (1973). *The prosecutor's screening function: Case evaluation and control.* National Center for Prosecution Management.

National District Attorneys Association (NDAA). (1976). *National prosecution standards* (1st ed.). Chicago.

Nugent, M. E. (2004a). *The changing nature of prosecution: Community prosecution vs. traditional prosecution approaches.* Alexandria, VA: APRI.

Nugent, M. E. (2004b). *What does it mean to practice community prosecution? Organizational, functional, and philosophical changes.* Alexandria, VA: APRI.

Pound, R., & Frankfurter, F. (1922). *Criminal justice in Cleveland: Report of the Cleveland Foundation survey of the administration of criminal justice in Cleveland, Ohio.* Cleveland: The Cleveland Foundation.

President's Commission on Law Enforcement and Administration of Justice. (1967a). *The challenge of crime in a free society.* Washington, DC: U.S. Government Printing Office.

President's Commission on Law Enforcement and Administration of Justice. (1967b). *Task force report: The courts.* Washington, DC: U.S. Government Printing Office.

President's Commission on Law Enforcement and Administration of Justice. (1967c). *Task force report: The police.* Washington, DC: U.S. Government Printing Office.

Remington, F. J. (1993). The decision to charge, the decision to convict on a plea of guilty, and the impact of sentence structure on prosecution practices. In L. E. Ohlin & F. J. Remington (Eds.), *Discretion in criminal justice* (pp. 73–133). Albany: State University of New York Press.

Remington, F. J., & Logan, W. A. (1991). Frank Miller and the decision to prosecute. *Washington University Law Quarterly, 69(1),* 159.

Skogan, W. G. (1990). *Disorder and decline: Crime and the spiral of decay in American neighborhoods.* New York: Free Press.

Smalley, S. (2005, October 5). Police struggle with shrinking force, resources. *Boston Globe.* Retrieved May 26, 2006, from http://www.boston.com/news/specials/menino_record/police_struggle_with_shrinking_force_resources/.

Sviridoff, M., Rottman, D., Ostrum, B., & Curtis, R. (2000). *Dispensing justice locally: The implementation and effects of the Midtown Community Court.* Amsterdam: Harwood Academic Publishers.

Thompson, A. C. (2002). It takes a community to prosecute. *Notre Dame Law Review, 77(2),* 321–372.

Tumin, Z. (1990). *Summary of proceedings: Findings and discoveries of the Harvard University executive session for state and local prosecutors at the John F. Kennedy School of Government, 1986–1990.* Cambridge, MA: Harvard University Press.

U.S. National Commission on Law Observance and Enforcement (Wickersham Commission). (1931). *Report on prosecution.* Washington, DC: U.S. Government Printing Office.

Walker, S. (1992, March). Origins of the contemporary criminal justice paradigm: The American Bar Foundation Survey, 1953–1969. *Justice Quarterly, 9, 1,* 47–76.

Walker, S. (1993). *Taming the system: The control of discretion in criminal justice, 1950–1990.* New York: Oxford University Press.

Wilson, J. Q., & Kelling, G. L. (1982, March). Police and neighborhood safety: Broken windows. *The Atlantic Monthly,* 29–38.

Wolf, R. V., & Worrall, J. L. (2004). *Lessons from the field: Ten community prosecution leadership profiles.* Alexandria, VA: APRI and Center for Court Innovation.

Chapter Ten

Community Prosecution

Rhetoric or Reality?

M. ELAINE NUGENT-BORAKOVE
and PATRICIA L. FANFLIK

Introduction

In the late 1980s and early 1990s, a few pioneering prosecutors' offices in Manhattan, New York, Portland, Oregon, Kings County, New York, and Montgomery County, Maryland, implemented a new community-oriented approach to crime known as community prosecution (for more information on the chronology of community prosecution, see Goldkamp, Irons-Guynn, & Weiland, 2002). In Portland, prosecutors were deployed into the neighborhood in response to concerns about quality-of-life crimes in the business district (Boland, 1998). Kings County, New York, and Montgomery County, Maryland, reorganized their offices to have prosecutors assigned to cases by geographic areas, allowing them to build relationships with their communities (Goldkamp et al., 2002).

The idea behind community prosecution was that prosecutors could use the legal resources of the office to help address neighborhood crime and public nuisance issues, departing from the more traditional methods of prosecution to a more integrated solutions-based approach to eradicate crime. The community prosecution approach brings prosecutors together with residents to identify quality-of-life issues (such as graffiti, vandalism, trespassing, prostitution, drug solicitation, aggressive panhandling, etc.) in an attempt to develop long-term strategies to address community concerns (Coles, 2000).

By 2001, community prosecution had taken hold in offices of all sizes, not just large urban offices. In fact, in 1990, only a handful of offices (approximately 1%) were known to practice community prosecution. By 2001, the number of offices engaged in community prosecution increased to nearly half (Nugent & Rainville, 2001).

This phenomenon has been called a paradigm shift—a significant change in the way prosecutors do business (Boland, in press; Coles & Kelling, 1998). Some have argued, in fact, that community prosecution is a "redefinition of the prosecutor's role in crime prevention, crime control, and the maintenance of public order" (Heymann & Petrie, 2001, p. 27). With so many offices practicing community prosecution, at least in part, it would seem that it is indeed a new evolution for local prosecution. Some researchers contend that community prosecution is not necessarily a paradigm shift but rather a natural and logical extension of the prosecutor's work (Roth, Gaffigan, Koper, Moore, Roehl et al., 2000, as cited in Heymann & Petrie, 2001). Still others raise significant questions about the appropriateness of a community prosecution focus (Clear & Karp, 1998; Forst, 2000). However, much of the research in support of a paradigm shift has been largely qualitative (Boland, 2001, 1998; Coles & Kelling, 1998; Gramckow, 1997).

Whether or not there is a paradigm shift, the question of why prosecutors have moved in this direction is important. Is it an attempt on the part of prosecutors to build on the successes of community policing, or is it an attempt to build system capacity for crime control or fill the gaps left by failed social institutions to address the root causes of crime and disorder (Tumin, 1990)? It also is possible that community prosecution represents a realization on the part of prosecutors that crime prevention is a legitimate and necessary goal of their work, and that they are in a unique position to form partnerships toward these ends (Jacoby, 1995). Perhaps the movement toward community prosecution represents nothing more than an attempt to gain political capital (Forst, 2000). This chapter attempts to answer these questions to determine whether community prosecution is a reality or just rhetoric by examining the elements of community prosecution, its implementation, how it differs from traditional prosecution, and evidence of whether or not community prosecution is a new, and lasting, approach to crime control.

Elements of Community Prosecution

Community prosecution has generally been described as a grassroots approach to justice, involving citizens, law enforcement, and other government agencies in problem-solving efforts to address the safety concerns of the local jurisdiction (Boland, 1998). Early research emphasized how community prosecution differed from traditional prosecution because of its focus on community involvement in identifying crime and related problems, and in the formulation of solutions (Gramckow, 1997). As initially conceptualized, six operational elements were at the core of community prosecution:

1. an integrated approach to crime involving both reactive (e.g., prosecuting crimes identified by the police) and proactive strategies (e.g., anticipatory actions aimed at addressing problems at their root cause *will be both reactive and proactive.*
2. a clearly defined geographic target area
3. an emphasis on problem solving, public safety, and quality-of-life issues
4. partnerships between the prosecutor, the community, law enforcement, and others to address crime and disorder
5. use of varied enforcement methods (i.e., use of tools other than criminal prosecution to address problems)
6. use of long-term strategies to address problems at their source (American Prosecutors Research Institute, 1995) *proactive needs long-term strategies.*

Goldkamp et al. (2002) further operationalized seven dimensions of community prosecution strategies to include the problem(s) targeted, the type of target area, the role of the community in the strategy, the type of response to community problems, organizational adaptations in the prosecutor's office, case processing adaptations, and interagency collaboration. A census of prosecutors conducted by the American Prosecutors Research Institute was designed to empirically test the various dimensions of community prosecution and compare the differences between those offices claiming to practice community prosecution and those claiming to have a traditional prosecution approach.

The study found that, in fact, there are only three defining elements of community prosecution: (1) partnerships with a variety of government agencies and community-based groups, (2) use of varied enforcement methods, including problem-solving techniques to address crime and public safety issues, and (3) community involvement (Nugent, Fanflik, & Bromirski, 2004). These elements are interesting in that they suggest real change in prosecutors' offices and their focus. In fact, although "traditional" offices also reported partnerships with a variety of agencies, use of varied enforcement methods, and community involvement, their application of these elements is qualitatively and statistically different than community prosecution offices. Community prosecution offices were, on average,

1. almost five times more likely than traditional offices to form partnerships with community groups
2. three times more likely to partner with private organizations, special interest groups, housing authorities, and health organizations

2x 3. nearly two times more likely to create partnerships with school groups, advocacy groups, youth service organizations, and businesses

3x 4. three or more times as likely to meet with other government agencies and community members to develop solutions to problems, to meet with residents to discuss public safety concerns, and to assign nonattorney personnel to work with communities

9x 5. almost nine times more likely to view the community as a partner in the identification of public safety problems and formulation of solutions as opposed to simply the recipient and beneficiary of prosecutorial efforts (Nugent et al., 2004)

The results of this census of prosecutors on the differences between community prosecution and traditional prosecution further showed that community prosecution offices were statistically more likely to view their roles as somewhat different from those offices that did not embrace these three elements. Although both community prosecutors and traditional prosecutors felt prosecuting crimes was their primary role, community prosecutors were more likely to rank crime prevention and crime reduction as secondary roles, whereas traditional prosecutors ranked punishing criminals as a secondary role (Nugent et al., 2004).

The research is clear in its distinction between community prosecution and traditional prosecution in terms of focus. What is less clear, however, is the extent to which these distinctions actually influence practices in prosecutors' offices.

Continuum of Implementation

If community prosecution represents more than a passing fad fueled by the availability of significant government grant funds, then there must be discernible changes in how prosecutors approach their day-to-day activities. Nugent (2004) proposed a continuum of implementation that tracked community prosecution through three phases: (1) the program phase, (2) the strategy phase, and (3) the philosophical phase. As shown in Figure 10.1, under each phase different "models" are practiced, moving progressively over time to the final phase, during which a "full" community prosecution model is practiced.

Based on survey results and case study data, the program phase is most prevalent in years 0 through 2, the strategy phase in years 3 to 5, and the philosophical phase in year 6 and beyond. The program phase consists of the initial implementation of community prosecution. In the first 2 years of implementation, the practice of community prosecution is generally limited to a few staff members, who may occasionally meet with community members in

Community Prosecution Program	Prosecution Strategy	Philosophical Change in Prosecution
Initial Implementation	Intermediate Implementation	Full Implementation
Program Elements *(Initial Implementation)*	*Strategy Elements* *(Intermediate Implementation)*	*Philosophy Elements* *(Full Implementation)*
• Specific personnel assignment • Single geographic location • Attendance at community meetings • Outreach to community • Problem identification • Traditional responses • Limited nontraditional responses • Grant funded • Community prosecution in addition to regular caseload	• Creation of unit • Multiple locations • Written guidelines/job descriptions • Establishment of partnerships • Supplemental/matching funding secured • Involvement in non-CP cases • Trained personnel • Ongoing dialogue with communities • Use of nontraditional responses in conjunction with traditional responses	• Office-wide utilization of community prosecution • Organizational changes • Policy/procedural changes • Incorporated into operating budget • Recruitment changes • Ongoing monitoring • Institutionalized relationships with citizenry • Established network of agencies for addressing problems • Community involvement in prioritization of resources and case dispositions

FIGURE 10.1

The Community Prosecution Continuum of Implementation

addition to handling their "traditional" case processing assignments. The partnerships formed with the community tend to be more informational in nature and not collaborative. Although there may be some development of problem-solving activities, the activities are more likely to be more "traditional" in nature (i.e., the creation of diversion programs).

Once offices reach the strategy phase (years 3 to 5), community prosecution becomes more robust and systematic. Assigned personnel may now work in specialized units, have fewer traditional case processing responsibilities, have increased authority to exercise their own discretion in formulating solutions to problems, and work more closely with community groups and various agencies to identify problems, establish priorities, and develop solutions to identified problems. In addition, at this stage, management and policy issues begin to take shape, such as the creation of flexible work schedules, community prosecutor performance assessment, and number and type of cases for which community prosecutors are responsible.

The final stage, the philosophical stage (generally years 6 and beyond), represents the full shift from a traditional case processing model to a community-oriented model. The full implementation of community prosecution is characterized by significant organizational, managerial, and cultural changes. Changes in written policies and procedures, recruitment and staff performance evaluations, promotional paths, and case processing are common. Priorities for the office are established with input from the community and other partners in the community prosecution effort, and targeted efforts in specific neighborhoods tend to spread over the entire jurisdiction. While traditional case processing remains critical to the organization, prosecutors are more connected to the community in terms of the impact of the crime(s) and more informed about interrelated community problems. In addition, financial support for community prosecution tends to be institutionalized with multiple sources of support, not just a single grant.

Based on recent case study research focusing on several large offices with population sizes ranging from 1.3 million to more than 5 million, there is some empirical evidence to suggest that a handful of offices (San Diego, California; West Palm Beach, Florida; Chicago, Illinois; Indianapolis, Indiana; Detroit, Michigan; Dallas, Texas; and Seattle, Washington) are making a philosophical shift from traditional prosecution to a more holistic, community-oriented approach to crime (Fanflik, Budzilowicz, & Nugent-Borakove, in press). From the case study information, there were discernable changes in how prosecutors approach day-to-day activities and case processing. For example, in some of the offices studied, community prosecutors were frequently called upon to assist in case processing when a case required detailed information regarding the community. Typically, office prosecutors relied on the community prosecutor to assist in drug and gang-related cases, as community prosecutors can add pivotal information relating to gang associates, drug dealers, and problematic properties in the community. Additionally, in these offices, community prosecutors had strong ties to police departments in their communities and acted as liaisons between the police and the prosecutors' offices. In these instances, community prosecutors provided case intelligence that would otherwise be unknown to the office. Information sharing in regard to the community resulted in a more integrated, cohesive relationship with office prosecutors and the community prosecutor.

Funding for a community prosecutor is another example of how these offices have fully integrated community prosecution. In the offices examined, community prosecution was treated as a necessary and vital component in the office. As such, community prosecution positions were included as part of an office's annual budget. Most offices had all or some part of their community prosecution unit and corresponding activities funded through the internal budget.

Organizational Structure

The change in emphasis from case processing to problem solving almost inevitably requires a change in the organizational structure of the prosecutor's office (Goldstock, 1992). To facilitate the implementation of community prosecution, prosecutors' offices have adopted a variety of organizational structures driven in part by the size of the office and the availability of resources but also by the phase of implementation (Goldkamp et al., 2002; Nugent, 2004). As defined in the continuum, changes in the organizational structure generally do not occur before the third year. Based on preliminary conceptualizations of community prosecution, which seem to have remained constant throughout its evolution, and early case study work, there are three distinct organizational compositions for community prosecution: (1) individual, (2) specialized unit, and (3) decentralized (Boland, 2001, 1998; Nugent, 2004; Coles, 2000; Coles & Kelling, 1998).

In keeping with the proposed continuum, in its infancy community prosecution programs tend to have individuals assigned to community-related activities, whereas in the latter years, specialized units, consisting of both attorneys and nonattorney staff, are the norm. In its fullest implementation (the philosophical stage), ideally community prosecution would spread from a specialized unit to the entire office. Although not yet fully studied, the handful of offices that have been practicing community prosecution for more than 6 years appear to be moving toward a more decentralized structure, or at a minimum, increasing the number of staff assigned to community prosecution (Nugent, 2004; Fanflik et al., in press).

Management of Community Prosecution

The experiences of the most well-developed community prosecution initiatives indicate that traditional prosecution management strategies are not necessarily applicable in a community prosecution setting and in fact pose a number of challenges for the chief prosecutor and/or supervisory staff:

Examples:

1. how to recruit and retain attorneys with community-based, problem-solving skills
2. how to supervise community-based staff
3. how to evaluate the performance of community prosecution and community prosecution staff
4. how to avoid potential ethical issues

In addition to allowing community prosecutors discretionary authority to problem solve, there must be uniformity and consistency across all areas of community prosecution (Gramckow, 1997). Despite the obvious importance of community prosecution management, it remains largely unexamined on an empirical level, with the exception of qualitative case study research (Fanflik et al., in press).

Traditionally, the management of a prosecution office focuses on case processing. Should full implementation occur under a community prosecution model, where case processing is less of a focus for individuals, specialized units, or office-wide, the emphasis shifts to the recruitment and retention of community-oriented personnel, training, supervision of noncase-related activities, and performance assessment.

Perhaps one of the greatest lessons learned in community prosecution, and one of the most significant challenges, is addressing staffing issues of recruitment and retention. As public servants, young prosecutors often face huge law school debt and low salaries, making recruitment difficult for local prosecutors (National District Attorneys Association, 2006). To further confound the issue, community prosecution requires a community-oriented person, not necessarily a litigator (Wolf & Worrall, 2004). Law schools do not train attorneys to be community-based problem solvers. Time and again, interviews conducted by Wolf and Worrall (2004) with leaders in the field of community prosecution revealed the need to train staff to be community prosecutors.

To address training needs, some offices practicing community prosecution now require a community prosecution rotation during which new prosecutors spend time in the community to learn the basic principles of community prosecution. This strategy also has been modified to include the entire office. In this case, the community prosecutor spends a predetermined amount of time in the community and then rotates back to the main office. However, before doing so, she or he is "shadowed" by the next prosecutor, so that some continuity within the community can be achieved. This strategy allows the entire office to be trained in community prosecution.

Offices experienced in community prosecution also have implemented recruitment standards that focus on candidates' commitment to and experience in problem solving and working in community-oriented initiatives (Coles & Kelling, 1998). Some offices have opted to place more seasoned prosecutors into the community (Boland, 1998), whereas others recruit personnel outside of the legal profession to handle community-related activities (Coles & Kelling, 1998). Where community prosecution is fully implemented, the office as a whole recognizes the importance of a community-based response to crime, so for these offices recruitment from within the office is not difficult. Although this has made recruitment somewhat easier, finding a prosecutor with personal characteristics suited for community prosecution is still problematic. As a result, some offices have tailored their recruiting styles to focus specifically on personnel from within the main office so that personal characteristics have already been evaluated.

Community prosecutors often are given the authority to exercise their own discretion in solving problems, which creates the potential for a number of management problems. First, as suggested by Gramckow (1997), the potential exists for inconsistency in problem solving resulting in different qualities of service being provided to communities. To resolve this issue, some offices opt for regular reporting to supervisors of complaints received, actions taken, level of effort, and outcomes. Others turn problem solving into actual programs, such as drug dealer evictions or prostitution red zones, to ensure consistency.

Second, community-based prosecutors must be accountable to the communities they serve and also must be held accountable for their performance. Part of the difficulty with measuring performance to ensure accountability to the public is the lack of tested performance measures in community prosecution. Because of the unique nature of the problems facing communities, it is long been believed by communities prosecutors that there cannot be a single set of measures that can be applied universally. However, if one considers the overall intent of community prosecution (i.e., to reduce crime, to hold violent and low-level offenders accountable, etc.), then a set of measures can be defined and applied.[1]

At the individual level, performance assessments that traditionally focused on case processing do not allow for the supervision and evaluation of how well community prosecutors perform. The more experienced community prosecution offices have attempted to redesign personnel performance assessments to account for the different assignments and intended outcomes required of community prosecutors. Some offices have community leaders participate in the evaluation process by filling out an evaluation form or survey that will be used in conjunction with the manager's evaluation (Fanflik et al., in press). Offices that are closely linked to the community can get direct feedback on a community prosecutor's performance. In addition, some offices evaluate performance based on the number of meetings, presentations, and contacts in the community. The quality and extent of the professional relationships developed in the community also are examined. Interestingly, for some offices, managers have developed strategies to retain, supervise, and evaluate prosecutors that mirror the basic components of community prosecution. As community involvement is a defining element of community prosecution, many management strategies also include the community.

Taking prosecutors out of their traditional domain (i.e., the courtroom) and placing them in direct and daily contact with community members and other government agencies can raise a number of ethical issues, of which management must be cognizant and prepared to address:

1. Impartiality: Community prosecutors must remain impartial in addressing the problems of communities.
2. Treating similarly situated defendants similarly: Defendants identified through community prosecution efforts must not be singled out for disproportionate treatment—coercive force must be applied uniformly.
3. Due process: Information collected by community prosecutors that is used for criminal prosecution may face legal challenges related to *Miranda*, when custody begins, and permissible investigative tactics.
4. Immunity: Prosecutors do not have absolute immunity from civil actions when acting beyond the scope of their traditional responsibilities, and as a result of their relationships with community members, prosecutors must be mindful not to provide legal advice to private parties about civil matters.
5. Displacement: Problem solving in targeted areas often results in the problem moving from the target location to another location, and community prosecutors must be ready to respond to citizens' requests for assistance from these other locations.
6. Abuse of prosecutorial resources: Community prosecutors must limit their use of problem solving to conditions of disorder and criminal acts and not be tempted to become involved in neighborhood disputes.
7. Political pandering: The goal of community prosecution must remain focused on addressing neighborhood problems that prosecutors are legally permitted to address, and not to increase the visibility of the office for political purposes. (Kuykendall, 2004)

To overcome or, at a minimum, to guard against potential ethical issues, managers in community prosecution offices incorporate ethics discussions into training programs and monitor the activities of community prosecutors. In addition, managerial decisions regarding geographic coverage and the line prosecutors' ability to respond to the entire array of disorder and crime in the jurisdiction can help protect the office from ethics claims.

Functional Changes

One of the main features of community prosecution is that it takes prosecutors out of the courtroom and into the community to use nontraditional methods to deal with crime and public safety issues. However, like most community justice initiatives, a one-size-fits-all approach, simply is not possible. Community prosecution may look very different from one community to another. Part of the argument against the one-size-fits-all model is that the activities of community prosecutors are driven by the unique problems facing the communities they serve. However, despite the types of problems the community and community prosecutors are working to resolve, the fact remains that the overall approach is the same:

1. Community prosecution offices all work in partnership with community members and groups, other government agencies, and law enforcement.
2. Community prosecution offices all employ some form of nontraditional enforcement techniques to address community problems.

The question is: "Do the functional changes that occur with community prosecution drastically change the role of the prosecutor?" Forst (2000) asserts that the implementation of community prosecution may take away valuable resources from the prosecution of violent offenders. Empirical studies, to date, have not supported this criticism. Coles and Kelling (1998) found that one of the main functional changes that occurs is a refinement of the core capabilities to enhance the prosecution of violent and repeat offenders. This refinement of prosecutorial capabilities is a direct outgrowth of partnerships with government and community groups; the adoption of both traditional and nontraditional enforcement methods, such as saturation arrest, prioritization of cases based on community input, use of civil remedies such as drug dealer eviction programs, and nuisance abatement strategies; and a more educated juror pool (Nugent, 2004).

Moreover, prosecutors themselves report that despite the community focus, the prosecution of criminals remains a central function of the office (Nugent et al., 2004). Although some larger offices with available resources have opted to place dedicated attorneys in the community and to not allow them to carry a caseload, other offices may have community prosecutors vertically prosecute cases that come from their assigned neighborhood (Goldkamp et al.,

2002). Community prosecutors that do carry caseloads handle a variety of cases; in fact, 80% of offices report that prosecutors assigned to community-related activities handled drug cases, violent crimes (65%), juvenile crimes (63%), property crimes (62%), and public-order crimes (46%) (DeFrances, 2002). Thus the notion that community prosecution takes away valuable resources from the prosecution of violent offenders does not appear to have merit.

Community Prosecution Tenets in Practice

Most of the research on community prosecution consistently indicates that under community prosecution, the goals of prosecution change to include preventing and reducing disorder and crime, restoring victims and communities, and empowering citizens (Coles & Kelling, 1998). Comparisons of prosecutors' responses to different types of crime problems and the driving force behind the response do not demonstrate that the goals have changed dramatically. In fact, both traditional office and community prosecution offices report that prosecuting crimes is the number one priority for their offices, and that the most important outcomes of their responses are the prevention of future crime and improved quality of life for community members (Nugent et al., 2004).

The key difference between community prosecution offices and traditional offices is that while they may support the same goal, the strategies employed differ. In addition, community prosecutors have more discretionary power than traditional prosecutors to identify and implement solutions to address crime and disorder. Community prosecutors generally work more closely with communities to address concerns in addition to the prosecution of both serious and less serious offenses than do traditional offices. Moreover, for certain types of offenses (generally lower-level offenses and quality-of-life crimes), community prosecutors use tools other than criminal prosecution or traditional enforcement methods to address the problem, whereas offices that do not practice community prosecution rely more heavily on increased enforcement.

As community prosecution focuses intensely on community involvement, community prosecutors often use community-based groups to help develop problem-solving approaches to address crimes that do not include traditional enforcement techniques or prosecution. Community prosecutors frequently build partnerships with community leaders, groups, and other non-law enforcement groups and city agencies, such as sanitation, fire, or health departments, to address problematic issues in the neighborhood. Community groups work together with the prosecutor to identify and eradicate troublesome issues. For example, in a large urban community, the community prosecutor, business owners, and local high school administrators worked together to stop students from loitering in front of busy commercial businesses. Business owners were complaining, because customers were unable to enter their businesses unobstructed, due to large groups of students. The students also were observed leaving copious amounts of litter on the sidewalk and storefronts. The community prosecutor worked together with each group to find a solution to the problem. To minimize loitering, business owners organized a fund-raiser to collect money and also donated a proportion of their sales to start an after-school program, while school administrators worked with the county to arrange a facility. As a result of their efforts, students were given an alternative place to come together with friends that did not interfere with downtown businesses. In addition, they were offered an opportunity to volunteer after school in the community for school credit.

Community prosecutors also have used civil code enforcement to address problematic crime issues in the community. Civil laws regarding zoning, housing, and health codes have been employed as an alternative method of enforcement. For example, in one neighborhood, community members complained of an old dilapidated housing structure that was used by drug dealers to distribute drugs. Instead of addressing the problem using traditional enforcement and prosecution, the community prosecutor worked with code enforcement officers to impose housing regulations. The owner of the housing structure was subsequently found in violation of several housing codes. As a result, the owner was given an ultimatum; clean up the property and bring it up to code so that the criminal element will disperse, or face harsher penalties.

Different from traditional prosecution, community prosecutors often adapt their own style of doing business, as traditional methods of enforcement typically are not effective for low-level or quality-of-life offenses. Often, community prosecutors take a bottom-up approach in determining priorities and solutions that involve regular contact with partners and stakeholders but that also require an in-depth understanding of the needs of the community. In order to be successful, community prosecutors must adapt and learn new and innovative methods that fit the needs of a particular community. For this reason, what works in one community may not work in another. Community prosecutors often are faced with a variety of issues requiring prosecutors to think outside of the box in terms of enforcement.

Evidence of a Paradigm Shift

The elements of community prosecution are clearly distinguished from the more traditional case processing model, but does it represent a paradigm shift? One measure is the extent to which community prosecution has taken hold across the country. Prior to 1995, only a handful of offices (10 to 20, or about

1%) had been identified as practicing community prosecution. By 2001, 49% of prosecutors' offices reported practicing community prosecution (Nugent & Rainville, 2001). By 2003, the number of offices either identifying themselves as community prosecution offices or engaging in the practices associated with community prosecution had only increased slightly to 55% which would not necessarily indicate that community prosecution has been embraced fully among all prosecutors.

Nonetheless, among those offices practicing community prosecution, a number of relevant factors can be considered in answering the question of whether or not a paradigm shift has occurred. These factors include:

1. the degree to which experienced offices have progressed along the continuum of implementation
2. budgetary resources in support of community prosecution activities
3. the degree of community involvement
4. a willingness to assess effectiveness and level of accountability to the public
5. motivation for implementing community prosecution

One would expect that if community prosecution represented a paradigm shift, then the most experienced offices would have institutionalized the practices and adopted the community orientation office-wide, as suggested by the continuum of implementation. To date, there is mixed evidence as to the extent of implementation. The most experienced offices, having practiced community prosecution for more than a decade, have institutionalized aspects of community prosecution, but the majority have not achieved office-wide implementation. Consider Multnomah County (Portland), Oregon, thought by many to be the leader in the field of community prosecution. Having implemented community prosecution before it was in vogue, and over time increasing coverage to nearly all parts of the county, one would expect that the practices would become institutionalized and spread throughout the office's practices, which is not the case. In fact, in recent years, faced with a significant decrease in funding, the chief prosecutor began "recalling" the prosecutors from the community and placing them back into a case processing function.

The experience of the Portland District Attorney's Office then raises another issue with regard to whether or not a paradigm shift has occurred, which is the budgetary support for community prosecution. In the 1990s, millions of dollars in federal grant funds were used to spread the implementation of community prosecution. Grants were given to hundreds of prosecutors' offices to plan for and ultimately implement community prosecution. Additional grants were awarded to 10 of the most experienced community prosecution offices (called leadership grants) to allow them to expand their scope and serve as models for prosecutors trying to move toward community prosecution. Interestingly, most of the leadership site implemented community prosecution without the support of federal grant funds. However, for those offices new to community prosecution (i.e., implementing the effort in the late 1990s and early 2000s), the implementation of community prosecution seems to be directly related and more importantly dependent on the availability of grant funds. Much of the focus of training and technical assistance provided to these sites was on securing funding for community prosecution. If community prosecution does indeed represent a new way of doing business, then one would expect that its implementation would not be reliant on limited grant funds but rather incorporated into the overall operational budget for the prosecutor's office.

In terms of the functional elements of community prosecution, the involvement of the community is paramount. Goldkamp et al. (2002) operationalized eight different modes of community involvement, including recipients of prosecutorial services, advisors to the prosecutor's office, core partners in problem-solving efforts, and core participants in the implementation of community prosecution. Because community involvement is a defining element of community prosecution, evidence that a paradigm shift is occurring would include increased community involvement with the prosecutor's office as full partners. Rainville and Nugent (2002) did not initially find support for the notion that prosecutors work more closely with community members under a community prosecution model; however, a subsequent study did find that community prosecutors were significantly more likely to view the community as a partner in their efforts than traditional offices (Nugent et al., 2004). In fact, 90% of community prosecution offices report that community members serve as full partners in the identification and resolution of problems.

One indication that prosecutors are truly undergoing reform is a willingness to rigorously assess the effectiveness of community prosecution and, more importantly, to make the findings available publicly (Forst, 2000). The notion of outcome measurement and performance measurement in community prosecution is one that challenges even the most experienced offices. With the exception of a few outcome evaluations, there is little effort on the part of prosecutors to assess the effectiveness of prosecution. However, as an indication of a paradigm shift, it is important to note that the dearth of rigorous assessment is not a result of prosecutors' unwillingness to critically examine community prosecution but rather a lack of empirically based outcome measures that can be applied in different types of offices.

Forst (2000) maintains that community prosecution has only marginal effects on crime and in fact only offers political advantages to the prosecutor rather than any true benefit to the community. There is little available research that allows for a determination of motivation—most raises it as a question (Rainville & Nugent, 2002). Only self-reported information about factors that influence prosecutors' decisions about how to respond to crime problems is available to help shed light on this issue.

Both "traditional" offices and community prosecution offices tend to point to the same factors as their motivation for a particular response (i.e., to increase feelings of safety, to reduce crime, and to deter future crime). However, community prosecutors were twice as likely to report that their motivation was to gain media attention and to increase the visibility of the office, perhaps to raise awareness of the problem or their response to it, or to build political capital (Nugent et al., 2004).

Anecdotal information from prosecutors' offices indicates that community prosecution is increasingly becoming a topic in prosecutors' election campaigns, raised by opponents. In fact, in the early days of community prosecution, challengers to incumbents criticized community prosecution. It is more common now for challengers to run campaigns based on "more" community prosecution, which would provide some support for the notion that community prosecution is at least in part used to build political support.

Perhaps the single greatest test of a paradigm shift is the extent to which prosecutors have aligned the priorities of the more traditional-based court system and its emphasis on enforcement and punishment with the priorities of the communities served, often focusing on less serious crimes and addressing public nuisances and disorder (Jacoby, 1995).

For community prosecutors, traditional enforcement and punishment efforts are combined with more proactive techniques that act to interrupt or prevent more serious criminal behavior. Intelligence gathered by community prosecutors about the nature of criminal activity in the community and the solid working relationships developed with community members become useful tools in case screening, preparation, and adjudication. Moreover, the work of the community prosecutor can help increase the community's understanding and trust of the criminal justice system, thereby improving traditional enforcement efforts.

The manner and degree that community prosecutors involve the community is in stark contrast to how prosecutors have traditionally done business. Involving the community prior to any criminal activity is fundamentally different, in that community prosecutors act to prevent crime rather than intervening once the crime has already occurred. For instance, typically prosecutors wait for a crime to occur and then are tasked with determining if a case will be charged. In traditional offices, the prosecutor often is reactive to crime issues in the community rather than proactive. In order to be more proactive, community prosecutors involve neighborhood residences in identifying which crime issues are of greatest concern for the community; this is a key difference in their approach. To do this, often community prosecutors will send surveys to community members, interview leaders in the community, or attend neighborhood or town hall meetings to meet residents and garner opinions regarding the crimes community members believe are the most important to address. Community prosecutors have established groups such as crime advisory boards or neighborhood problem-solving coalitions specifically designed to target crime issues in the community. Community prosecutors do not work in isolation to eradicate a particular crime but rather as members of a proactive team.

There also is a movement in community prosecution toward reentry efforts whereby the community prosecutor and neighborhood residences are involved when newly released offenders are returned to the community. Whereas most traditional offices are superficially involved when an offender is released, some community prosecutors are now taking steps to keep communities safe by instituting programs designed to assist newly released offenders. One community prosecutor brings together local, state, and federal law enforcement officers for a monthly, all-day meeting for newly released offenders. This gives released offenders an opportunity to ask questions and also to receive services they may not have otherwise received. This meeting is designed as well to alert an offender to the notion that the community is aware of the offender's presence in the community, and that criminal activity will not be tolerated.

In addition, for community prosecutors, not only are neighborhood residents involved in the front and back end of many crime issues in the community, but a handful of community prosecution programs are implementing community-based courts that include community residents. Typically these courts are designed to hear only low-level juvenile or nuisance crimes. By having community members participate in these courts, residents are fully invested and committed to the process.

Conclusion

Community prosecution clearly represents innovation in the field of prosecution. By implementing community prosecution, prosecutors are adopting a more holistic approach to crime, focusing not only on punishment but also on addressing the social and environmental conditions that lead to crime. However, it is not yet clear that community prosecution represents a paradigm shift.

No state or local prosecutor's office has moved completely beyond the use of specialized units to work collaboratively with communities to solve crime and disorder problems. Nor does it appear that the majority of offices that adopted community prosecution have institutionalized funding to maintain community prosecution efforts (with a few exceptions, such as Marion County [Indianapolis], Indiana, and the City Attorney's Office in Dallas, Texas).

Moreover, comparisons of community prosecution offices to traditional offices do not show a marked difference in their overall priorities and goals as one would expect if this phenomenon represented a paradigm shift. Both types of offices cite case processing and the prosecution of offenders as the primary focus of the office. There are only marginal differences in the relative weight and importance that each places on crime prevention, crime reduction, and punishment.

On the other hand, it does appear that community prosecution is more than just rhetoric. Even those offices that claim not to practice community prosecution report engaging in a number of activities indicative of a community prosecution approach. Moreover, while community prosecutors are more likely to report that gaining media attention and increasing visibility are motivating factors for how they respond to crime and disorder problems, the outcomes of political campaigns and whether or not community prosecution continues to be a focus for those candidates who claim that more needs to be done will help shed light on the real motivation for adopting community prosecution.

The next decade or so will be very telling for the future of community prosecution. Without the support of federal grant funds and with decreasing state and local budgets, prosecutors will be hard pressed to continue problem-solving efforts with empirical evidence of their effectiveness. For many of the large offices that have practiced community prosecution for some time, the focus on community partnerships and problem solving will likely continue at some level. However, based on the current evidence, it does not appear that community prosecution will result in a changed set of goals and objectives for these offices. Moreover, the medium-to-small-size offices that initiated community prosecution with the support of federal funding are likely to disband their efforts and redirect their attention to case processing. In short, community prosecution is not just rhetoric for many offices—it is a real and an important part of their everyday business; it has not yet, however, become a paradigm shift.

Note

1. For more information on performance measures, see "Performance Measures and Accountability," chapter 5 in this book.

References

American Prosecutors Research Institute. (1995). *Community prosecution implementation manual.* Alexandria, VA: American Prosecutors Research Institute.

Boland, B. (1998). Community prosecution: Portland's experience. In D. R. Karp (Ed.), *Community justice: An emerging field* (pp. 253–277). Lanham, MD: Rowman & Littlefield.

Boland, B. (2001). *Community prosecution in Washington, DC: The U.S. Attorney's Fifth District pilot project.* Washington, DC: National Institute of Justice.

Boland, B. (in press). *The effect of Multnomah County district attorneys on crime: 1990–2005.* Alexandria, VA: American Prosecutors Research Institute.

Clear, T., & Karp, D. (1998). The community justice movement. In D. R. Karp (Ed.), *Community justice: An emerging field* (pp. 3–28). Lanham, MD: Rowman & Littlefield.

Coles, C. (2000). *Community prosecution, problem-solving, and public accountability: The evolving strategy of the American prosecutor* (Working Paper No. 00-02-04). Cambridge, MA: Harvard University, J. F. Kennedy School of Government.

Coles, C., & Kelling, G. (1998). *Prosecution in the community: A study of emergent strategies.* Cambridge, MA: Harvard University, J. F. Kennedy School of Government.

DeFrances, C. (2002). *Prosecutors in state courts, 2001.* Washington, DC: National Institute of Justice.

Fanflik, P. L., Budzilowicz, L., & Nugent-Borakove, M. E. (in press). *Management strategies for community prosecution.* Alexandria, VA: American Prosecutors Research Institute.

Forst, B. (2000). Prosecutors discover the community. *Judicature, 84,* 135–141.

Goldkamp, J., Irons-Guynn, C., & Weiland, D. (2002). *Community prosecution strategies: Measuring impact.* Philadelphia, PA: Crime and Justice Research Institute.

Goldstock, R. (1992). The prosecutor as problem-solver. *Criminal Justice, 7,* 3–9, 48–49.

Gramckow, H. (1997). Community prosecution in the United States. *European Journal on Criminal Policy and Research, 5,* 9–26.

Heymann, P., & Petrie, C. (2001). *What's changing in prosecution? Results of a workshop.* Washington, DC: National Academy Press.

Jacoby, J. (1995). Pushing the envelope: Leadership in prosecution. *The Justice System Journal, 17,* 291–307.

Kuykendall, M. (2004). *From the courtroom to the community: Ethics and liability issues for the community prosecutor.* Alexandria, VA: American Prosecutors Research Institute.

National District Attorneys Association. (2006). Law school loans and lawyers in public service. *The Prosecutor, 40,* 6.

Nugent, M. E. (2004). *What does it mean to practice community prosecution? Organizational, functional, and philosophical changes.* Alexandria, VA: American Prosecutors Research Institute.

Nugent, M. E., Fanflik, P. L., & Bromirski, D. (2004). *The changing nature of prosecution: Community prosecution vs. traditional prosecution approaches.* Alexandria, VA: American Prosecutors Research Institute.

Nugent, M. E., & Rainville, G. (2001). The state of community prosecution: Results of a national survey. *The Prosecutor, 35,* 26–28, 30–33.

Rainville, G., & Nugent, M. E. (2002). Community prosecution tenets and practices: The relative mix of "community" and "prosecution." *American Journal of Criminal Justice, 26,* 149–164.

Roth, J. A., Ryan, J. F., Gaffigan, S. J., Koper, C. S., Moore, M. H., Roehl, J. A., et al. (2000). National evaluation of the COPS program—Title I of the 1994 Crime Act. Washington, DC: National Institute of Justice.

Tumin, Z. (1990). *Summary of proceedings: Findings and discoveries of the Harvard University executive session for state and local prosecutors at the John F. Kennedy School of Government, 1986–1990.* Unpublished manuscript, Harvard University, John F. Kennedy School of Government.

Wolf, R. V., & Worrall, J. L. (2004). *Lessons from the field: Ten community prosecution leadership profiles.* Alexandria, VA: American Prosecutors Research Institute.

Chapter Eleven

Prosecutors in
Problem-Solving Courts

JOHN L. WORRALL

Introduction

All mean the same

A profound development is occurring on the American court scene: problem-solving courts (a.k.a., specialized courts, special jurisdiction courts, or boutique courts) are being added in significant numbers (Petrila, 2003). These courts are not unlike traditional limited jurisdiction courts, such as those aimed at traffic violations. They differ, however, in terms of the range of problems they target. Drug courts were among the first problem-solving courts; then came community courts and domestic violence courts. More recently, problem-solving courts have started to address problems ranging from gun violence and drunk driving to homelessness, mental illness, and family matters (Berman, Feinblatt, & Glazer, 2005; Berman & Feinblatt, 2001).

The problem-solving court movement is not just significant because of its focus on specialized justice. Some such courts are redefining the role of criminal courts altogether. Certain problem-solving courts, homeless courts being a prime example, do not adjudicate new offenses, yet they are considered courts. Many problem-solving courts are but one part of a larger collaboration aimed at a specific problem, such as domestic violence. In this sense, they move away from a linear progression of justice, from arrest to prosecution, trial, and sentencing. Some problem-solving courts effectively collapse the otherwise linear progression into something of a one-stop shop. What is more, the actors involved in such courts, especially prosecutors and judges, have assumed nontraditional roles.

The purpose of this chapter is, specifically, to call attention to the role of prosecutors in problem-solving courts. It begins with a short history of the problem-solving court movement. Then it discusses the distinguishing features of problem-solving courts, the role of prosecution in problem-solving courts (compared to traditional courts), and the literature concerned with the effectiveness of problem-solving courts. More generally, this chapter's purpose is to call attention to a significant transformation in criminal justice. The problem-solving court movement is but one example of what this author calls the "amalgamation of justice," the fusion of various steps in the criminal process, justice systems, and professional roles in the name of crime control and prevention.

The Emergence of Problem-Solving Courts

Problem-solving courts—like problem-oriented and community policing—were arguably put into motion by two key forces, Goldstein's (1979) problem-oriented policing article in *Crime and Delinquency* and Wilson and Kelling's (1982) broken windows article in the *Atlantic Monthly*. Other developments in and out of the criminal justice system also were certainly responsible to some extent. Berman and Feinblatt (2001, pp. 5–6) pointed to six "social and historical forces" that "helped set the stage for problem-solving innovation:

(1) breakdowns among the kinds of social and community institutions (including families and churches) that have traditionally addressed problems like addiction, mental illness, quality-of-life crime and domestic violence; (2) the struggles of other government efforts, whether legislative or executive, to address these problems . . . (3) a surge in the nation's incarcerated population and the resulting prison overcrowding . . . (4) trends emphasizing the accountability of public institutions . . . (5) advances in the quality and availability of therapeutic interventions, which have given many within the criminal justice system greater confidence in using certain forms of treatment . . . and (6) shifts in public policies and priorities—for example, the way the "broken windows" theory has alerted perceptions of the importance of low-level crime.

Not long after "problem oriented" and "broken windows" become criminal justice buzzwords, Philadelphia implemented a "Protection from Abuse Court," in which a judge oversaw all of the civil protection orders in one courtroom, and Cook County, Illinois, established a domestic violence calendar in one of its criminal courts. These two projects were largely overshadowed by Dade County's (Florida) drug court that opened in 1989. The court was the first to sentence drug offenders to judicially supervised drug treatment.

In 1991, Alameda County, California, established the second drug court, and shortly thereafter Dade County started a specialized domestic violence court. In 1993, the first community court, the Midtown Community Court, opened in Times Square. The court was among the first to combine punishment and assistance to offenders and victims, focusing largely on minor offenses. In 1994, Congress passed the Violent Crime Control and Law Enforcement Act of 1994, authorizing the attorney general to fund drug courts across the country. By the end of that year, 42 drug courts could be found across the country. The Violence against Women Act also was passed in 1994, providing funding to states and local communities in the name of combating domestic violence and all of its variations.

In 1995, the Drug Courts Program Office was established in the U.S. Justice Department. From 1995 to 2000, it oversaw the creation of more than 275 drug courts. Other problem-solving courts began to emerge around that time. In 1996, Marion County, Indiana, started its Psychiatric Assertive Identification Referral/Response (PAIR) program, what amounted to the nation's first mental health court. In the same year, Brooklyn, New York, started the first domestic violence court that processed felony cases.

By 1997, several states had started drug courts for juveniles. In the same year, Broward County implemented the first court formally called a "mental health court." By 1998, the Drug Courts Program Office reported that nearly 100,000 offenders entered drug treatment as a result of drug court participation. The Hartford Community Court also opened in the same year. In 1999, the Office of Justice Programs, in the U.S. Department of Justice, funded nine "reentry courts." Reentry courts currently assist parolees in reentering the community. Drug courts continued to expand during that time, and in 1999 San Diego implemented the first homeless court, focusing on assistance to the homeless rather than just the traditional adjudication of criminal offenses.

Since 2000, problem-solving courts have experienced continued growth. Drug courts, domestic violence courts, and mental health courts are largely staples on the criminal justice scene. The less prominent courts, such as homeless courts, also are beginning to gain a foothold. San Bernardino, California, is currently working on starting a homeless court. Teen courts, where teens assume the roles of judge and other courtroom actors, with adult supervision, have gained in popularity. Community courts, such as that found in Brooklyn's Red Hook Community Justice Center, also are becoming more common. What makes this progression so interesting is not just the number of problem-solving courts but what they are doing to redefine the role of the court. The following section highlights some of the features of problem-solving courts relative to their traditional criminal counterparts.

Therapeutic Jurisprudence

A distinguishing feature of many problem-solving courts is the practice of so-called "therapeutic jurisprudence," which amounts to seeing law as a helping—as opposed to law enforcement—profession (Stolle, Winick, & Wexler, 2000). It stems from mental health law where, traditionally, there was a focus on the legal rights of mental health patients rather than on their treatment needs. Therapeutic jurisprudence also is concerned with how the law can detrimentally affect social relationships. Law is viewed not as an abstract set of rules but as a social process that influences people.

Therapeutic jurisprudence closely parallels the military's "don't ask, don't tell" policy—as long as recruits do not talk about their sexual orientation, the military is not permitted to ask about it. But this approach to addressing sensitive issues of sexuality may have unanticipated consequences. It could lead gay people to feel that their sexual orientation is a taboo topic, and they may be disinclined to talk about it altogether. This possible "side effect" of justice is what therapeutic jurisprudence is intended to overcome.

The therapeutic jurisprudence approach is routinely relied upon in the domestic violence context, where the focus is on issues of victim safety and offender accountability. Traditionally, if an abuser was arrested, then he or she (usually he) may have retaliated against a partner upon returning home by inflicting additional abuse. Domestic violence courts seek to minimize such harmful outcomes that can result from, for instance, mandatory arrest. In short, ". . . the therapeutic jurisprudence approach focuses on offender accountability and victim safety, and it requires those who are making decisions to consider the potential benefits and consequences of their decisions on those involved" (Fritzler & Simon, 2000, pp. 1–2).

Distinguishing Features of Problem-Solving Courts

The Center for Court Innovation (CCI) has identified six principles and practices that make problem-solving courts different from traditional courts (Berman & Feinblatt, 2001). The first is a focus on case outcomes, as opposed to the process. As one well-known community court judge, who often deals with drug addiction and related problems in her courtroom, has observed ". . . outcomes—not just process and precedents—matter. Protecting the rights of an addicted mother is important. So is protecting her children and getting her off drugs" (Kaye, 1999, p. 13).

Judicial monitoring also separates problem-solving courts from traditional courts. Traditionally, judges hand down sentences and wash their hands of the case. In contrast, problem-solving court judges stay involved in the cases from beginning to end. This is especially true of drug court judges, who closely supervise offenders who participate in treatment. Closely related to judicial monitoring is the third principle, informed decision making. Problem-solving courts rely on on-site staff to keep judges more informed about what is happening in the lives of offenders who come before the courts. In some community courts, for example, on-site caseworkers evaluate defendants' needs so judges can tailor appropriate sentences aimed at achieving meaningful results.

Other problem-solving court principles include collaboration, nontraditional roles, and systemic change. First, problem-solving courts often work with officials from several public and private agencies, many of whom are often stationed in the courthouse. With respect to nontraditional roles, perhaps the most distinguishing feature of problem-solving courts is a movement away from the adversarial system. Instead of having prosecutors and defense attorneys working against each other, some problem-solving courts see extensive cooperation between both parties. Finally, systemic change refers to the lessons that problem-solving courts have learned and to the changes they urge other public agencies to take.

Thinking in terms of collaboration, judicial participation, and citizen involvement, the CCI has described problem-solving courts in this fashion:

> Instead of adversarial sparring, prosecutors and defenders in some problem-solving courts work together to encourage defendants to succeed in drug treatment. Instead of embracing the tradition of judicial isolation, judges in problem-solving courts become actively involved in their communities, meeting with residents and brokering relationships with local service providers. Perhaps most importantly, instead of being passive observers, citizens are welcomed into the process, participating in advisory boards, organizing community service projects, and meeting face to face with offenders to explain the impact of crimes on neighborhoods. (Center for Court Innovation, n.d.)

Prosecution in Problem-Solving versus Traditional Courts

Particularly relevant to this book is the role of prosecutors in problem-solving courts. To the extent that prosecutors charge offenders and represent the state in problem-solving courts, their role does not differ markedly from their role in a traditional court. But when problem-solving courts are viewed as part of a larger movement toward personalized justice and achieving meaningful results for offenders, the prosecutor's role is quite different than it once was. According to the American Prosecutors Research Institute, the prosecutor's role in problem-solving courts specifically, and in community prosecution more generally, consists of six operational elements, including:

(1) A focus on problem-solving, public safety, and quality-of-life issues; (2) inclusion of the community's input into the criminal justice system, including the courtroom (e.g., admission of community impact statements to be considered at sentencing); (3) partnerships with the prosecutor, law enforcement, public and private agencies, and the community; (4) varied prevention, intervention, and enforcement methods (e.g., use of tools other than criminal prosecution to address problems); (5) a clearly defined focus area, which has traditionally been defined as a targeted geographic area; and (6) an integrated approach involving reactive (e.g., prosecuting crimes identified by the police) and proactive strategies (e.g., anticipatory actions aimed at addressing problems at their root cause. (Nugent, 2004, p. 7)

These six elements are not necessarily unique to prosecution in problem-solving courts. For example, partnering can—and does—take place outside of the courtroom. Likewise, approaches that seek to avoid court altogether cannot be considered part of the problem-solving court movement. There remain, however, certain prosecutorial roles in problem-solving courts that differ to a large extent from the traditional prosecution role. The traditional role has been described as consisting of "representing the state in criminal matters, seeking justice, holding offenders accountable, imposing appropriate penal sanctions, reducing crime, ensuring social control, deterring future crime, and rehabilitating offenders" (Nugent, 2004, p. 16). Those roles are of course still critical, but they are increasingly being augmented with "increasing the use of nontraditional civil remedies, introducing specialized units, adopting innovative approaches to prosecution, increasing investigative powers, expanding discretionary powers, and implementing technological and scientific advances" (Nugent, 2004, p. 16).

Of course some of these "nontraditional roles" can find a home outside of the problem-solving court context. For example, scientific advances help prosecutors in *all* courts. What, then, makes prosecution in problem-solving courts different from traditional criminal courts? One answer that many commentators have pointed to is that there is less adversarialism; prosecutors and defense attorneys work together to achieve results. The authors of a study of New York's drug courts describe the process in this way: "Because of the reduced emphasis on litigation, many practitioners describe proceedings in these courts as distinctly less adversarial, with the prosecution and defense working toward the same goal of defendant sobriety" (Knipps & Berman, 2000).

Prosecutors who work in problem-solving courts, especially community courts, routinely handle low-level offenses. Fresh out of law school, most prosecutors have aspirations of trying felony cases. Some regard minor problems, misdemeanors, community disputes, and the like as not interesting. Indeed, given that many prosecutors' offices are strapped for resources, serious felonies are given priority. Problem-solving courts turn much of this thinking on its head. Prosecutors in community courts, such as in Brooklyn's Red Hook Community Justice Center, do nothing more than target low-level problems. In doing so, their goals are not punishment but rather problem solving. Thus community service and other less punitive sanctions are the norm in these courts.

Above all else, prosecution in problem-solving courts is a collaborative affair. When offenses are adjudicated, it is true that prosecutors more or less perform their traditional role of representing the state, but with an awareness that certain problem-solving courts house multiple services in the same building, prosecutors often offer sentencing recommendations to the effect that such services are regularly tapped. To some, this gives the impression that problem-solving courts are soft on crime. But by realizing that most such courts do not handle serious felonies and by realizing that the overarching goal is one of achieving meaningful results for offenders, it becomes apparent that they are not soft on crime. With respect to drug courts, some offenders may see them as even more punitive than a traditional court because of the extensive monitoring that goes along with a sentence to participate in treatment.

To dwell much more on the role of prosecutors in problem-solving courts would be to miss the boat concerning the changing role of the American prosecutor. To a large extent, prosecutors in problem-solving courts perform many of the same duties as traditional prosecutors. This is not unlike community policing, where most officers still perform traditional roles of making arrests, investigating crimes, issuing citations, and so forth. Viewed as part of a larger movement, however, prosecution in problem-solving courts is but one piece of a larger community prosecution puzzle. Many activities in which community prosecutors are engaged are intended to avoid trials altogether. The approaches and programs discussed in the previous two chapters provide clear evidence of this.

Do Problem-Solving Courts Work?

The research on problem-solving courts' effectiveness is biased toward the courts that have been around the longest, namely, drug courts. Since they have been in operation for several years now, much research is available. Comparatively little research is available concerning the effectiveness of more recently developed problem-solving courts. Even so, the available research is encouraging. Problem-solving courts appear to represent an effective alternative to traditional adjudication.

Drug Court Research

Drug courts generally operate in one of two ways. First, some offenders are diverted out of the formal criminal process for participation in treatment. Successful completion of treatment means that the offender will not carry the stigma of a criminal record. Second, postadjudication programs either defer sentencing or suspend it in exchange for successful completion of a treatment program. Whichever approach is used, the court will closely monitor the offender during the treatment period. Frequent hearings will be held, where the judge inquires about the offender's progress in treatment. The first drug court was established in Dade County, Florida, in 1989. Since then, drug courts have become quite common (General Accounting Office, 2002). One reason probably owes to the effectiveness of such courts.

It would be impossible in this limited space to review all, or even several, of the drug court evaluations currently in print. Instead, it is useful to consider review studies and meta-analyses. The first of these, published in 1997 by the General Accounting Office, summarized 20 drug court evaluations:

> Some studies showed positive effects of the drug court programs during the period offenders participated in them, while others showed no effects, or effects that were mixed, and difficult to interpret. Similarly, some studies showed positive effects for offenders after completing the programs, while others showed no effects, or small and insignificant effects. (General Accounting Office, 1997)

Belenko, who has conducted several drug court evaluations, more recently summarized 37 separate drug court evaluations (Belenko, 2001). He concluded that "[D]rug courts have achieved considerable local support and have provided intensive, long-term treatment services to offenders with long histories of drug use and criminal justice contacts, previous treatment failures, and high rates of health and social problems" (p. 1). However, Belenko also expressed some reservations about the current state of the research in this area. For example, he was dissatisfied with the scant attention researchers paid to outcomes such as recidivism. Moreover, he was disturbed by many studies' failure to track offenders' records over the long term.

The General Accounting Office (GAO) and Belenko simply summarized the literature. More recently, Wilson and his colleagues conducted a meta-analysis of drug court effectiveness. After analyzing the results of 42 separate drug court evaluations, they concluded, tentatively, that ". . . drug offenders participating in drug court are less likely to reoffend than similar offenders sentenced to traditional correctional options, such as probation" (Wilson, Mitchell, & MacKenzie, 2002, p. 20). Like the researchers before them, though, they expressed concern over research designs used to evaluate drug courts. Like Belenko, however, they also were concerned that many of the evaluations ". . . made no attempt to statistically control for differences between drug court and comparison participants, and a common comparison group, drug court drop-outs, has a bias favoring the drug court condition" (ibid.).

While these literature reviews and meta-analyses are generally supportive of drug courts, the most sophisticated studies in this area paint a more complex picture (see, e.g., Gottfredson & Exum, 2002; Deschenes, Turner, & Greenwood, 1995). Add to that the complication that drug court participation is often voluntary, and selection bias issues invariably creep up (e.g., Gottfredson, Najaka, & Kearly, 2003).

Research on Other Problem-Solving Courts

Researchers have started to turn their attention to the effectiveness of domestic violence courts as well. One researcher recently described the advent of domestic violence courts in this way:

> . . . domestic violence courts seek to coordinate with medical, social service, and treatment providers and establish special procedures and alternative sentencing options to promote effective outcomes. Success necessitates system-wide collaboration and the ongoing commitment of judges, health care professionals, the police, prosecution, and citizens who witness violent acts. (Ostrom 2003)

Drug courts are of course more common than domestic violence courts, but a recent survey conducted by the National Center for State Courts revealed that there were some 200 domestic violence courts in 1998 (Karan, Keilitz, & Denaro, 1999). A more recent study suggests that nearly 300 courts nationwide are giving specialized attention to domestic violence cases (Keilitz, 2000). Some of these courts, however, are not stand-alone courts; they reserve time for specialized processing of such cases (Levey, Steketee, & Keilitz, 2001).

Some research suggests that domestic violence courts secure more convictions (Hartley & Frohmann, 2003), but in terms of recidivism, only one study appears to have been published. Gover and her colleagues recently concluded that such courts may reduce recidivism (Gover, MacDonald, & Alpert, 2003). More specifically, they found that offenders who were processed through the domestic violence court were 50% less likely to be rearrested.

Community courts also have come to the attention of evaluators. Unfortunately, though, most statements concerning the effectiveness of community courts have been anecdotal (e.g., Chase, Alexander, & Miller, 2000). As of this writing, only one outcome evaluation appears to have been published (Svirdoff,

Rottman, Weidner, Cheesman, Cortis, Hansen, & Rottman, 2002). Part of their evaluation entailed a recidivism analysis, wherein it was found that offenders who went through community court had fewer arrests during a 3-year follow-up period, and that longer stays in treatment were associated with additional reductions in arrest. The evaluation had no control group, however, making its conclusions somewhat uncertain.

Other problem-solving courts are starting to team up with evaluators, but this developing area in criminal justice needs a great deal more attention than it has already received. For example, only one homeless court evaluation appears to have been published, and it was concerned only with the number of cases resolved following implementation (Kerry & Pennell, 2001). Over 700 cases (for 266 homeless people) were resolved between October 1999 and February 2001, but whether homeless courts help their clients secure employment or services remains unclear. Likewise, mental health courts have received only scant attention. An evaluation of the King County (Washington) mental health court revealed that those who participated in the program spent less time in detention and were booked on fewer new offenses (Trupin, Richards, Wertheimer, & Bruschi, 2001). An evaluation of Broward County's mental health court revealed that offenders brought before the court were much more likely to receive mental health treatment than offenders in a comparison group (Boothroyd, Poythress, McGaha, & Petrila, 2003).

Theorizing Problem-Solving Courts: The Amalgamation of Justice

Earlier in this chapter it was suggested that problem-solving courts emerged on the heels of community policing developments and a pervasive concern in the 1980s with targeting low-level, quality-of-life offenses. This may be true insofar as community courts are explained. However, domestic violence courts and drug courts surely emerged for other reasons. Some such reasons readily come to mind, including inefficiency of traditional approaches and a lack of continuity and follow-up in the criminal process. Likewise, a certain degree of specialization is needed in trials for such offenses, hence the emergence of courts aimed specifically at targeting them. But problem-solving courts are but one part of a larger movement in criminal justice, calling for role integration, multiagency and intergovernmental collaboration, and a combination of previously distinct functions. This amalgamation of justice is happening throughout prosecution, courts, corrections, policing, juvenile justice, and beyond.

Examples of amalgamation in criminal justice are appearing more and more frequently. For example, juvenile justice reforms, such as waivers, are beginning to make the juvenile system resemble the adult system. As another example, police are starting to partner with probation officers to help them engage in supervision duties (or, viewed differently, probation officers can help police circumvent the Fourth Amendment by acting as stalking horses). In the case of drug courts, judges are involving themselves more and more in the supervision of offenders, a task historically left to probation officers. Collaborations between federal and local law enforcement, such as many of those occurring under Bush's Project Safe Neighborhoods program, are starting to blur the lines between levels of government when it comes to crime control and prevention responsibilities. What explains this trend? The answer lies in the insights of some thinkers in the postmodern tradition.

As O'Malley (1999, pp. 175–176) has put it, "[T]here is currently a bewildering array of developments occurring in penal policy and practice, many of which appear mutually incoherent or contradictory. Disciplinary obedience versus enterprising autonomy, incapacitation and warehousing versus correctional reform, punishment and stigmatization versus reintegration, formal criminalization versus informal victim/offender settlements—these inconsistent and sometimes contradictory couples may all be used to describe elements that make up the diversity and incoherence of contemporary penal policy and practice." Likewise, Hallsworth (2002, p. 146) has stated, "In recent decades penal regimes across the western world have embarked upon a process characterized by relentless expansion and volatile and contradictory patterns of innovation and development" (see also Garland, 1996; Simon, 1995). This incoherence, coupled with the blurring of traditional and comfortable role distinctions, offers some insightful reasoning into the emergence of problem-solving courts. At a glance, they have emerged to cope with real problems. Upon further examination, though, they may have emerged on the criminal justice landscape out of a response to rapid developmental changes characterized by late modernity.

Conclusion

Problem-solving courts have grown in both number and scope. Drug courts have been around the longest, but other courts are now targeting a host of different crime problems. Problem-solving courts have different goals than traditional criminal courts; some avoid adjudication altogether. Likewise, prosecutors' responsibilities in these courts are nontraditional, focusing largely on closing the revolving door that characterizes the traditional model of offense processing. While problem-solving courts have surely emerged out of a need for specialization in certain areas, some theorists would place this development in a camp with other recent penal reforms characterized by contradiction, incoherence, and the blurring of role distinctions and traditional boundaries of responsibility.

References

Belenko, S. (2001). Research on drug courts: A critical review, 2001 update. *National Drug Court Institute Review, 4,* 1–60.

Berman, G., & Feinblatt, J. (2001). *Problem-solving courts: A brief primer.* New York: Center for Court Innovation.

Berman, G., Feinblatt, J., & Glazer, S. (2005). *Good courts: The case for problem-solving justice.* New York: The New Press.

Boothroyd, R. A., Poythress, N. G., McGaha, A., & Petrila, J. (2003). The Broward mental health court: Process, outcomes, and service utilization. *International Journal of Law and Psychiatry, 26,* 55–71.

Center for Court Innovation. (n.d.). *Problem-solving courts.* New York: Center for Court Innovation. Available at http://www.problem-solvingcourts.org.

Chase, D. J., Alexander, S., & Miller, B. J. (2000). Community courts and family law. *Journal of the Center for Families, Children, and the Courts, 2,* 37–59.

Deschenes, E. P., Turner, S., & Greenwood, P. W. (1995). Drug court or probation: An experimental evaluation of Maricopa County's drug court. *The Justice System Journal, 18,* 55–73.

Fritzler, R. B., & Simon, L. M. J. (2000). Principles of an effective domestic violence court. *American Judges Association Court Review, 37,* 1–2.

Garland, D. (1996). The limits of the sovereign state. *British Journal of Criminology, 36,* 173–215.

General Accounting Office. (1997). *Drug courts: Overview of growth, characteristics, and results.* Washington, DC: U.S. General Accounting Office.

General Accounting Office. (2002). *Drug courts: Better DOJ data collection and evaluation efforts needed to measure impact of drug court programs.* Washington, DC: U.S. General Accounting Office.

Goldstein, H. (1979). Improving policing: A problem-oriented approach. *Crime and Delinquency, 25,* 236–258.

Gottfredson, D. C., & Exum, M. L. (2002). The Baltimore city drug court: One-year results from a randomized study. *Journal of Research in Crime and Delinquency, 39,* 337–356.

Gottfredson, D. C., Najaka, S. S., & Kearly, B. (2003). Effectiveness of drug treatment courts: Evidence from a randomized trial. *Criminology and Public Policy, 2,* 171–196.

Gover, A. R., MacDonald, J. M., & Alpert, G. P. (2003). Combating domestic violence: Findings from an evaluation of a local domestic violence court. *Criminology and Public Policy, 3,* 109–132.

Hallsworth, S. (2002). The case for a postmodern penality. *Theoretical Criminology, 6,* 145–63.

Hartley, C. C., & Frohmann, L. (2003). *Cook County target abuser call (TAC): An evaluation of a specialized domestic violence court, revised final report.* Washington, DC: National Institute of Justice.

Karan, A., Keilitz, S. L., & Denaro, S. (1999). Domestic violence courts: What are they and how should we manage them? *Juvenile and Family Court Journal, 50,* 75–86.

Kaye, J. (1999). Making the case for hands-on courts. *Newsweek, 134,* 13.

Keilitz, S. L. (2000). *Specialization of domestic violence case management in the courts: A national survey.* Washington, DC: National Center for State Courts.

Kerry, N., & Pennell, S. (2001). *San Diego homeless court program: A process and impact evaluation.* San Diego, CA: San Diego Association of Governments.

Knipps, S. K., & Berman, G. (2000). New York's problem-solving courts provide meaningful alternatives to traditional remedies. *New York State Bar Journal, 72,* 8–10.

Levey, L. S., Steketee, M. W., & Keilitz, S. L. (2001). *Lessons learned in implementing an integrated domestic violence court: The District of Columbia experience.* Washington, DC: National Center for State Courts.

Nugent, M. E. (2004). *The changing nature of prosecution: Community prosecution vs. traditional prosecution approaches.* Alexandria, VA: American Prosecutors Research Institute.

O'Malley, P. (1999). Volatile and contradictory punishment. *Theoretical Criminology, 3,* 175–196.

Ostrom, B. J. (2003). Domestic violence courts: Editorial introduction. *Criminology and Public Policy, 3,* 105–108.

Petrila, J. (2003). An introduction to special jurisdiction courts. *International Journal of Law and Psychiatry, 26,* 3–12.

Simon, J. (1995). They died with their boots on: The boot camp and the limits of modern penality. *Social Justice, 22,* 25–49.

Stolle, D. P., Winick, B. J., & Wexler, D. B. (2000). *Practicing therapeutic jurisprudence: Law as a helping profession.* Durham, NC: Carolina Academic Press.

Sviridoff, M., Rottman, D. B., Weidner, R., Cheesman, F., Curtis, R., Hansen, R., & Ostrom, B. J. (2002). *Dispensing justice locally: The impact, costs, and benefits of the Midtown Community Court.* New York: Center for Court Innovation.

Trupin, E., Richards, H., Wertheimer, D. M., & Bruschi, C. (2001). *Mental health court evaluation report.* Seattle, WA: University of Washington.

Wilson, D. B., Mitchell, O., & MacKenzie, D. L. (2006). A systematic review of drug court effects on recidivism. *Journal of Experimental Criminology, 2,* 459–487.

Wilson, J. Q., & Kelling, G. (1982, March). Broken windows: The police and neighborhood safety. *Atlantic Monthly,* 29–38.

PART V

Future Challenges

Chapter Twelve

The Future of Local
Prosecution in America

JUDITH N. PHELAN
and MICHAEL D. SCHRUNK

Introduction

Local prosecutors occupy a small but critical niche in the criminal justice system. In 2003, less than 4% of the 2.1 million state and local justice employees were employed in prosecutors' offices (Perry, 2006). Of the interdependent organizations that make up the criminal justice system, none may be as essential to the continuing operation of that system as the office of the elected prosecutor. The domain of the prosecutor can vary from jurisdiction to jurisdiction. Some prosecutors are responsible for misdemeanors, felonies, and child support enforcement; other jurisdictions may divide prosecution responsibilities between the elected district attorney, who covers felony matters, and the appointed county or city attorney, who is responsible for misdemeanors. The focus in this chapter is on the men and woman who are the elected prosecutors, all of whom bear responsibility for the prosecution of felony criminal behavior.

No one has a crystal ball that can conjure up a clear vision of what the future holds for prosecution in the United States. What we do have is a rich history of the development of public prosecutors in the United States, an understanding of the role of the prosecutor, and glimpses of how that role is evolving, expanding, and changing.

In 2005, the Bureau of Justice Statistics (BJS) surveyed a sample of the 2,344 local prosecutors' offices in the United States. The prosecutors in charge of the 42 largest offices, those serving populations of over 1 million, tend to be the prosecutors in the news. In actuality, the majority of prosecutors, 2,302 of them, live and work in smaller jurisdictions. There are 213 offices that serve populations between 250,000 and 1 million. The remaining 2,089 offices serve populations of less than 250,000, and half of those offices serve populations of 36,500 or fewer (Perry, 2006). In 1990, only half of the chief prosecutors occupied full-time positions (DeFrances, 2003). By 2005, 75% of the chief prosecutors served in full-time positions (Perry, 2006).

These prosecutors, no matter the size of their jurisdiction, are defined by statute as the chief law officer or one of the chief law officers of their jurisdiction, and they are part of the executive branch of government. Each office represents a legal jurisdiction, or a combination of jurisdictions, and in all but a few the prosecutors are elected by the local citizenry—a critical distinction. This sets them apart from other prosecutors in the Western world. It also creates a unique relationship with the local community. The people who elected the prosecutor vest broad powers in the office. Prosecutors have the power and authority to bring a criminal charge and to decide the level and seriousness of the charge, and they can terminate a charge (Jacoby, 1980, p. 29). These powers remain at the heart of the role of the prosecutor and form the priority for the prosecutor in his or her most fundamental role as a case processor.

The role of the prosecutor cannot be narrowly defined as one of just processing cases. The National District Attorneys Association (NDAA) National Prosecutor Standards specify that the primary responsibility of prosecution is to see that justice is accomplished (NDAA, 1991, p. 9). Prosecutors in practice rank their primary role as one of prosecuting crime and punishing criminals. However, reducing crime and preventing crime also were included among prosecutors' top priorities (Nugent, Fanflik, & Bromirski, 2004, p. 1). The American Bar Association (ABA) Standards for Criminal Justice Prosecution Function and Defense Function, published by the ABA Criminal Justice Standards Commission, spell out that ". . . the duty of the prosecutor is to seek justice, not merely to convict" (ABA, 1993, p. 4). By all accounts the pursuit of justice involves more than determining the guilt or innocence of an individual.

The Pursuit of Justice

The question "What is justice?" is as old as Socrates (Phillips, 2004, p. 99). In 2003, King County (Seattle, Washington) District Attorney Norm Maleng wrestled with this very question when he faced defendant Gary Ridgway, the Green River Killer. For 20 years law enforcement officials had been investigating a string of homicides that grew to include close to 50 women. It was through DNA and the testing of old evidence with advanced forensic technology that Ridgway was finally identified, arrested, and charged with a handful of the homicides. Initially, DA Maleng signaled that Ridgway deserved the death penalty. Public sentiment was in agreement. Here was a defendant who had for at least 20 years viciously preyed on vulnerable women. An article in *The Prosecutor* (May–June 2004, p. 30) featured this case and DA Maleng's decisions about it. "He had enough evidence to convict Ridgway of seven murders, but this would leave the other victims in what he called 'the dark shadows,' with their families never knowing what happened to them." DA Maleng believed that the families of the other known victims deserved justice as well. He decided that if Ridgway would provide the details of the murders and plead guilty to 48 charges of aggravated murder, the prosecution would not seek the death penalty.

In announcing his decision, DA Maleng issued a public statement that included these words. "Gary Ridgway does not deserve our mercy. He does not deserve to live. The mercy provided by today's resolution is directed not at Ridgway, but toward the families who have suffered so much and the larger community. . . . They (the families) are deserving of answers; they are deserving of truth; they are deserving of mercy. . . . Finally the face of justice reflects our whole community. . . . Justice and mercy: for the victims, the families and the community. That is why we entered into this agreement" (*The Prosecutor*, May–June 2004, p. 31).

This is a stark example of the complexity and types of the decisions prosecutors must make and the degree to which cases involve so much more than the criminal act by the defendant. On a daily basis cases involve victims, families of victims, witnesses, and the community. Prosecutors are always in the position of having to make choices, choices that impact the defendants, the victims, the families of both, witnesses, community members, law enforcement personnel, and all of the components of the criminal justice system. The actions they take, as well as the actions they decline to take, reverberate throughout the criminal justice system and the community. With this perspective it is understandable that the Kennedy School of Government at Harvard University held a series of meetings in the mid-1980s through the early 1990s to examine the various roles prosecutors play. These meetings, the Executive Sessions on State and Local Prosecution, brought together a group of elected district attorneys, researchers, and other criminal justice professionals. Their discussions led to the identification of the five major roles prosecutors fill; the case processor, the sanction setter, the problem solver, the strategic investor, and the institution builder (Tumin, 1990).

Prosecutors also have other roles to fulfill that flow from their status as elected officials—the role of the politician and, from their position in charge of an organization, the management role. This layering of roles and the complexity of relationships within their organization, the justice system, and the community contribute to a dynamic, ever-changing, platform from which prosecutors must operate.

The Case Processor

The case processor role, cited as the prosecutor's primary role, is responsible for the fair, evenhanded, and efficient review of cases. The prosecutor can decide to decline a case, a decision requiring as much thought and preparation as issuing charges on a case, or the prosecutor can decide that there is legal sufficiency to pursue the case through to prosecution and resolution. The great majority of cases are resolved by negotiated pleas. The case processor role is fundamental to maintaining the peace and ensuring the safety of a community by enforcing the rule of law. It is the rule of law, and its consistent and equitable enforcement, that keeps a democratic society stable.

To achieve equitable case processing it is essential to have clear, objective standards. The NDAA has published a set of model standards to which prosecutors can look for guidance as they set policies and operating procedures within their organizations. These NDAA standards form a basis for the discussion that needs to take place among prosecutors as their organizations and responsibilities expand in order to meet changes in and the demands of the local community. Having objective standards gives prosecutors a consistent end product and credibility in the eyes of the public. The best insurance a prosecutor could have regarding concerns over bias would be clear and transparent standards to provide a measure for prosecutors to use when weighing the information and evidence available to them in making the crucial decision either to charge or not charge, and when entering into plea negotiations, the method by which most criminal cases are resolved. Without consistent and objective standards, the potential exists for arbitrary, discriminatory, capricious, or inconsistent application of the rule of law. Pamela Utz, in her study of prosecutors' offices, found that ". . . abuses of prosecutorial discretion are not inherent in discretions; rather, they are contingent upon the context and the manner in which discretion is exercised" (Utz, 1979, p. 119). It is the responsibility of prosecutors to clearly articulate the standards that can guide their organizations in exercising that discretion.

The key check on prosecutorial discretion is the public, the constituency the prosecutor serves. As an elected officer of the state, the prosecutor must answer to the public. If the constituency of the jurisdiction is not satisfied with the performance of the elected prosecutor, then there is an opportunity, depending on the electoral cycle of the jurisdiction, to make changes. If egregious acts are committed, then immediate remedies are needed. Prosecutorial misconduct does take place, and there are established processes to handle such situations. But it is the public nature of the office, where the prosecutor's track record is available for all to see, that serves as the ultimate check on prosecutorial discretion.

A prosecutor's credibility is dependent upon the transparency of the office and his or her effectiveness as a case processor. Without performing this function of enforcing the rule of law fairly, impartially, and expeditiously, the prosecutor could not effectively perform the other roles outlined by the Kennedy School's Executive Sessions on Prosecution. All of these roles are intertwined; they overlap and support each other. To think of them as discreet functions, independent of each other, would fail to appreciate how they build on and impact one another. Prosecutors are employing different strategies and techniques, always adapting to new circumstances as they fulfill these roles. Greg Berman, director of the Center for Court Innovation and coauthor of *Good Courts, Bad Courts*, sees that for the future ". . . prosecutors will be light on their feet and must adapt to changing conditions on the ground" (personal communication, February 21, 2006).

Intertwining Roles—The Sanction Setter

The sanction setter role is closely tied to the case processor role. Prosecutors must consider sanctions at the earliest stages of issuing a criminal case. Because the criminal justice system is composed of ". . . a sequence of serially interdependent organizations whose combined efforts result in various products" (McDonald, 1979, p. 16), whatever the prosecutor decides filters through the entire system. The charging decision by the prosecutor affects the entire criminal justice system.

The introduction of judicial sentencing guidelines has led to an increase in the prosecutor's influence in the sentencing process. Judicial sentencing guidelines came about for a number of reasons—the need for legislative control of criminal justice budgets and greater predictability in forecasting state budgets and the desire to eliminate bias and inequality in sentencing as well as the perception of any disparity in sentencing. Judicial discretion to depart from the guidelines is limited. Consequently, the charges issued and plea agreements reached by the prosecutor will, in large part, determine the sentence the judge will assign to the defendant. This places the prosecutor even more firmly in the center of policy development around resource allocation for the criminal justice system.

Many prosecutors' offices and other components of the criminal justice system are almost completely funded by their state legislatures. Legislatures have exerted control over criminal justice spending by instituting sentencing guidelines, defelonizing certain crimes and decriminalizing others, and setting sanctions and reducing budgets for the agencies that provide those sanctions.

It is not unusual to see, as Oregon has experienced, the costs of jails and prisons squeezing out the funding for sanctions and services. When felony offenders who previously served time in state prisons were transferred to county jails, the result was an increase in local jail costs, which took a toll on the service side of the local corrections departments, thereby reducing their ability to provide sanctions. The unintended consequences of many of these types of legislative changes result in felonies being treated as misdemeanors due to decreases in the funding of sanctions. When the aim has been to reduce penetration into the costly criminal justice system, the result has been a reduction in penalties for offenders and an erosion of the credibility of the criminal justice system.

Because of the reductions in penalties that accompany these legislative changes, the prosecutor must pay close attention to setting sanctions in order to maintain the credibility of the criminal justice system. Prosecutors are challenged daily to keep sanctions in synchronicity with offenses so that less serious offenses do not receive harsher penalties than serious offenses. This is a particular challenge in the smaller jurisdictions with limited resources and alternatives. Calhoun County (Hardin, Illinois) District Attorney Charles Burch, who has been the elected district attorney since 1976, sees disparity in sanctions as a major problem for prosecutors. His one-man office serves a population of just over 5,000. He receives 95% of funding from the state. In his view, actions by the state legislature have contributed to disparity in sanctions. He cites burglary as an example of a felony offense having been virtually decriminalized due to the lack of availability of a jail sanction, while penalties for alcohol use by juveniles are more severe than juvenile marijuana use (personal communication, January 25, 2006).

Disparity in sanctions is not limited to small jurisdictions. Larger jurisdictions may have a jail option available, but due to the practice of releasing convicted offenders, based on a matrix and population limits, such as exists in Multnomah County, Oregon, the early release of the offender essentially eliminates the intended sanction. This has pushed prosecutors into the arena of policy development, which focuses on the broader issues of resource allocation for the entire criminal justice system as well as those agencies that provide assistance and services to the offender populations, such as health, mental health, and employment systems.

Prosecutors and Resource Allocation

Developing alternatives to jail and setting appropriate and incremental sanctions is one of the priorities for prosecutors now and in the future. The prosecutor is the only component of the justice system that touches all of the other components (Heymann & Petrie, 2001, p. 24). This unique positioning provides a broader base from which prosecutors can view the impact of policies regarding resource allocations. This encourages them to engage the other components of the criminal justice system, as well as other publicly funded services, in policy determinations that can provide incremental sanctions designed to foster system integrity. The need for cooperation and collaboration among the component agencies becomes even more critical as competition for resources increases.

It is particularly important that prosecutors are closely attuned to developing sanctions that are important to the local community. They have learned that the order and maintenance offenses, such as prostitution, low-level drug crimes, public disorder, and thefts and burglaries, often fueled by the need to support drug habits, are the crimes that affect the daily quality of life in a community. Setting appropriate and meaningful sanctions for these crimes is an ongoing challenge to prosecutors. In order to have effective sanctions, prosecutors need to have a broad understanding of how resources are distributed across not just the criminal justice system but the public and private sector as well, because their policy decisions can have drastic effects on all of these systems. If a prosecutor declines to intervene in cases involving public disorder in parks, then local community members lose the resource of the park. If a prosecutor declines to intervene in public disorder in a business district, then the customer base can dry up and businesses can fail. Prosecutors need to be aware of budgets for and services from the health, mental health, housing, employment, and transportation sectors and understand how their services contribute to and can be a part of their plea negotiations and sentencing recommendations. Lack of services in these systems can result in an offender ending up in jail by default because the local systems could not provide the needed services. Prosecutors' policy decisions can and do affect resource allocations for all of these systems.

Collaboration on Resource Allocation, Public and Private

In recent years, specialty courts have emerged as a way to deal with the challenges to the criminal justice system of the mentally ill, the drug addicted, the victims and perpetrators of domestic violence, and maintenance and order offenses. Drug treatment courts and community courts are two examples of the results that can be achieved when the components of the criminal justice system and private-sector organizations cooperate, collaborate, and share resources. Their focus is not simply on adjudicating and disposing of the case but on seeking justice for the defendant and the community. For years, police, prosecutors, and the courts have been performing their functions independently, arresting, prosecuting, and sentencing those who committed low level drug crimes and quality-of-life offenses. For the resources expended, the results were not acceptable. The criminal justice system was recycling the same offenders without long-term, positive effects, and the community continued to be victimized by the offenders. A different approach was needed, and in 1989, Miami launched the first drug treatment court. Word of its success in enrolling and keeping addicts in treatment rapidly spread to other jurisdictions. According to the Center for Court Innovation Web site there are now over 1,600 drug courts in operation or being planned. They handle cases involving substance-abusing offenders, and they monitor their progress through supervision, drug testing, and treatment and provide sanctions and incentives. In February 2005, the GAO released a report on drug court evaluations. It concluded that there was less recidivism for both new arrests and new convictions among drug court participants and a reduced recidivism for a period of time following drug court completion (Casey, 2005).

The Midtown Community Court in Manhattan, launched in 1993, was the first of its kind to target cases involving quality-of-life offenses: prostitution, shoplifting, public disorder, illegal vending, fare evasion, and graffiti. Community courts sanction the offender, often by requiring a stint of community service or some other penalty appropriate for the offense. They also look at the individual defendant and connect defendants to social services, mental health treatment, employment, or other services to counter the underlying causes of the offenses that brought them to the attention of the justice system. Like drug treatment courts, community courts can provide sanctions appropriate to the offenses without utilizing the costlier penalties of long-term probation or jail sentences. Though far fewer in number than drug treatment courts, there are about 30 community courts operating or in planning stages. These courts, such as the ones in Portland, Oregon, Hartford, Connecticut, and West Palm Beach, Florida, offer models of how communities can deal constructively with public disorder offenses and cut back on repeated offenses.

Kings County (Brooklyn, New York) District Attorney Charles J. Hynes, when interviewed by the Center for Court Innovation, said: "The easiest thing we do is put people in jail. That is not a difficult thing, if you've got your prosecutors trained well. The real challenge is to keep public safety at a level that is acceptable to the people you represent, and I believe that fundamentally you do that by recidivism reduction. Every time you reduce recidivism you knock down another layer of crime problems" (Center for Court Innovation, 2006).

Both the drug treatment courts and the community courts focused on specific types of offenses, and the people who commit those offenses, aiming to reduce recidivism and restore men and women as contributing members of the community. As prosecutors examine the kinds of community and crime issues that affect public safety, they take on different roles, especially as characterized by the Harvard Executive Sessions, the problem solver role.

The Problem Solver Role and Community Prosecution

The problem solver role requires prosecutors to focus on more than the sanctions and penalties necessary to preserve system credibility. It looks to early problem identification and an array of possible solutions, including crime prevention and control. The problem-solving prosecutor digs deeper into the social, environmental, and other community conditions that allow both nuisance and serious crime to flourish (Nugent et al., 2004, p. 3). The traditional prosecutor reacts to the individual criminal act as a case processor. The problem-solving prosecutor also performs the case processor role but in addition will work with the community to identify problems so that effective strategies can be developed to alter or amend the conditions that allow crimes to occur. In problem solving the prosecutor does not limit strategy development to law enforcement personnel but includes business and community members and local organizations in crafting solutions to community safety issues.

Just as law enforcement offices that engage in problem-oriented policing activities call their work community policing, prosecutors engaging in problem-solving activities refer to this function as community prosecution. In one APRI survey of prosecutors' offices, 49% of the offices reported that approximately half of the respondents said they practice community prosecution, and 64% of the larger offices, those serving populations over 250,000, reported practicing it (Nugent & Rainville, 2001). In the BJS 2005 survey, 66% of all the offices reported using tools other than prosecution to solve community problems, 40% of the offices self-identified as community prosecution sites, and over half of the offices stated that they involved the community in identifying crime or problem areas (Perry, 2006). The BJS 2005 survey was the first time prosecutors were asked to self-identify as a community prosecution site. The inclusion of that question in the survey is in itself an acknowledgment of the increasing use of community prosecution as a legitimate function of the elected prosecutor. Prosecutors who have adopted the problem-solving role have experienced success in managing some of their most entrenched community safety problems, many of which are order and maintenance offenses.

In Portland, Oregon, the district attorney's office took on the problem-solving role in earnest, beginning in one geographic area that was undergoing redevelopment. The neighborhood and business associations in the area wanted the community to be a safe place to live and work and the problems of theft from cars, public disorder, and illegal camping eliminated. Taken individually, the criminal acts were considered minor incidents of low-level criminal behavior; taken collectively, they interfered with daily living and commerce. The groups involved in redevelopment wanted public safety expertise to be part of the planning, and in 1990, a deputy district attorney was assigned to work with the group. What developed from that first step, and similar first steps in other jurisdictions, has become known as community prosecution.

One of the first issues addressed stemmed from district residents and businesses consistently complaining about unlawful camping and its accompanying problems of litter, petty vandalism, and aberrant street behavior. The transient population, with its problems of homelessness and substance abuse, fueled the problem. The city of Portland was spending up to $60,000 a year cleaning up the affected areas, and the police were citing and arresting persons for illegal camping. These traditional responses to the crimes were temporary measures but not long-term solutions to the problem. In an effort to eliminate the negative impact these behaviors had on the local district, the prosecutor met with residents, businesses, the police, representatives of the homeless populations, and others, and together they devised a strategy that they set in motion following a costly cleanup by the city. It involved posting signs in the affected areas specifying that camping was prohibited but listing resource information for anyone who wanted services. Volunteers monitored the areas and notified police by fax of any illegal camping. Officers leaving the precinct on the next shift were able to respond immediately and advised campers that they were not allowed to remain. Within a year the incidence of camping was virtually eliminated, with only an occasional occurrence. The benefits to the strategy are positive in every way; no displacement of the problems to adjacent areas, increased livability in the district for residents and businesses alike, and no further need for costly cleanups or police or prosecutor resources (Multnomah County District Attorney, 2006).

Placing prosecutors in the community also allows them to see problems close at hand without the filter of the police report. No longer was it one case of a low-level drug sale on a dimly lit street. They began to understand the impact of the repeated low-level drug sale, night after night of a parade of cars lining the street to pick up drugs, car doors slamming every few minutes, the dash to the front door, the quick exchange and back to the car, and the gunning of the engine and the screech of tires as the cars peeled away into the night. The magnitude of the problem could not be denied, and the police had limited ability to control the problem in terms of search-and-seizure practices. The best results came from the collaboration among the citizens, the police, and the prosecutor. The prosecutor was able to bring the rule of law directly to the citizens and provide law enforcement personnel with clear guidance on what citizens could and could not do. The prosecutors then got creative— working in the neighborhoods, they came up with new city ordinances and approaches to dealing with prostitution and drug crimes. They proposed the establishment of the citizen-driven warrant, the drug-free zone, and the prostitution-free zone ordinances for the affected geographic areas. These instruments have gone through multiple reviews, extensive public hearings, revisions, and court challenges, only to be upheld as legally sufficient methods to control the negative impacts of criminal activity on neighborhoods. These would never have been developed if prosecutors had not looked beyond the individual case and toward methods to long-term solutions to prevent and control crime (Multnomah County District Attorney, 2006).

In Howard County, Maryland, former district attorney Marna McLendon (January 1995–January 2003) assigned prosecutors to serve as liaisons to neighborhood groups and schools; in Atlanta, Georgia Deputy District Attorney Wanda Dallas shut down drug houses, rehabbed them, and brought up neighborhood property values in the process; and in Dallas, Texas, Assistant City Attorney Roxanne Pais marshaled code enforcement officers to eliminate hot-spot crime areas in structures housing criminal activity. Through community prosecution and problem-solving activities, prosecutors are directing their energies toward disrupting, reducing, and eliminating criminal activities, moving beyond the boundaries of individual case processing and sanction setting to the broader issues of problem identification and crime control.

These prosecutors and others like them are doing what former Marion County (Indianapolis, Indiana) district attorney Scott C. Newman described when he said "I also try to emphasize an ethos throughout everything I do in the office that we're not just case processors, we're law enforcement strategists" (Center for Court Innovation, 2006). As strategists, prosecutors are looking toward what they can do to increase the capacity of the criminal justice system and their local communities to deal effectively with public safety problems. They are becoming strategic investors.

The Strategic Investor

Taking on problem-solving approaches moves prosecutors from the micro, the individual case, to the macro, the context in which the case developed. They move beyond problem solving to what the Harvard Executive Sessions identified as the strategic investor role. In times of ever-tightening budgets, prosecutors have had to create new ways to add capacity and new tools for citizens, the police, themselves, and the courts; in doing so, they have enhanced the credibility and capacity of the criminal justice system. Since 9/11 there have been limited opportunities for new programs to develop through federal and state grants. In the past, prosecutors and other criminal justice agencies had been able to develop innovative programming with financial support from state and federal government grants. When grant funding expired, the programs that proved to be effective were incorporated into ongoing budgets funded by the local or state government. In this way, criminal justice professionals were able to experiment with innovative and effective program concepts. This is how drug treatment courts developed so rapidly. With the reprioritization of federal resources following 9/11, prosecutors and others have had to create other methods to increase system capacity by acting as strategic investors.

Prosecutors also have been successful in obtaining grants from private foundations and philanthropic institutions as a way to test new program ideas. Hennepin County (Minneapolis, Minnesota) former prosecutor, now senator, Amy Klobuchar established a strong partnership with the Target Corporation Foundation, which enabled her to expand its community prosecution functions. The Philadelphia Community Court, opened in 2002, provides additional capacity for sanctioning public disorder and similar-type crimes and has strong backing and financial support from the Pew Charitable Trust. Prosecutors who engage in problem solving are creating new partnerships that open different doors and offer new options for resource acquisition and sharing. But prosecutors are looking beyond grants in aid and developing other methods to expand capacity.

Partnerships with other public agencies are another avenue to increase capacity. This has been effectively achieved with multijurisdictional task forces involving law enforcement agencies from the local, state, and federal levels. Buchanan (1989) highlighted the advantages of cooperation and collaboration between law enforcement from various jurisdictions and prosecutors using this approach. The multijurisdictional task forces he studied targeted high-level drug dealers and included Multnomah County, Oregon, as well as task forces in Maine, New York City, and Laconia, New Hampshire. He found that through greater collaboration and a sharing of resources, both prosecutors and the police were successful in meeting their goals for arrests and convictions.

Some prosecutors have developed partnerships with private businesses to add capacity to criminal justice programming. The Portland Business Alliance (PBA), an organization composed of local businesses dedicated to promoting economic growth for the region, is a key partner in the Neighborhood District Attorney Unit and the Westside Community Court. The services the PBA provides include staff support and supervision of community service projects, thereby expanding the capacity of both program areas in a significant fashion. Similarly, the Lloyd Center Business District Association provides financial support for the Neighborhood District Attorney Unit. Early concerns that big business was buying prosecution services have proved to be without foundation. These partnerships have brought greater information sharing and an even broader dissemination of information with the public and have increased the transparency of the case processing function.

Three prosecutors who have been highly successful in adding capacity to their local criminal justice systems are former Jackson County (Kansas City), Missouri, prosecutors Albert Reiderer and Claire McCaskill (now Senator McCaskill), and the current state attorney for Winnebago County (Rockford, Illinois), and 2005 president of the NDAA, Paul Logli. In 1989,

Reiderer, in collaboration with his colleagues in the criminal justice system, presented the voters with the Community Backed Anti-Drug Tax (COM-BAT), a quarter-cent sales tax, the proceeds of which would support not only law enforcement but prevention and treatment programs. The tax passed and has generated $15 to $20 million each year since its approval. Senator McCaskill, during her tenure as Jackson County prosecutor, further developed and expanded COMBAT (Coles & Kelling, 1998) The program continues, and in August 2003, voters extended the tax through March 2011 (Join Together, 2006).

State Attorney Logli, along with the Winnebago county sheriff and other local officials, advocated for a referendum for an additional one-cent sales tax to build and manage a new jail. Crime rates had soared. Winnebago County had the highest crime rate in Illinois in 2001 and a 29% increase in serious felony crime in the first quarter of 2002 (Sweeney, 2002). The referendum passed, and in the first year approximately $25 million was raised. This allowed the county to build new jail and administrative facilities, add staff support, and fund much-needed private social service programs.

Through strategic investment, prosecutors, in collaboration with other partners, have been able to add capacity to local criminal justice systems and strengthen institutions and services in their communities. In building these partnerships, they have expanded their realm of influence by playing influential roles in determining policies and resource allocations within their jurisdictions. The results are clear—substantial improvements in their local justice systems and in their local communities.

The Institution Builder

For prosecutors to be successful in problem-solving and strategic investment roles, they have had to leave the confines of their courthouse offices and meet directly with community and business leaders, listening to their views of what the community safety problems are and working with them to accurately identify priority issues. They have had to cede some of their authority and power to the group and work in collaboration with law enforcement professionals, businesses, and community organizations. Travis County (Austin, Texas) District Attorney Ronald Earle calls this "sharing the power" of the district attorney with the community. In his words, increasing community involvement in the justice system is ". . . reweaving the fabric of community" (personal communication, December 9, 2005). DA Earle views the community as the basic building block of society. He speaks frequently on this topic and of his belief that the true safety in communities lies in the close relationships among individuals who make up the community and its institutions. He has formalized partnerships among community members and justice system personnel by establishing a local justice council that is charged with setting policy for the Travis County criminal justice system.

Other prosecutors and justice system professionals see the potential dangers of engaging citizens' and victims' advocates in policy-setting roles. Judge Andrew Sonner, Montgomery County, Maryland, Special Appeals Court judge, and almost 30-year veteran as Montgomery County state attorney, cautions prosecutors in ceding too much authority to individual groups, such as victim advocacy groups, and ending up with biased policies. He cites that the real danger for prosecutors in the future is diluting due process (personal communication, December 8, 2005).

The roles of the case processor, sanction setter, problem solver, strategic investor, and institution builder blend together. It often is difficult to distinguish where problem solving ends and institution building begins. Larger jurisdictions, with higher case volumes and staff numbers, may be able to adapt their operations and experiment in these areas to a greater degree than smaller jurisdictions. Prosecutors who have broken out of the habit of responding to problems the same way over and over again have had to develop a different set of tools and learn how to use them effectively. There is a wide range of new tools available to prosecutors, including specialized units, multi-jurisdictional task forces, drug-free zones and other new ordinances and codes, good neighbor agreements, the broader use of civil remedies, specialty courts, and a variety of alternative remedies. Prosecutors have discovered that they can achieve positive results that meet community expectations by expanding their role beyond simple case processing. They are learning that ". . . wielding unconventional tools just might improve their effectiveness" (Greg Berman, personal communication, February 21, 2006).

The Need for Data Analysis and Research

In the past, prosecutors have worked in isolation. The new paradigm involving community prosecution, with its close cooperation with other systems and the private sector, will further encourage prosecutors to become more savvy about the importance and use of data sharing and analysis with these groups. Prosecutors who already have been successful in developing and using unconventional tools and strategies have one thing in common—they have made effective use of data to analyze and better understand the problems facing them. The absence of consistent data collection and analysis is one of the most glaring omissions within the field of prosecution. Prosecutors need dramatic improvement in this area in order to meet future demands.

Data analysis, objective research, and evaluation are clearly lacking in the field of prosecution. The National Research Council's Law and Justice Committee (Heymann & Petrie, 2001) has stated, "Prosecution is notable . . .

for the lack of rigorous social science research that has been conducted on it, in contrast to these other sectors of the criminal justice system." Brian Forst, a longtime advocate for greater emphasis on data collection and analysis by prosecutors, has urged prosecutors to make use of data analysis to improve their operations. "Now statistical information on prosecution and sentencing is beginning to accumulate, and D.A.s and chief judges are tending to shift their thinking from the single-case litigation perspective instilled by conventional legal training to an orientation that considers the aggregate information in the context of the goals of prosecution and sentencing" (Forst, 1984, p. 34).

These observations are more important today than ever before. The police have opened their doors to researchers and have had success with using data effectively to analyze, pinpoint, and monitor criminal activity and the impact of their enforcement efforts. The New York Police Department's use of Compstat (computer-assisted statistical analysis) and the use of similar data analysis efforts in other jurisdictions have brought greater accountability and transparency to police operations. Prosecutors can benefit from the lessons learned by the police. They are in a better position now, due to improved technologies and management information systems available to them, to follow law enforcement's lead. Many jurisdictions have data readily available that can be utilized to assist prosecutors in better understanding the dynamics of crime and the context in which it takes place. Prosecutors who have adapted quickly to advanced technologies in trial work, such as DNA, are only beginning to make effective use of new technology in terms of their own organizations. Quality data analysis will provide prosecutors with the ability to be openly accountable to the public and to offer comprehensive and objective results of alternative approaches to crime control and other initiatives. For the future, this means that prosecutors will need to continue to build and develop personnel with the necessary legal skills but also to acquire additional skill sets through training and hiring.

The situation can only get better with the ever-improving management information systems. Prosecutors can look at the individual and overall performance of the organization and work with other jurisdictions to develop standardized data collection efforts that will bring much-needed, greater transparency to the functions that prosecutors perform. Now and in the future, prosecutors need to pay close attention to individual performance within the organization, aggregate performance of the organization, and external data pertinent to community safety and crime control problems. The American Prosecutors Research Institute's "Prosecution in the 21st Century" identifies a model framework to guide prosecutors in the development of objective outcome measures for prosecution. The critical questions are the following: What are prosecutors trying to achieve? How do they plan to achieve it? How can they measure whether or not they are achieving what they have set out to do? What things have helped achieve it? (Nugent et al., 2004, p. 5). Partnering with researchers and universities, as police agencies have been doing to improve law enforcement practices, may be the most effective route that prosecutors can take to improve office practices and problem-solving activities.

Some prosecutors have brought technological and scientific advances into the everyday operations of their organizations. They have embraced advances in computer technology and software systems that enable them to keep track of cases and outcomes. They have improved their collection of data related to managing their own organizations and are utilizing data analysis to monitor and improve their procedures and operations. This has enabled them to become more efficient in the daily processing of routine cases and to pinpoint problems and focus resources on emerging problems. This ability to break down data to smaller and smaller units, thereby isolating problems and working on solutions specific to these problems, is a technique that holds much promise for the future. But until there is more consistency in the use of data by a greater number of prosecutors throughout the profession, prosecutors will have limited ability to meet future demands.

Will Resources Drive Policy?

Former Denver district attorney, and now Colorado governor, William Ritter, sees the clash between ideology and the fiscal imperative, brought on by escalating operational costs and tighter budgets, as the greatest future danger for prosecutors (personal communication, December 14, 2005). In his view, the real challenge for prosecutors will be guarding against ideology being driven by finances. With the technological advances available to prosecutors, they now have, as never before, the information and ability to monitor and review their operations. Prosecutors who take advantage of these increased capacities to perform data analysis and who utilize the information to craft responses to local public safety issues will be in a stronger position to formulate well-reasoned strategies and operations.

The anticipated increases in the elderly population are likely to yield increases in crimes against the elderly. The societal problems of illegal drug and alcohol abuse, the flood of the mentally ill in the justice system, and juvenile crime are areas of ongoing concern for prosecutors. There is a need for prosecutors to gather improved data on these population groups and on how the criminal justice system can deal more effectively with them. Without objective outcome measures, the elected prosecutor cannot build a budget that can stand up to capricious political winds or support the retention of trained personnel.

Attracting, training, and retaining skilled attorneys are keys to the effective and successful operation of a prosecutor's office. Judge Andrew Sonner sees that the emphasis on training and professionalism by the National District Attorneys Association, coupled with the availability of training through the National College of District Attorneys and the National Advocacy Center at the University of South Carolina, has helped prosecutors improve their practice and increase their professionalism. Continuing support for high-caliber training is essential to advance the professionalism of prosecutors.

Conclusion

Prosecutors are employing a wider variety of strategies in their pursuit of justice. They have moved from a strict crime sanction advocacy role to employing more complex strategies that involve the full array of partners from not only the criminal justice system but from across the public and private sectors. Some strategies involve civil remedies, such as injunction relief, asset forfeiture, and civil abatement procedures. Prosecutors have partnered with city attorneys and other regulatory offices to pursue these approaches. They have established prosecutorial work units to focus on specific crime problems, such as drugs, guns, gangs, child abuse, and domestic violence. They have formed alliances with businesses, community groups, and neighborhood associations, working to construct innovative approaches to achieving solutions to local problems. The future challenge is to institutionalize these practices.

Crime will continue to be a priority for communities, and local prosecutors must remain transparent and accountable to their constituencies. The problems that prosecutors now face will be part of what they will face in the future. What they can count on is that the future will bring new issues and opportunities. What prosecutors have demonstrated over the years is an ability to identify trends and adapt to them. They have stepped up to take on the role of community leaders and public policy makers. They have pioneered innovative ideas and embraced technology to solve crimes and community safety problems. They have worked collaboratively with other components of the criminal justice system and the community, bringing the private sector into public policy development. They have professionalized the role of the prosecutor and have continued to expand their knowledge. Prosecutors are turning problems and issues into new opportunities in achieving their primary responsibility ". . . to seek justice, not merely to convict" (ABA, 1993, p. 4). This is their past, and it is what is demanded of them for the future.

References

American Bar Association (ABA). (1993). *Standards for criminal justice prosecution function and defense function* (3rd ed.). Washington, DC: American Bar Association, Criminal Justice Standards Commission, Criminal Justice Section.

Boland, B. (1998). Community prosecution: Portland's experience. In D. R. Karp (Ed.), *Community justice: An emerging field* (pp. 253–277). Lanham, MD: Rowman & Littlefield.

Buchanan, J. (1989). Police-prosecutor teams: Innovations in several jurisdictions. *The Prosecutor, 23*, 31–36.

Casey, P. (2005, Spring). Drug court evaluations: Looking at the trend line. *Problem-Solving Reporter, 2*, 1. Retrieved January 4, 2007, from http://www.ncsconline.org/Projects_Initiatives/ProbSolving/vol2No1.htm.

Center for Court Innovation. (2006). Retrieved November 27, 2006, from http://www.courtinnovation.org/index.cfm?fuseaction=document.listDocument&documentTopicID=26&documentTypeID=8.

Coles, C., & Kelling, G. (1998). *Prosecution in the community: A study of emergent strategies.* Cambridge, MA: Harvard University, J. F. Kennedy School of Government.

DeFrances, C. J. (2002). *Prosecutors in state courts, 2001.* Washington, DC: U.S. Department of Justice, Office of Justice Programs, Bureau of Justice Statistics.

DeFrances, C. J. (2003). *State court prosecutors in small districts, 2001.* Washington, DC: U.S. Department of Justice, Office of Justice Programs, Bureau of Justice Statistics.

Dillingham, S., Nugent, E. M., & Whitcomb, D. (2004). *Prosecution in the 21st century: Goals, objectives, and performance measures.* Alexandria, VA: American Prosecutor Research Institute.

Forst, B. (1984). Prosecution and sentencing. *The Prosecutor, 18*, 30–37.

Heymann, P., & Petrie, C. (2001). *What's changing in prosecution?: Report of a workshop.* Washington, DC: National Research Council, Committee on Law and Justice.

Jacoby, J. (1980). *The American prosecutor: A search for identity.* Lexington, MA: Lexington Books.

Join Together. (2006). Retrieved November 27, 2006, from http://www.jointogether.org/news/headlines/comminitystories/2003/mo-voters-extend-tax-to-fund.htm.

McDonald, W. F. (1979). The prosecutor's domain. In W. F. McDonald (Ed.), *The prosecutor* (pp. 9–49). Beverly Hills, CA: Sage Publications.

Multnomah County District Attorney. (2006). *Neighborhood District Attorney Program.* Retrieved November 27, 2006, from http://www2.co.multnomah.or.us/cfm/da/NDAP/index.cfm?fuseaction=strategies&menu=43&title=illegal%20Camping, and http://www2.co.multnomah.or.us/cfm/da/NDAP/index.cfm?fuseaction=strategies&menu=19&title=Drug%20Free%20%Zones%20%28DFZ%29.

National District Attorneys Association (NDAA). (1991). *National prosecutor standards* (2nd ed.). Alexandria, VA: National District Attorneys Association.

National District Attorneys Association. (2004). Maleng's toughest call: Charging the Green River Slayer. *The prosecutor, 38(3)*, 30–31.

Nugent, E. M., Fanflik, P., & Bromirski, D. (2004). *The changing nature of prosecution: Community prosecution versus traditional prosecution approaches.* Alexandria, VA: American Prosecutors Research Institute.

Nugent, M. E., & Rainville, G. (2001). The state of community prosecution: Results of a national survey. *The Prosecutor, 35*, 26–28, 30–33.

Perry, S. (2006). *Prosecutors in state courts, 2005*. Washington, DC: U.S. Department of Justice.

Phillips, C. (2004). *The six questions of Socrates: A modern-day journey of discovery through world history*. New York: W.W. Norton & Co.

Rockford Register Star. (2002, August, September).

Sedgwick, J. (2006). Prosecutors meeting today's challenges with limited resources. *The Prosecutor, 40*, 40, 47.

Sweeney, C. (2002, November 10). Tax revenue must be retained for public safety, Rockford Register Star website. Retrieved January 21, 2007, from http://nl.newsbank.com/nl-search/we/Archives?p_action=list&p_theme=gannett&s_site=rrstar&p_product=RRSB&p_topdoc=21.

Tumin, Z. (1990). *Summary of proceeding: Findings and discoveries of the Harvard University executive session for state and local prosecutors at the John F. Kennedy School of Government, 1986–1990*. Cambridge, MA: Harvard University.

Utz, P. (1979). Two models of prosecutorial professionalism. In W. F. McDonald (Ed.), *The prosecutor* (pp. 99–124). Thousand Oaks, CA: Sage Publications.

Contributors

STEVEN BELENKO is a professor in the Department of Criminal Justice, Temple University. He is also affiliated with the University of Pennsylvania School of Medicine as adjunct professor of psychology in the Department of Psychiatry, and senior scientist at the Treatment Research Institute (TRI), and he is a research affiliate at the Center for Mental Health Services and Criminal Justice Research at Rutgers University. Prior to joining the TRI in 2002, Belenko was a CASA Fellow at the National Center on Addiction and Substance Abuse at Columbia University, a Senior Research Fellow at the New York City Criminal Justice Agency (where he also held the positions of research director and acting executive director), a senior research associate at the New York City Office of the Mayor and the Vera Institute of Justice, and a research psychologist at Mathematica Policy Research. Belenko has conducted extensive research on substance abuse and crime, the impact of drugs on the adult and juvenile justice systems, adolescent substance abuse, prescription drug abuse and diversion, HIV risk behaviors and related service needs for offenders, and the integration of treatment and other services in criminal justice settings, including drug courts, diversion programs, and prisons. He has published numerous articles and book chapters and is the author of two books, *Crack and the Evolution of Antidrug Policy* (winner of the American Library Association's Choice Magazine Academic Book of the Year Award) and *Drugs and Drug Policy in America: A Documentary History*. Belenko earned his BS in applied mathematics and PhD in experimental psychology from Columbia University.

ROBERT CHESNEY is an associate professor of law at Wake Forest University School of Law, where he teaches and writes on the topic of national security law. Chesney's scholarship examines the manner in which legal systems respond to national security threats including, in particular, the threat of terrorism. His work has appeared recently in the *Stanford Law Review*, the *Michigan Law Review*, and the *Southern California Law Review*, among others. Chesney has served as chair of the Section on National Security Law of the Association of American Law Schools, and currently serves as editor of the American Bar Associations' *National Security Law Report* and the book review editor for the *Journal of National Security Law and Policy*. Chesney is a member of the American Law Institute and a graduate magna cum laude of Harvard Law School.

CATHERINE M. COLES, JD, MA/PhD (anthropology), is a visiting scholar at the School of Criminal Justice, Rutgers University-Newark. Previously she was a researcher in the Program in Criminal Justice Policy and Management, JFK School of Government, Harvard University; project ethnographer/director of Evaluation for the Newark Safer Cities Initiative, School of Criminal Justice, Rutgers University-Newark; and faculty member in Local Government Studies at Ahmadu Bellow University, Zaria, Nigeria (1979–1981) and Anthropology and African Studies at Dartmouth College (1983–1990). Coles writes on prosecution, the courts, constitutional and criminal law, community justice, and public policy in these areas. She has studied the changing roles of police and prosecutors through several projects funded by the National Institute of Justice. She is the coauthor (with George Kelling) of *Fixing Broken Windows: Restoring Order and Reducing Crime in Our Communities* (The Free Press, 1996); the author of case studies of community policing in Savannah (Georgia) and Saint Paul (Minnesota) for the National COPS Evaluation (1998), and has published numerous articles on prosecution. She has served as a consultant on community prosecution, criminal justice, and community collaborations nationally and internationally.

SCOTT H. DECKER is professor and director in the School of Criminology and Criminal Justice at Arizona State University. He received his BA in social justice from DePauw University and his MA and PhD in criminology from Florida State University. His main research interests are gangs, juvenile justice, criminal justice policy, and the offender's perspective. His most recent books include *European Street Gangs and Troublesome Youth Groups* (winner of the American Society of Criminology, division of International Criminology Outstanding Distinguished book award, 2006) and *Lessons from the Inside: Drug Smugglers on Drug Smuggling* (Philadelphia: Temple University Press, 2008).

CAROLINE R. DONHAUSER, JD, is an assistant district attorney in the Office of the District Attorney of Kings County (Brooklyn), New York. Since

2005, she has been the associate counsel to the district attorney and legislative secretary of the New York State District Attorneys Association. Previously she worked for many years in the office's Appeals Bureau, briefing and arguing numerous appeals in state and federal courts and rising to the level of senior appellate attorney. She then became a deputy chief of the office's Alternative Programs Bureau, focusing on the operation and expansion of several diversion programs, including the Drug Treatment Alternative-to-Prison Program and the Treatment Alternatives for Dually Diagnosed Defendants Program. Donhauser received her BA from Princeton University and her JD from Columbia Law School. From 1983 to 1985, she was a U.S. Peace Corps volunteer in Morocco.

RODNEY L. ENGEN received his BS in psychology and his MS in sociology at the University of Wisconsin-Madison, and his PhD in sociology at the University of Washington. He is currently associate professor of sociology at North Carolina State University where he teaches courses in criminology, juvenile delinquency, and formal social control. Engen is a former research investigator at the Washington State Sentencing Guidelines Commission and technical consultant to the North Carolina Sentencing Policy and Advisory Commission. His research examines the implementation of sentencing reforms, the exercise of judicial and prosecutorial discretion under sentencing guidelines, racial and ethnic disparities in case processing, and the effects of social and organizational forces in prosecution and sentencing. His published research appears in journals including *American Journal of Sociology*, *Criminology*, *Justice Quarterly*, the *North Carolina Law Review*, and *Social Problems*.

PATRICIA L. FANFLIK is deputy director of research and evaluation at the National District Attorneys Association's American Prosecutors Research Institute. She has more than 10 years of applied research experience in the social sciences. Her areas of specialization include the criminal justice system and mental health, social psychology, and deviance. She is currently involved in several research studies, including a national community prosecution initiative, the effectiveness of sexual assault nurses' exams on the prosecution of sexual assault cases, aggression and lethal violence encountered by prosecutors, drug prosecution and prevention programs, forensic interviewing and child sexual abuse, prosecutor involvement in reentry programs for formal incarcerated persons, and vicarious trauma experienced by prosecutors. Fanflik's experience also includes specialized training as an individual and family therapist. She has been invited as a guest lecturer to discuss the interface of law and psychology and the importance of research in the criminal justice system. She has coauthored a number of peer-reviewed journal articles, and she has presented her work at several regional and national conferences across the country.

BRIAN FORST is professor of justice, law, and society at the American University's School of Public Affairs, Washington, D.C. He came to American University in 1992, after 3 years on the faculty at George Washington University. Prior to that, he was research director at the Institute for Law and Social Research (1974–1985) and research director at the Police Foundation (1985–1989). His research on prosecution and sentencing, the deterrent effect of the death penalty, and policing is widely cited by scholars and criminal justice practitioners. His book, *Errors of Justice: Nature, Sources, and Remedies* (Cambridge University Press, 2004), was named book of the year for 2006 by the Academy of Criminal Justice Sciences. He has a BS (statistics) and an MBA (quantitative methods) degrees from the University of California at Los Angeles, and a PhD (information and decision systems) from George Washington University.

KAY LEVINE holds a JD from Boalt Hall School of Law and a PhD in jurisprudence and social policy, both from the University of California at Berkeley. She is currently an associate professor of Law at Emory University, where she teaches courses on criminal law, criminal procedure, gender and sexuality, and victimless crimes. Levine's recent research, which explores numerous issues relating to prosecutorial discretion and the enforcement of statutory rape, has been published in the *Emory Law Journal*, the *Fordham Urban Law Journal*, the *Wake Forest University Law Review*, the *American Criminal Law Review*, *Law and Social Inquiry*, and *Studies in Law, Politics, and Society*. Before joining the academy she served as both a prosecutor and a criminal defense attorney in California.

JACK McDEVITT is associate dean for research and graduate studies at the College of Criminal Justice at Northeastern University. He also directs the Institute on Race and Justice and the Center for Criminal Justice Policy Research. He is the coauthor of three books: *Hate Crimes: The Rising Tide of Bigotry and Bloodshed*, *Hate Crime Revisited: American War on Those Who Are Different* (both with Jack Levin), and *Victimology* (with Judy Sgarzy). He has also coauthored a number of reports on racial profiling including a monograph for the U.S. Department of Justice and statewide reports from Rhode Island and Massachusetts on the levels of disparity in traffic enforcement. He is coprincipal investigator with Dr. Amy Farrell of a national evaluation of the recent Police Integrity Initiative of the U.S. Department of Justice's Office of Community Orientated Policing Services (COPS). Over this period he h as published numerous articles on a wide variety of topics in criminal justice. He has spoken on hate crime, racial profiling, and human trafficking both nationally and internationally, and has testified as an expert witness before the Judiciary Committees of both U.S. Senate and the U.S. House of Representatives and as invited expert at the White House.

M. ELAINE NUGENT-BORAKOVE is a senior project director with the Justice Management Institute (JMI). Prior to joining JMI, she served as the director of Research and Evaluation at the National District Attorneys Association's American Prosecutors Research Institute. For nearly 20 years, she has conducted national studies on criminal and juvenile justice issues. Over the past decade, her work has focused on the nation's local prosecutors. Nugent-Borakove is credited with the development of a quantitative method for assessing prosecutorial workload and has conducted extensive research on community prosecution and performance measurement for prosecutors. Numerous other studies include examinations of sexual assault nurse examiner programs, local prosecutors' role in homeland security and terrorism, prosecution of hate crimes, and identity theft. Her work has been published in a series of special-topic monographs for prosecutors as well as several peer-reviewed journals.

JUDITH N. PHELAN, trainer and organizational consultant, retired from the Multnomah County District Attorney after serving from 1984 to 2004 as staff assistant to the district attorney. In that role she was instrumental in planning, developing, and implementing several innovative programs including the Neighborhood District Attorney Project, Portland's Community Courts, the Multnomah County Drug Court, the Regional Organized Crime/Narcotics Task Force (ROCN), and the Regional Drug Initiative (RDI). Phelan is the author of several reviews and articles. She has been a speaker at national conferences in the United States and Thailand, and a trainer for businesses and organizations, including the National College of District Attorneys, the National Advocacy Center, the American Prosecutors Research Institute, and the National Institute of Corrections. Phelan holds a master's degree in social work from Portland State University in Portland, Oregon, where she also has served as an adjunct professor. She completed her undergraduate work at the College of St. Teresa in Winona, Minnesota.

MICHAEL D. SCHRUNK has held the office of district attorney in Multnomah County, Oregon, since January 1981. Schrunk is a graduate of the University of Oregon Law School. He has extensive experience in the prosecution of criminal cases. While in private practice, he represented plaintiffs and defendants in civil litigation and defended criminal cases. He served as a captain in the U.S. Marine Corps in Vietnam and is past president of the Multnomah County Bar Association and the Oregon District Attorneys Association. Schrunk has been a leader in several innovative justice initiatives including: the Neighborhood District Attorney Program in 1990, the drug Court in 1991, and Portland's Community Court Project in 1998. Schrunk currently chairs the Regional Organized Crime Narcotics Task Force and is a member of Multnomah County's Public Safety Coordinating Council. He has served as a lecturer for the National District Attorneys Association, the American Prosecutors Research Institute, the National College of District Attorneys, and the Drug Enforcement Administration. He also has served as a consultant for the American University and for a federal justice program/U.S. Department of Justice, Zagreb, Croatia. He has provided articles and reviews for the Bureau of Justice Assistance and the National Institute of Justice and has served nationally and internationally as a consultant on criminal justice policy and operations. Schrunk is the recipient of several national awards, including the U.S. Department of Justice's Public Service Award for Community Leadership and the Lecturer of Merit Award from the National College of District Attorneys.

HUNG-EN SUNG received his doctoral degree from the State University of New York at Albany and has been an associate professor of criminal justice at John Jay College of Criminal Justice since the fall of 2006. Prior to his current appointment, Sung served as a research associate at the National Center on Addiction and Substance Abuse at Columbia University, where he led projects on drug abuse treatment, religious faith, and reentry of offenders funded by public and private agencies. His research interests are coerced treatment for drug-abusing offenders and comparative research on crime and justice. His recent publications have appeared in the *Journal of Substance Abuse Treatment, Journal of Offender Rehabilitation, Social Forces, Journal of Contemporary Criminal Justice,* and *Journal of Research in Crime and Delinquency.*

ANNE J. SWERN, a prosecutor for 26 years, was appointed first assistant district attorney by Charles J. Hynes, district attorney for Kings County (Brooklyn, New York). She is the executive in charge of the nationally acclaimed drug Treatment Alternative-to-Prison (DTAP) program, dedicated to diverting prison-bound nonviolent predicate felons into residential substance abuse treatment. She also is the district attorneys office's senior executive supervising Brooklyn's three substance abuse treatment courts, the Red Hook Community Justice Center, and the Mental Health Court. As the district attorney office's executive in charge of mental health issues in the criminal justice system, she supervises the Treatment Alternatives for the Dually Diagnosed (TADD) program, which diverts mentally ill defendants into treatment as well. Swern is the author of the Brooklyn DTAP *Annual Report.* She serves on the Judiciary Committee of the Brooklyn Bar Association and the Prosecution Function Committee of the American Bar Association. She currently serves as the ABA's liaison to the Joint Committee on Administration of Criminal Justice, pursuant to Senate Concurrent Resolution No. 117, in developing an effective legislative approach to high incarceration rates and related fiscal issues in post-Katrina, Louisiana. She is a member of the board of directors of the National District Attorneys Association. She served on the New York State Commission on Drugs and the Courts and assisted in the preparation of a report to Chief Judge Judith Kaye in 1999, *Confronting the Cycle of Addiction and Recidivism*. Swern was selected as the 1999 Humanitarian of the Year by the Education and Assistance Corporation and the 2000 Prosecutor of the Year by the Kings County Criminal Bar Association. She also received the 2006 Thomas E. Dewey Medal from the Association of the Bar of the City of New York. Swern is an adjunct associate professor at Brooklyn Law School and John Jay College of the City University of New York.

JOHN L. WORRALL is an associate professor in the Criminology Program at the University of Texas at Dallas. He received his PhD in political science from Washington State University in 1999. Worrall is the author of several books, the most recent of which is *Crime Control in America: An Assessment of the Evidence, 2nd ed.* (Allyn and Bacon, 2008). His work has appeared in a number of journals, including *Criminology, Evaluation Review*, and *Justice Quarterly*, and he is the coauthor (with Robert V. Wolf, Center for Court Innovation) of *Lessons from the Field: Ten Community Prosecution Leadership Profiles* (American Prosecutors Research Institute, 2004). He is also editor of the journal *Police Quarterly*.

Index

criminal process *(continued)*
  grand jury, 6
  preliminary hearing, 10, 17, 97, 100
  speedy trial laws, 10

death penalty cases. *See* capital cases
defendants, 40, 43, 52, 54, 55, 56, 57,
    61, 63, 67, 68, 74, 80, 81, 99, 100,
    102, 114, 115, 120, 121, 122, 124,
    130, 150, 151, 159, 160, 163, 164,
    166, 167, 168, 220, 235, 249, 251,
    253, 254
  criminal history, 82
deferred prosecution, 115, 117, 119, 120,
    123, 130–31
deferred sentencing, 119, 120, 123,
    130–31
deterrence, 68, 93, 94, 101, 188
  gun crimes, 153 (*see also* Project Safe
    Neighborhoods)
discretion, prosecutorial, 5, 9, 11, 14, 15,
    17, 43, 53–54, 55, 58, 75, 77, 80,
    81–82, 84–87 passim, 92, 102,
    112, 178, 181–86 passim, 194,
    202, 250–51
  abuses of, 56, 67, 202
  accessibility to citizens, 196
  charging, 17, 81, 85, 99
  in community prosecution, 199, 216,
    218, 219, 222
  decision making, 12, 56
  power of, 9, 19, 51, 100, 236
  whether to prosecute, 53
district attorney, 3, 15, 16, 18, 19, 37, 45,
    113, 177, 185, 186, 193, 247
domestic violence. *See also* problem-solving courts
DNA evidence, 52, 66, 248, 261
drug-free zones, 256, 260
drugs, 77, 125, 130, 132, 189, 223, 256,
    263
  and community prosecution, 216
  connection to crime, 188
  drug offenders, 22, 78, 116, 232
  recidivism among drug offenders, 22,
    238

risk responsivity theory, 112
treatment (*see* drug courts)
drug courts, 22, 112, 113, 114–15, 116,
    128, 231, 233, 236–37, 239, 240,
    241
  alternative prosecution and adjudica-
    tion strategies, 111
  components of, 115
  diversion into treatment, 112
  evaluations of, 239
  funding for, 233
  for juveniles, 233
  number of drug courts, 115, 233,
    254
  operation of, 238
  studies of, 111, 115
  treatment, 115
Drug Enforcement Agency, 147
drug treatment alternatives program
    (DTAP), 22, 116, 118–32. *See also*
    treatment programs
  collaborative efforts, 129
  cost benefits, 126–27
  creation of, 116, 177
  dilution of effects, avoidance of,
    118
  effectiveness compared to incarcera-
    tion, 125
  eligibility criteria, 121
  employment rates, 126
  evaluation of, 118, 119, 122–28
  goals, 128
  job counseling and placement ser-
    vices, 119
  non-eligible defendants
  for nonviolent offenders, 120
  program failure, 124
  readmission of participants, 119
  recidivism, 124–25
  reducing drug use, 125
  for repeat felons, 117
  research on, 117
  retention rate, 118, 123
  screening, 121
  support for, 117
  treatment provision, 122